About *The Human Rights Culture . . .*

"Reams of books and articles have been written about human rights, but *The Human Rights Culture* is unique. It is the first comprehensive, sociological study of human rights in the contemporary period. With his characteristic erudition and graceful style, Lawrence Friedman addresses all the central topics: women's rights, minority rights, privacy, social rights, cultural rights, the role of courts, whether human rights are universal, and much more. This surprisingly compact book presents a balanced discussion of each issue, filled with fascinating details and examples. Friedman's core argument is that the recent rise of human rights discourse around the globe is the product of modernity — in particular the spread of the cultural belief that people are unique individuals entitled to respect and the opportunity to flourish. This terrific book will be informative not only to human rights experts and practitioners but also to people who wish to read a clear and sophisticated introduction to the field."

— Brian Z. Tamanaha
Professor of Law
Washington University

THE
HUMAN
RIGHTS
CULTURE

A Study in History
and Context

BY

LAWRENCE M. FRIEDMAN

Stanford University

Contemporary Society Series

qp

Quid Pro Books

New Orleans, Louisiana

THE HUMAN RIGHTS CULTURE

Published in 2011 by Quid Pro Books.

QUID PRO, LLC
5860 Citrus Blvd., Suite D-101
New Orleans, Louisiana 70123
www.quidprobooks.com

ISBN: 1610270711 (pbk)
ISBN-13: 9781610270717 (pbk)
ISBN: 1610270703 (hc)
ISBN-13: 9781610270700 (hc)
ISBN-13: 9781610270724 (Kindle)
ISBN-13: 9781610270731 (ePub)

Cover photograph courtesy of NASA and its project "The Visible Earth," used with permission. The project is found at *http://visibleearth.nasa.gov*.

Cover design and production by Ryan J. Carter.

Printed in the United States of America. Second paperback printing, January 2012.

Publisher's Cataloging-in-Publication

Friedman, Lawrence M.

The human rights culture: a study in history and context / Lawrence M. Friedman.

p. cm.

Includes index.

Series: *Contemporary Society*.

1. Human rights. 2. Human rights—History. 3. Human rights—Sociology. 4. Human rights—United States—History. I. Title. II. Series.

JC573.F33 2011   323.19'2—dc22

CIP

Contents

Acknowledgments..i

1. Introduction..1

2. On the Rule of Law; and on
       Consciousness of Rights................................19

3. A Small Dose of History....................................25

4. On Modern Religion...55

5. Is There a Culture of Human Rights?..................63

6. Universal and Particular....................................69

7. Women and Minorities......................................77

8. Privacy and Dignity..89

9. Social, Economic, and Cultural Rights................111

10. Sovereignty and Rights...................................139

11. Some Concluding Remarks..............................157

About the Author..165

Notes...167

Index...193

For Leah, Jane, Amy, Sarah,
David, Lucy, and Irene

Acknowledgments

I would like to thank Scott Shackelford, Andrew Shupanitz, Russ Altman-Merino, and David Oyer for their help with the research on this book. Also, as usual I had enormous help from the staff of the Stanford Law Library, including Paul Lomio, Erika Wayne, Kate Wilko, George Wilson, Sergio Stone, and Sonia Moss; and from my assistants, Mary Tye and Stephanie Basso. As the footnotes show, I have also used and depended on dozens of scholars who have worked in this field, and I am grateful to them. They include, among others, my colleagues Helen Stacy and Jenny Martinez. Jenny Martinez also made extremely careful, extensive, and valuable comments on the manuscript.

— L.M.F.

THE
HUMAN
RIGHTS
CULTURE

1

Introduction

We live in the age of human rights. An age of constitutions, declarations, manifestoes, proclaiming the rights of man (and woman). An age of aspiration—an age of longing; for freedom, for equality. In country after country, human rights are high on the political and social agenda: what they consist of, how to defend them, and debates on all sides of many issues in which they figure. No discussion of international law and international politics can ignore the human rights movement. In some ways, we live in an age of human rights triumphant. But we also live in an age of turbulence and war; an age of suicide bombs and genocide, an age of good governments and bad governments and terrible governments and governments that are miserable failures. Yet even the worst of these governments *claim* to be committed to human rights. The human rights movement can be trampled on, distorted, manipulated; but (apparently) cannot be ignored.

Nor is it ignored — in the world of scholarship. There is a huge and daunting literature on human rights, whole shelves and libraries: books and books and books. Most of these are written by earnest, learned people. Almost all of them are animated by a passion for human rights.

It is an impressive body of scholarship. And yet, somehow, something is lacking. The problem in general is not quantity, but quality. Or at least quality in one particular sense. The literature is vast but surprisingly narrow. Philosophers, political theorists, and lawyers write most of the books and articles. This is not bad in itself; moreover, most of them care deeply about human rights, which is also not bad in itself. Undeniably, one can learn a lot by diving into the oceans of words that these scholars have written. One can learn a lot about the textual history of those declarations, treaties, manifestoes, and covenants that have sprouted like weeds since the second World War. The literature also tells us about great thinkers of the past and the present, and what they have had to say about the rights of humankind. There are illuminating debates on many important and controversial subjects.

But what is missing, on the whole, or in short supply, is what one might call the sociological dimension. The human rights movement—the social movement that has inspired this enormous literature—is a massive social fact. But where does it come from? Why has it been so successful (in places)? Where is it going, and why? Why, in this period, unlike all others, do we have a feminist movement, a gay rights movement, a movement of indigenous peoples, a revolt of the handicapped, the aged, prisoners, students, speakers of small languages, and so on?

THE HUMAN RIGHTS CULTURE

The sociological question nags at me. What is it about the late 20th century, and the early 21st, that has led so many millions of people, in developed countries, but elsewhere as well, to accept certain doctrines or dogmas, which then become central premises of the human rights movement? What led people to decide that all human beings are and should be equal in law and in society—women as well as men; people of all races and religions; minorities as well as majorities? To many of us, equality of this sort seems obvious, seems right, seems simply just and proper. But did any society in the past think this way? Does any traditional society, in the contemporary world, think this way? What, then, is it about modernity that pushes women—and men—in the direction of gender equality? What gives rise to the struggle—often more or less successful—for the other equalities at the base of the human rights movement?

It may seem as if there is no room for more books; but I hope this is wrong. I hope there is room for a book which explores the human rights revolution—I think we can call it that—historically and sociologically. This would be a minority approach. It would not exactly be new and untried. Still, I hope that I can add at least a nuance or two.

We can start off with a question of definition. What do we mean by human rights? Before we can talk about human rights or basic rights, or fundamental rights, we might want to specify what we mean by a right in the first place.

It would be hard to think of more common *legal* terms than "right" and "rights." These are very ordinary English words. Equivalent words meaning more or less the same in other languages are no doubt just as ordinary. Modern legal systems are all organized in terms of rights. Or, to put it another way, you can always describe the rules and doctrines of legal systems as clusters or networks of rights. I have a right to sue somebody who backed into my car in a parking lot. Adults have a right to get married—and a right to get unmarried. Landowners have the right to sell their land, inventors have a right to patent their inventions, and so on and so forth. We can indeed rephrase every rule or doctrine in terms of rights—rights of somebody or some group or some institution, rights of this or that type, rights against government, or against other people, rights for and rights against.

When we talk of "human rights," or fundamental human rights, or the like, we are talking about a subset of the cluster of legal rights. But exactly what subset? "Human rights" is, unfortunately, a vague and slippery phrase. It has a core and a periphery. Most people would probably recognize the rights at the core. Freedom of speech, they would say, is a basic human right. Freedom to vote for and against a government is another one. Freedom to choose your religion or no religion, is also fundamental. And people in modern countries would probably sense that these "rights" are different somehow, importantly different, from the right to sell a used car or foreclose a mortgage.

Freedom of speech, or religion, or the right to vote, or the right to travel, are just a few of the rights people might mention if you asked them to draw up a list of basic or fundamental rights. Perhaps no two people would come up with the identical list. And the typical list in, say, France might be different from the list in Finland or Japan. Moreover, the typical list today would obviously be quite different from the list that John Locke or Thomas Jefferson would have come up with in their day.

This last comment is a way of expressing a pretty banal fact: concepts of "human rights" or "basic rights" are social facts—ideas that people have and express. These concepts are culturally and historically contingent. They are not the product of pure reason, nor are they something handed down from time immemorial; they are not the inevitable result of some facet of basic human nature. Certainly, people in past societies would never have subscribed to our concepts of human rights. For the most part, these ideas are specifically modern—they are relatively recent in human history.

Recent; and, in addition, definitely on the march, as it were. In the club of wealthy, developed countries—mostly Western, but including Japan, for example—these concepts of basic rights, fundamental rights, are growing in legal and social significance. And there is a strong tendency for new "rights" to get added to the list. I referred to the club of wealthy developed democratic countries. But rights-consciousness is not confined to these countries. It is most in evidence in these societies. But it is found elsewhere as well, at least among some strata of society, and perhaps to some extent in every country in the world by now. For the last few decades at least, the human rights *movement* and human rights *consciousness* have been spreading throughout the world.

I am not going to draw up a list or catalog of basic human rights, as of now, or as of any time in the past. My idea is, instead, to try to explain them; to discuss where they fit, in contemporary society; where they came from; and why. The human rights idea has tremendous power and sweep. The cluster of ideas and institutions that animate the human rights movement have enormous legitimacy. There are people who devote their lives to the cause; or are even willing to die to advance human freedoms. Where does this power come from? This might seem like a foolish question. We tend to take the legitimacy, the value, the idealism of the human rights movement for granted. But this was not always the case. Far from it.

And what makes human rights such a seductive idea? Because the human rights idea is so seductive that even those who oppose it and despise it hesitate to do so openly. Scholars have pointed out that many awful regimes, repressive regimes, dictatorial regimes, sign their names to human rights treaties, without blushing—treaties which they have not the slightest intention of enforcing. Sudan and China, to take only two examples, have ratified a number of these treaties. Indeed, since the 1980's, "repressive governments have often been in the majority, ratifying the treaties more often than their liberal counterparts."[1] Treaty ratification is "not only . . . not associated with better human rights practices than otherwise expected," it is rather "often associated with worse practices."[2] As we will see, some evidence points in a different direction. For now, however, I only mention the paradox of good treaties signed by bad countries. And there are also good countries—the United States for one (and it is, whatever you think of it, a lot more respectful of human rights than, say, the Sudan or Saudi Arabia)—which are extremely reluctant to sign such treaties, and sometimes simply refuse.[3]

It would indeed strike many people as a kind of sadistic joke to find the signature of the Sudanese government on a human rights treaty. The citizens of that country would probably not find this joke very funny. Human rights are in extremely short supply in the Sudan. Many of us in the West—and not only in the West—certainly believe that every country *should* enforce these rights. These rights ought to belong to the Sudanese people, just as much as to anybody else; human rights, as Jack Donnelly has put it, are "the rights that one has because one is human."[4] The rights that one has—perhaps it would be more accurate to say, the rights that people think one *ought* to have; that everybody ought to have. But in fact, as is well known, they are violated all the time in some countries, and from time to time in almost every country.

A "right," including a "human right," implies some sort of law or rule, and one that can be enforced. These laws and rules are expressed in constitutions and in bills of rights. Each country has its own version. Is there something else—something beyond the positive laws of particular countries? Is "human rights law" part of a body of international law? International law, supposedly, is a reality; a group of customs that countries follow, and which is not the law of one country or some countries, but of all countries; or which ought to be. The trouble is that countries do not really follow "international law." Or rather, they follow it when it suits their interests, and ignore it when it does not. The Security Council of the United Nations can enforce its decisions, in some cases. But in general, there is no way to enforce "international law." It is, for the most part, "powerless rhetoric in the face of national interests."[5]

Certainly, human rights is not hard, positive law, insofar as this country or that lacks the framework of enforcement, or refuses to enforce these rights. In this case, it is little more than "empty promises."[6] But even "empty promises" sometimes have an impact. A growing literature starts out from the premise that even unenforceable promises can make a difference. Some scholars have tried to measure this impact. Human rights practice is hard to catalog or measure. As we said, most countries—rotten regimes and democratic ones alike—have a tendency to sign, sign, and sign some more (with notable exceptions). When a country signs and ratifies, does something change? The country has made a formal commitment, whether it intends to live up to it or not. Perhaps a process has been set in motion. Or has it? The research, on the whole, reaches mixed and inconclusive results.[7] The most elaborate test, by Beth Simmons, cautiously suggests a certain impact, in some countries. The treaties have an effect on internal politics. They "set visible goals for public policy and practice that alter political coalitions and the strength, clarity, and legitimacy of their demands." The treaties, to be sure, are "not a silver bullet through the heart of the world's dictatorial regimes." They do, however, "offer some leverage where repression itself can be contested."[8] Oona Hathaway calls the treaties and declarations a "powerful expressive tool." In liberal democracies at least, interest groups may "mobilize to pressure their government to comply."[9] And another study found "strong empirical support for the limited effect of the international law of human rights on state practice," even after controlling for a number of factors—like democracy and wealth—which admittedly make a difference.[10]

Thus the "powerless rhetoric" of all the treaties, declarations, and conventions is not always empty verbiage. The rhetoric, in any event, is mightily pervasive; and more so all the time. Governments can try to hide behind a screen of treaties, or manipulate these agreements cynically for their own ends, or simply ignore them; but often the population, as Simmons points out, may take the treaties and declarations more seriously. They inspire people; and they strengthen the hand of NGO's and other interest groups that battle for human rights. This is, in any event, a plausible hypothesis;[11] and, as we will see later on, a certain amount of evidence backs it up.

But perhaps we are asking the wrong question; or asking it backwards. The impact of treaties is almost impossible to measure—too many other things are going on, in every country. Yes, the treaties and conventions cannot be enforced from outside; yes, international law is a hollow reed (although there are signs of change). But the more basic question is this: Where did the treaties and declarations come from? Why do we have them? They have sprouted like mushrooms, in the late 20th century. Why is this? And why are they so seductive—not simply to governments, but to ordinary people? What are the social forces, the norms, the ideas, the cultural habits, that animate the human rights movement? What gives the public, and its organizations, so many hopes, dreams, and passions? The texts are, in a way, like dry, withered leaves, without life of their own. And how many people have actually read them? They *seem* to have vast power; but that might be an illusion. Something else has the power; and that something else is what has created the movement, and has also given rise to its texts.

Whichever way the arrow of causality points, the human rights idea has shown a tremendous capacity for growth—as a social ideal, and as part of the normative baggage of ordinary people in our times. The result has been a tendency—and more than a tendency—for human rights ideals to spill over into positive law and positive institutions. Constitutions have been growing like summer weeds. Constitutional courts sit and decide cases that would have been unthinkable in past generations. How and why have the *words* become so potent? How is it that what seems ghostly, unreal, a figment of the imagination, turns into something concrete and influential; what is it that gives this airy nothing, to borrow Shakespeare's phrase, not only a local habitation and a name, but a form, a body, a living, breathing self?

The human rights literature is enormous. More and more books pour out of the printing presses every year. The big bookstores have whole walls of shelves on the subject. There are thousands of journal articles—many of them in journals that are entirely devoted to human rights. There are programs, institutes, research centers. In the light of all this, is there anything new or different to be said? I rather timidly think so. The literature is a vast ocean in size; but as I said earlier, it is skewed in particular directions. Much of it is heavily theoretical and philosophical. The experts who write the books tend to be professors of philosophy or political theory or specialists in ethics. Legal scholars have also spilled oceans of ink on the subject. These two fields— philosophy (broadly conceived) and law—have dominated the literature.[12] The lawyers, like the philosophers, focus on texts and procedures; and tend to be highly normative. They have strong ideas about what *should* be the social and legal reality. Both literatures are useful. Lawyers, in particular, have to do the dirty work of drafting the documents, declarations, and treaties. They bring and manage the cases on human rights, whenever there are cases to be brought. But they have also played, as Michael Freeman argues, a dominant (and distorting) role in the academic study of human rights.[13]

What we have, as a result, is a lot of theory, a lot of philosophy, a lot of policy proposals, a lot of exhortation. A great deal of it is noble, fine, uplifting. Good people with good motives write most of the books. They are fighting a good, and necessary, fight. After all, the world is full of enemies of human rights. These enemies run much of the world. They have prisons and death squads and armies. Hitler wrote *Mein Kampf*; but most of our contemporary dictators do not bother to write books.[14] That is probably just as well. The books are written, on the whole, by high-minded men and women; humane men and women. Yet something seems to be missing. The work, on the whole, lacks the tough fiber of sociological reality. The research on *how* rights operate, and *why* they take certain forms, is relatively thin. There are some honorable exceptions—we mentioned, for example, studies which try to test the impact of human rights documents. There are also essays on the historical roots of the human rights movement; indeed, a fairly substantial literature on this subject.[15] There is also some literature on the sociology of rights— although surprisingly little. But on the whole, the normative stuff dwarfs the slim shelf of books which try not to exhort or condemn, but to explain.[16]

I am willing to be just as normative as the next person; and I confess that I have strong feelings about human rights. But this book is not about what is right and wrong with the human rights movement. Rather, it is about the concepts and practices of fundamental rights as social facts. That is to say, fundamental rights as notions and ideals in peoples' minds; and what people and institutions make of them. Or, to put it another way, I am concerned with what ordinary and not so ordinary people, in various places, think about the subject. I am also interested in the *practice*—the behavioral side of human rights. And also how courts and other institutions handle the subject; and how the language of the law and the lawyers, and the language of the ruling texts, reflect the norms that lie underneath the surface.

That conceptions of rights change over time is as obvious as anything can be. In Western countries, today, the law takes it absolutely for granted that men and women have equal rights; the equality of the sexes is also (to a degree) the ideal in social life as well. But this notion of gender equality was totally absent during most of human history. The American Declaration of Independence announced that "all men" were created equal. Not "all men and all women," but "all men"; and this was hardly accidental. The same is basic- ally true of the "rights of man" in its French revolutionary version. Not to mention the fact that, in the United States, "all men" really meant all *white* men.

There were, to be sure, rights that belonged both to men and women. A woman arrested in the United States or France, or in England, and charged with a crime, had as much access to a fair trial, probably, as a man had. She had religious freedom; and the right to express herself in print, and to give speeches (society frowned on such behavior, to be sure). But women could not vote, or hold office, and hardly anybody thought they should or could. In the common law system, a woman lost most of her power to control her property, the instant she got married. The power passed to her husband. African- Americans had even fewer rights than women. Most of them, up to the time of the Civil War, were slaves. Free blacks, south and north, were nowhere the legal equal of whites; and socially even less so. Yet De Tocqueville considered the United States a radical experiment in democracy. And it was, compared to most countries—countries without democratic elections, or who punished or persecuted religious minorities; or where only the nobility was truly free.

Hence even in the United States, where the law in, say, 1800 clearly recognized some basic human freedoms—freedom of speech and religion, for example—human rights meant something quite different than it does today. Even the most advanced thinkers of the Enlightenment, or of the age of the American Revolution, would be quite startled by today's menu of human rights. In scope and reach these rights are incomparably broader than any- thing in the past. Thomas Jefferson certainly believed strongly and firmly in freedom of speech. But he would surely be amazed, and horrified, at the notion that the right of freedom of speech covered emotional outbursts, or dirty words, or, for that matter, books about various positions of sexual intercourse. Basically, the founding fathers were thinking of political speech; and debates about religion (short of blasphemy). Not only have the classic rights expanded; but there are also distinctively modern rights, which Jefferson never dreamt of—privacy, for example. Many of the new constitu- tions also list a battery of so-called social rights—rights to education, housing, health care, and so on. There is also more and more recognition of language rights, of cultural rights in general, and the rights of indigenous peoples.

All this tremendous variation, over time and space, makes it possible to argue that the whole idea of fundamental rights lacks logical or philosophical sense.[7] But the people who walk the streets of New York or Tokyo or Stockholm are not philosophers or logicians; and ideas about human rights are firmly rooted in their mind-sets. People tend to believe quite strongly that there *are* fundamental rights, basic rights—sacred rights, untouchable and inalienable rights.

To be sure, popular opinion on the subject is no doubt incoherent, variable, and at times illogical. Yet a single basic premise, I think, does underlie most of the basic items on the menu of modern rights. (The word "modern" here is quite crucial). This is the dogma that all human beings are or ought to be absolutely equal in public policy and law: men and women, black and white, young and old, Christians and non-Christians, and so on. Every individual should count the same as every other individual. Jack Donnelly has put it succinctly. Human rights are "the rights that one has simply as a human being. As such human rights are equal rights, because we are all equally human beings." And these rights are "inalienable," because, whatever we do, and whatever is done to us, "we cannot become other than human beings."[8] In general, a "right to equality" is now "regarded as an essential feature of both national law and international human rights instruments."[9]

In life, of course, equality of this sort is miles away from reality. But it is the bedrock on which, I believe, people build their mental structure of human rights. In the real world there are majorities and minorities, in race, religion, language, political beliefs, sexual orientation, and so on. This is fact. But human rights in the Donnelly sense do not depend on majority status; at any rate, they are not *supposed* to depend on majority status. Majorities and minorities stand shoulder to shoulder in equality—legal equality; and equality in dignity and respect. Whether this is because of their common humanity, or some other reason, the general tendency is unmistakable. I call the underlying concept *plural equality*.

For more than a century, and probably longer, the concept of human rights has been moving in this direction, that is, toward plural equality. Or, to put it another way, the doctrines of human rights have expanded greatly. In the United States, this means, first of all, by reaching out to include all adult white men as full citizens, with the right to vote and so on. Then later, full citizenship—and not just in the technical sense—expanded to include women, African-Americans and other racial minorities, and equality of rights passed also to other ethnic groups, and to aliens, the elderly, illegitimate children, people who are blind or deaf or in a wheelchair, the so-called sexual minorities, and many other categories, all of which were supposed to share in the general harvest of dignity; and for whom discrimination in employment, and in life, was socially or legally forbidden, or both. Of course, plural equality never reaches the stage where it covers everybody. Certainly not people who are defined as criminals. Perhaps also not for very deviant religions, which people consider "cults," or for those people still considered truly immoral —

child pornographers or polygamists — and perhaps not for "terrorists" or people who have wild and radical views that are too far out of the mainstream. And countries still distinguish sharply between citizens and non-citizens. Non-citizens do not vote; and cannot cross the borders at will. And while there are rights for children, and indeed international covenants on children's rights, children never do have the same rights — voting rights, for example — that adults do.

The American story is hardly unique. Each country has its own story; and the differences are significant. Take women's rights, for example. *All* developed countries have given women the vote; and all of them have some kind of principle banning discrimination on the basis of sex. But these developments occurred at different times, at different paces; and with different political backgrounds. And the current status of women is not the same in all developed countries, no matter what the statute book says.

What is or should be a fundamental right has not only changed—and expanded—over time; it is very much still in flux. In the 19th century, there was a budding movement for women's rights; but no sign of a movement for gay rights—this is distinctly contemporary. In the United States, the civil rights movement in the 1950's and 1960's made a powerful impact on society. There was also a contemporary feminist movement. The movements to empower the native peoples, the elderly, and the handicapped, came later in the day. Each of these has equivalents in other countries, too. Some of the more recent developments would have surprised not only Jefferson, but even heroes of liberty like Martin Luther King, Jr. A strong sense of right is hard to limit; and the notion that some rights are "fundamental" shows distinct signs of swallowing up huge areas of "ordinary" law. The right of privacy, for example, has elbowed aside aspects of criminal law and the law of defamation; it has been definitely expansive in the United States, and even more so in Europe.

If one took a poll, or a survey of the public in various countries, and asked for a list of fundamental rights, some items—freedom of speech is a handy example—would be more or less on everybody's list. Others are peculiar to one country, or one group of countries. Some are quite controversial. Millions of people in the United States think the right to own a gun is about as precious a right as exists; they point to the second amendment to the Constitution (on the right of the people to bear arms). The Supreme Court, in a recent decision, has agreed to read this amendment rather expansively.[20] Millions of other people (even in the United States) would disagree; and many or most people in, say, Finland or Great Britain probably think of the American passion for guns as something quite weird and pathological. For Americans, the right to trial by jury is quite precious; yet most of the world's legal systems lack a jury system, and seem able to do justice despite this fact (or even because of it). Most American states allow the death penalty; and Texas seems inordinately fond of it. All members of the European Union have abolished the death penalty. Indeed, getting rid of the death penalty is a requirement of membership. Some countries recognize rights of sexual minorities, and even allow gay people to marry.[21] Other countries do not, and in all countries, large numbers of people consider gay marriage an abomination; large numbers may also disapprove of gay rights in general. The French told Muslim girls they could not wear headscarves in school. This would probably puzzle most Americans. Doesn't this rule interfere with freedom of religion? And anyway what harm can a headscarf do? Who does it bother, after all?

In short, nobody can draw up a definitive list of "basic" or "fundamental" rights. There is too much variability. This does not contract the *idea* of fundamental rights; or even the passion that surrounds the idea. The boundaries will probably always be in dispute. Formally and legally speaking, lists of fundamental rights appear in written constitutions, or charters of basic rights, although, of course, the *popular* view and the formal, legal view of what should be basic are not at all necessarily the same. To put some norm into the constitution does lend it a certain amount of gravitas. Basic human rights are not like ordinary rights, like the right to sue a careless driver who backed into your car. They have a different normative flavor. They are supposed to be inherent and untouchable. This means that they lie in some exalted region, beyond majority rule, and beyond normal politics. But this would be nothing but theory, unless they had special legal status. This is done by putting them in constitutions, or charters of fundamental rights. Only in this way can they be locked up and buttoned down, fenced off out of the reach of Parliaments, kings, presidents, prime ministers and governments generally; or, for that matter, beyond the reach of the general public. Government should be powerless to encroach on these rights, except maybe under extraordinary conditions, like times of war (and perhaps not even then). Moreover, there should be some power that can enforce the rights, and protect them from encroachment. This fact lies behind the tremendous development of constitutions, bills of right, constitutional courts, and judicial review in the period since the second World War. In Germany and many other countries, there is a separate constitutional court. In the United States, the Supreme Court has this duty (the power of judicial review), but the Court has other functions as well.

The special status of basic rights is not just a question of legal or political theory. If the special status of bills of rights and declarations of rights means anything, it must reflect a genuine social norm. It must correspond, in some rough way at least, to what people in modern societies want and aspire to. Or at least the people who count, the people whose voices are heard.

A Bill of Rights, and judicial review, were something of a novelty when the United States was young, in the late 18th century. Every schoolchild in the United States at some point learns about *Marbury v. Madison* (1803).[22] This famous decision, written by Chief Justice John Marshall, first asserted the power of the Supreme Court to strike down a solemn act of Congress. At the time, this decision had its share of critics. But the Supreme Court never backed down. The Court also asserted the (less controversial) power to review *state* statutes, and weigh them against the federal constitution.[23] It seems, then, that the United States has recognized the power of judicial review for more than 200 years. But this statement is, in a way, misleading. The Supreme Court of the United States made very little use of this power for much of the 19th century. The story of judicial review in the United States is, in fact, extremely complicated. In the late 19th century, the Supreme Court did make rather heavy use of judicial review. But the Court did not act to protect minorities, and guarantee their basic rights (unless you consider business corporations minorities). Cases that, for example, struck down race segregation in the schools, or voided laws that discriminated against women or the sexual minorities—these dramatic cases were entirely a product of the second half of the 20th century, the same period when judicial review was spreading like wildfire in Europe and Latin America.

At the present time, judicial review is almost universal in the developed world; certainly, in the democracies, and to a degree, at least formally, in other governments as well. In Germany, at the end of the second World War, the Allies more or less imposed judicial review on the Federal Republic. This was very much the case in Japan, under American occupation.[24] These are two important examples of constitutional force-feeding; but they hardly explain why there is a constitutional court and judicial review in Portugal and South Korea; or why Hungary and Estonia embraced judicial review when the Cold War ended.

The spread of judicial review has, of course, caught the eye of scholars—legal scholars, and very notably, political scientists. There is a rich literature on the constitutional movement and the rise of judicial review. Scholars have spun out various theories to explain this important social development. It is easy to see in the trend a healthy reaction against fascist, Nazi, and Communist dictatorships. Neal Tate links the movement to "the principle that individuals or minorities have rights that can be enforced against the will of... majorities"; and this principle increases the importance of judges "whose institutional location usually makes it easier for them to make rules that favor minorities."[25] Ran Hirschl, however, takes a somewhat more jaundiced view. He has suggested that "judicial empowerment through constitutionalization is best understood as the by-product of a strategic interplay between three groups"—political elites, trying to preserve their power; economic elites, who want to put "certain economic liberties" beyond the reach of majorities; and "judicial elites and national high courts" who want to "enhance their political influence and international reputation."[26] Thus, in South Africa, when apartheid collapsed, the white majority suddenly became terribly interested in protecting minority rights, including property rights.

Hirschl's account seems plausible—as far as it goes. In each country, judicial review has its own special history; and a purely Whiggish history would be extremely naïve. But in one sense, the theory goes too far, and in another sense, in my opinion, not far enough. In many ways, Hirschl's general narrative suits the late 19th century better than it suits the modern world. Constitutional courts today are strikingly vigorous in protecting underdogs—people on the margin, Gypsies, prisoners, aliens, the downtrodden, racial and religious minorities. Economic and political interests of a conventional sort do, no doubt, lie behind *some* aspects of the movement to create a system of judicial review. The attitudes of judges are also important. Judicialization, according to Neal Tate, develops when judges decide that they "should... participate in policy-making," and have the will to do so. Democracy is another prerequisite. As he puts it, it is "hard to imagine a dictator, regardless of...ideological stripe," who would allow judges to upset his plans and his arrangements.[27] So structures are important; and so are the mind-sets of judges. But beyond all this, there are very strong *cultural* and *normative* roots to the human rights movement. Forces from the bottom, as well as from the top. Or, if not from the bottom, at least from outside the halls of government, the corridors of the judiciary, and the boardrooms of giant corporations. A massive social movement lies at the very heart of the constitutional revolution.

The Bill of Rights of the United States is one of the oldest lists of fundamental rights. It is also one of the shortest. It mentions freedom of speech, freedom of religion, freedom of the press. There are provisions designed to guarantee fair criminal trials and police procedures—rules against unreasonable searches and seizures, rules about the right to remain silent, the right to counsel, rules outlawing double jeopardy. The more recent constitutions have longer lists of basic rights. The fundamental law (Grundgesetz) of the Federal Republic of Germany speaks of a right to "free development of personality." It prohibits discrimination on the basis of sex, race, national origin; it adds, too, that no one should be disadvantaged on the basis of a handicap.[28] These rights are much less explicit in—or are absent from—the American Constitution.

The South African Constitution is a strong example of a recent trend in the drafting of constitutions.[29] Chapter II, The Bill of Rights, contains a long list of such rights. It provides, for example, that all people have "the right to have their dignity respected and protected." Peoples' right to privacy includes the right "not to have their person or home searched, or the privacy of their communications infringed." There is also a right to freedom of movement, the right to leave the republic, the right to a passport, the right to choose a trade, occupation, or profession, the right to fair labor practices; a right to "adequate housing" and to health care services, sufficient food and water, and social security. Children have the right to basic nutrition, shelter, and social services, and a right to be protected from neglect or abuse. Basic education is a right; and there is also a right to use the language and live the cultural life of a person's choice. A long cluster of rules buttresses the right to fair trial.

Not all of these rights are absolute and some of them—the so-called social rights, like the right to housing, food, and education—are perhaps not enforceable in any practical sense. There is a tendency, however, to multiply such rights. The Hungarian Constitution (Article 70/B) gives everybody the "right to work"; and the "right to rest and free time for recreation, and regular paid holidays." The Constitution of Chile gives the "right to live in an environment free from contamination." Easier said than done. Still, these constitutions do express very vividly at least the symbolic importance of a great many "fundamental" rights in a modern polity. Some of these modern rights, even though the U.S. Constitution fails to mention them, are none-theless part of the American constitutional system. The Supreme Court has read them into the Constitution, over the course of the years. This is true, for example, of the so-called right of privacy, and the right to travel.

Most Americans are aware of the Supreme Court, and have at least some notion of what it does. Probably in most country the elites are aware of their high courts; and these courts enjoy, in general, a good deal of support, though this support may not go very deep; and it surely varies a good deal from country to country.[30] Support for the institution is not the same as support for what the institutions do. How deep is the support for the rights themselves? It is easy to make exaggerated claims; easy, too, to underestimate the depth of the feelings for human rights.

We will discuss the evidence on both sides later. For now, I simply want to assert that there is strong evidence of a major trend in social and political history, toward more powerful *institutions* and structures of human rights. The spread of constitutions and constitutional courts, the rise of international organizations and international human rights courts, the growth of NGO's like Amnesty International, and Human Rights Watch: all of these *structural* facts suggest an underlying social phenomenon, a genuinely popular, and powerful, human rights movement; and this in turn must rest on a genuinely popular, and powerful, human rights *consciousness*. That all movements, trends, ideo-logies, and social facts are ragged and multiform is important, and undeniable; but in a sense beside the point.

Can we be more explicit about the boundary between an ordinary right—for example, the right to sue somebody for breaking a contract—and most "human rights," like freedom of speech? Perhaps we can. Ordinary rights are usually against a particular person or company—the firm that never delivered a carload of lumber, the man whose car crashed into mine, and so on. But the right of free speech is a right against the government, against other people, and against the whole world, so to speak. Not that this distinction is as clear-cut as one might want. Even ordinary rights have to be enforced through some legal institution. This makes somewhat artificial any distinction between A's right against B, and A's right against everybody, including the govern-ment.[31] Unless you have a legal right (to collect damages for that carload of lumber or the damage to the car), and unless that right is enforceable in court, that is, through a state institution, it can hardly be called a real right. A landlord's right to collect rent is also dependent on the state; the landlord is unable to throw the tenant out without getting a court order. Nor is it quite accurate to say that the landlord has a right only against Joe, his tenant; while the right of free speech is a right that everybody in society has to respect. The landlord's right is, after all, not just a right against Joe. Since the landlord "owns" the property, this means he has a right not only against Joe, but against Mary, Sam, and everybody else in society—they have to respect his ownership rights just as much as Joe does.

But the right of free speech, or the right to vote, unlike ordinary rights, is in theory *unbounded* and unlimited in quantity. It cannot be rationed. It exists in infinite supply. This is what we mean when we say that grown-ups have the right to register and vote in elections. If more people register, then more people vote. The government cannot say: sorry, the register of voters is full. Free speech has the same quality. My right to speak is not supposed to be limited or rationed. If more people want to speak, then more people *can* speak. There is no limit to the amount of free speech; and the right never expires or dies out. Most other rights depend on the supply of courts, judges, and the like; and are time-bound—they can lapse, for example, if one waits too long.

These are remarks about the *subjective* sense of a fundamental right. Objectively, however, things are more complicated. In fact, everything is rationed. There is no free lunch, and there is no unlimited right. This is true even of free speech. Naturally, it is not and cannot be absolute; nobody has the right, to use the old chestnut, to shout fire in a crowded theater. Or to slander other people. Or to market a poison without labeling it as such. But even with regard to plain, ordinary speech, certain facts of life, certain expectations, will always limit the right to express oneself. Suppose millions of people decided to go to Times Square in New York City, and make a speech. Each of them in theory has this right; and ordinarily in practice as well. But if millions tried to do so at the same time, they would quickly discover the limits. They simply won't all fit in Times Square. And the millions of people would create problems of safety and sanitation that the government could and would take steps to resolve.

Of course, we could say that in this situation one right—free speech—conflicts with other rights, or with public safety; hence there has to be some sort of balance. In fact, any time a right is exercised in a way that goes far beyond expectations, it conflicts with some other right, or some powerful norm or fact of law or policy; or some practical barrier. If too many people decide to vote, the polling-places might be swamped, and they might run out of ballots. Human rights are subjectively absolute. Objectively, they hardly can be. Nonetheless, the subjective sense is crucial—a crucial social fact.

In reality, too, claims of right are often in conflict; and, more often, *lead* to social conflict. When many more people than expected assert a claim, the system becomes overloaded. That much is obvious. If a society moves toward gender equality, more women will get jobs as doctors, lawyers, and business executives. This means fewer jobs of these kinds for men, unless the market expands greatly, which does not normally happen. This is one reason why "affirmative action" is, to many people, unpopular. No doubt many people who, in the abstract, approve of rights for minorities and women, find it uncomfortable to lose their own privileges. "Basic" rights can sometimes collide with each other. If we give indigenous groups more power, more authority to run their own affairs, more scope for their traditions, these traditions, we might discover, are in conflict with the rights of women or outsiders. We will deal with this particular problem in a later chapter. In general, tension between the *theory* of rights, and facts on the ground, seems unavoidable.

What are the social origins of the human rights movement—and of the concept of human rights in general? This, of course, is an enormously complex question; and surely there is no single answer. The human rights movement is firmly lodged in modern legal, social, and political culture. It might not be possible to give a full, complete, and satisfying account of why modern society, modern culture, and modern personality structures lead to a flowering of human rights. Later on, I will try to explore in somewhat more detail the social facts that lie at the base of the modern movement. For now, I want to mention only a few main points. The first is that the human rights movement depends on a culture that is strongly individualistic.

Law and society emphasize *individual* rights; and this corresponds with the way people feel about themselves—as unique individuals, with unique lives, destinies, strengths and weaknesses, desires and habits. Any account of modern culture, moreover—of the culture in which the human rights movement, and individualism, flourish—must pay attention to certain leading aspects of modern history. These include the industrial revolution, the rise of capitalism, and that other revolution, the scientific and technological revolution. One must mention also the growth of affluence in the developed world; and the role of *leisure*, which makes it possible for ordinary people to pursue their individual wants, tastes, and dreams.

A further point: I lay enormous stress on modern individualism. The basic human rights are all *individual* rights. Of course, they only exist in a social context. But they are nonetheless individual rights. There is a lot of loose talk about group rights. The claims of women, minorities, and ethnic groups certainly *look* like claims that depend on group membership: rights asserted on behalf of everybody who is black or Muslim or deaf or gay or a member of the Hopi people or the Maoris of New Zealand. There is much discussion and debate about the rights of cultural, ethnic, and linguistic minorities; and these too seem like group rights. There is a large literature on group rights, including notable attempts to bring some conceptual clarity to the issue.[32]

But the whole idea of group rights strikes me as, in part at least, misleading. Human rights are almost always profoundly *individual*. The right of a woman to be a police officer (or not), or to receive pay equal to a man's pay, is an individual right. The essence of human rights is their individual quality; but this individual quality often *depends* on empowering groups, that is, it depends on removing barriers and prejudices against groups. Removing these barriers allows the individual members to exercise choice. But the need to remove group disabilities is what gives the illusion of "group rights." To say this, is not to deny that sometimes the *solution* to a problem of discrimination has to be a group solution. There are powerful reasons to think that this is the case. "Affirmative action," which is so controversial in the United States, can be justified as a group solution to problems that bedevil, and hinder, the progress of many individuals.[33]

A similar point can be made about ethnic and religious minorities. As Rory O'Connell has pointed out, human rights law "speaks of the rights of *persons belonging to minorities*" and not about the rights of minorities themselves, which may indicate that "only human individuals should be rights holders."[34] This seems correct to me. Empowering a minority is, again, a group solution to individual problems. The right to have Basque taught in elementary schools, or to worship a particular faith, is an individual right that can be made real only through giving rights to people in a certain category, and who wish to exercise specific rights.[35]

"Individualism" is a difficult word, easily misunderstood. It is easy to equate it with neo-liberalism, that is, a leaning toward libertarianism and the laissez-faire state. Libertarians think the state has no business interfering with individuals, telling them what to do, beyond what is absolutely basic (libertarians are not against burglary laws). Laissez-faire people, or free-marketeers, think the government should regulate the economy as little as possible. How little regulation that implies is, of course, a matter of controversy.

This brand of individualism is controversial, and can easily seem selfish and callous. It flies in the face of the way we would like human beings to behave. It seems to fit poorly with the dominant ethos of many cultures, past and present. Does it fit the ethos of the human rights movement? "Individualism" of this type seems to assume a narrow, warped view of human nature—a "me first" conception of our species. It is the attitude that makes conservative economists seem like such misanthropes. "Communitarianism" would be more to the taste of thinking and feeling people, at least as an ideal.

What we are discussing here, however, is individualism not as a theory or a philosophical position, or even as an ideology. Mostly what we mean is individualism as a way of describing some aspects of today's world—describing how people feel, and to a degree how they behave. It is a social fact that family, clan, and group ties seem to have weakened. It is a social fact that more of modern life is organized around the idea of free choice; and that this is what people want and expect. I have already entered some caveats. Nonetheless, individualism, whatever its limitations as reality and ideal, is a true social norm of our times, meaning that in important ways it reflects ideas and values that millions of people hold. I will expand on this point in the concluding chapter.

One trait of the human rights movement, which flows logically from aspects of the movement we have already mentioned, is that it has an international character. If people feel, and believe, that some basic rights are inherent and inalienable, and if these rights apply to everybody everywhere, and to everyone the same, then it follows that no government should be able to impair these rights, and no statute, law, or decree can violate them legitimately. A government that tortures its citizens, or denies freedom of speech, cannot claim legitimacy for its actions. And national sovereignty ought to be no defense. At the famous Nuremberg trials, just after the second World War, the victorious allies put the Nazi leaders on trial; they were accused of waging aggressive war, and committing "crimes against humanity." This was an important step toward making human rights international. Such texts as the UN declaration of human rights, and various regional treaties, have also assumed and spread this revolutionary idea: human rights transcend national borders.

Human rights in general are primarily rights against a citizen's own government. This is only natural. But the very theory of human rights makes them global, or universal. Law and practice are moving in this direction. In more recent years, this trend has become if anything more salient. The fate of General Pinochet, former dictator of Chile, is a particularly striking example. Pinochet was arrested while visiting England; a Spanish judge had demanded his arrest and prosecution. We will discuss the international aspects of this case in chapter 10. It is enough here to mention that there are now international tribunals, and indeed a new International Criminal Court. The international courts assert the right to try and punish men and women who were guilty of atrocities in their own countries—atrocities which, technically, may not have been against the law. It was no defense at Nuremberg that genocide was not illegal in Hitler's Germany; indeed, it was state policy to kill the Jews, Gypsies, and the mentally ill.

This introductory chapter has contained some rough general notes—notes toward a sociology of human rights. I stressed a number of factors—individualism, capitalism, modern affluence, leisure, and the like—factors which are, obviously, common to all the developed countries. They are not specific to the West. Freedom of speech is not out of place in Japan or Thailand or South Korea. The human rights movement is global; and it is both a cause and effect of a powerful trend toward *convergence* of legal culture, all over the world, though most obviously in the democratic, developed world.

This claim about convergence may seem a bit strange or paradoxical, in view of the almost frantic emphasis on diversity, roots, cultural differences, cultural rights, rights of indigenous people and ethnic minorities, and so on, that is so obvious in modern politics. "Assimilation" has become a dirty word. Some would almost equate it with cultural genocide. Multiculturalism, on the other hand, is in. Many countries—Canada is a good example—are *officially* multicultural. Yet there is good reason to be skeptical about cultural "diversity" in developed societies. As Boli and Elliott suggest, "much of the worldwide celebration and promotion of diversity is the construction of façades that obscure underlying similarity and homogeneity."[36] My view is that Boli and Elliott are exactly right.

I will return to this theme, too, in chapter 9. For now, I say only that the human rights movement is a kind of exhibit A for the general thesis of convergence. It claims to be universal. It claims to trump particular cultural claims. Of course, this aspect of the human rights movement is sharply contested. Human rights doctrine insists on equality of men and women. Reality is far different; and this "equality" flies in the faces of many cultural traditions, which insist on radically different roles for men and women. This usually means male dominance. This conflict—between the human rights ethos, and claims of cultural sovereignty—is not easy to resolve. As a practical matter, Saudi Arabia can do as it likes in its own country; it can keep women from driving cars and holding down male jobs. But what happens when people from traditional societies move to Italy or Spain? What happens when their cultures collide with the culture enshrined in the local constitution? In some regards, this is one of the thornier issues confronting the human rights movement. In chapter 9, this subject will be dealt with in more detail.

2

On the Rule of Law; and on Consciousness of Rights

There is an obvious, and close, connection between the human rights movement and democracy; and also to what is usually called the rule of law. There is a huge literature on this vague and troubled phrase. There is no general agreement on how to define the rule of law. The term itself is, roughly, the equivalent in English of what is called the Rechtsstaat, in German-speaking countries, or the estado del derecho, in Spanish-speaking countries, to mention only two versions of the phrase.

All of these have slightly different nuances, to be sure. But with regard to all of them there do seem to be two rather distinct basic meanings (or sets of meanings). Perhaps the most fundamental idea is the idea of a body of rules, or laws, which limit the power of the state, the government, the administration.[37] Legal rules are or ought to be very general; are or ought to be applied equally and impartially, and are or ought to be knowable in advance. When we say a country lacks the rule of law, or is deficient in this regard, we are often referring to problems in the legal and political systems. In some countries, the judges are corrupt and incompetent. Or they may be creatures of the regime, without true independence. They might take bribes. Government decisions might be arbitrary, even whimsical. Nobody can be sure what the real rules are, or whether the bureaucracy will abide by the rules. There may be one law for the rich and another for the poor; or a law for one ethnic group and a different (and lesser) law for other ethnic groups. A government of this type is definitely not a "government of laws and not of men."

Corrupt and arbitrary law is bad for business; and particularly bad for potential foreign investors. Businesses and investors like to know where they stand, they like to confront clear rules, and to feel that they can get an honest, unprejudiced decision in courts and within the civil service. In particular, they like to feel that they can enforce their contracts; and that there is security for their property rights. A large body of scholarship, chiefly by economists and political scientists, has tried (with variable success) to connect the rule of law with economic growth or development.[38] It seems plain common sense that corrupt and inefficient societies are less likely to develop economically, compared to societies that enjoy the "rule of law." And, in general, the richer the society, the less arbitrary and corrupt its government and its legal system. This hypothesis seems intuitively correct, though the evidence is much shakier than one might think. It is particularly shaky if one equates the rule of law with Max Weber's concept of formal rationality: a fairly rigid, fixed, mechanistic, and predictable body of rules. Indeed, Frank Upham has argued that the economic success of the Asian tigers may be due to a *lack* of formality; these economies demonstrate "that the strict judicial enforcement of property and contract rights is not necessary to economic growth."[39]

In any event, in many countries, there are flaws and gaps in the legal system, and life falls far short of the ideal-typical Rechtsstaat; and yet, in some of these countries, businesses are extremely adept at finding ways to cope. This may include their own techniques of bribing and corrupting. Legal systems, like societies, are extremely complex; and the informal economy, with all its tricks and its leeways, plays an important role in quite a few countries.

But it is official doctrine, in organizations like the World Bank, that countries must have "the rule of law" if they are ever going to make progress. These organizations put money into schemes and proposals for fixing defects in the rule of law. Almost everybody is in favor of the rule of law, under one definition or another. Even countries like China talk incessantly about strengthening the rule of law. What they have in mind, most likely, is improving the legal climate for foreign investors, and perhaps for local businesses as well. It is possible for quite authoritarian societies to enjoy the "rule of law" in this sense. Modern Singapore is perhaps a good example. Singapore is hardly a model democracy (there are, and have been, a lot worse societies, to be sure), but there is apparently not much corruption; and the climate in Singapore is exceedingly friendly to business. The courts, moreover, do an honest job; and the legal system tends to live up to expectations. And Singapore is a very rich, very successful society. One might add Hong Kong to this list; and perhaps even (in some regards) China itself.

Yet people often talk about the "rule of law" in quite a different sense—not the Singapore sense at all. They mean a society that respects fundamental rights. There is no rule of law in a society where police knock on the door at night and drag people off to prison; or where people "disappear" without a trace; or where it is risky to criticize the government. The "rule of law" can also mean that fundamental rights are rigorously enforced. The two senses of the phrase are quite distinct; but they do have one thing in common: the rule of law is lacking, if the legal system operates in an arbitrary way; and there are few reliable rules to guide conduct. And it is hard to see how you can have security of property rights, if there is no personal security. At least in this sense, the rule of law has to imply more than rights to contracts and property.

Clarity and predictability imply a "strong formal legal system, underwritten by a set of political checks on state power and corruption."[40] But scholars who study law and society, and probably many other people as well, know enough to be skeptical. The living law is always full of ifs and buts; it is always, to a degree, unpredictable. It changes in subtle or not so subtle ways from day to day. The law on paper is never the same as the law in action. Between the ideal and the real there are enormous gaps. Even the most formal and Teutonic of legal systems has important gray areas. In any system, even fields of law and subfields that seem clean, clearly marked in black and white, can suddenly change to a mottled gray, as the times change, and new understandings arise.

Predictability is thus a matter of more or less. But it is important not to exaggerate the indeterminacy of the legal system. Rules *do* give more predictability in Singapore—or Finland—than they do in mainland China, or in contemporary Russia, or in the many countries which are, alas, run by satraps and despots, rife with bribery and cronyism; or in failed states without a real, functioning government and no civil service to speak of.

"Political checks on state power" are also vital. An economic argument can be made—and has been made—for constitutional checks on lawmakers; devices to keep them from running wild and overturning settled arrangements.[41] This may have played a role in the tremendous growth of judicial review in the last two generations. It is not necessarily a progressive development. Ran Hirschl, as we have seen, is a skeptic; and he has put the case strongly—constitutions and rights of judicial review are important for elites, and for the status quo.[42] One of his examples is South Africa, where, he argues, the break-up of apartheid frightened the rich white minority, and led them to demand constitutional protection. Makau Mutua has made a similar point: the "democratic...rights-based state has ironically turned out to be an instrument for the preservation of the privileges and the ill-gotten gains of the white minority."[43] There is, no doubt, something to these arguments. But I think much more is at stake than the protection of the status quo. The thesis hardly fits such converts to judicial review as Spain or Hungary. And many of the new constitutional courts have done exciting work, not about property rights or contracts or business law in general, but about human rights, and the rights of minorities—about the "rule of law" in the second sense, rather than the first. The movement to buttress human rights through constitutional structures has been the product of a social movement as well as a political and economic movement. Perhaps the social movement deserves priority.

World organizations have spent a lot of money, trying to bring the rule of law to countries that do not seem to have it. Some think the money has been largely wasted. Others object to the whole notion, on the grounds that standard concepts of the rule of law are incurably Western, unsuitable for third world countries. Imposing the so-called rule of law on these countries, then, is a form of neo-imperialism. We will look at this claim in a later chapter. A more cogent objection is that you cannot really export the rule of law; and you certainly cannot transport it as if it were some sort of cargo, or by flying in a gaggle of so-called experts who draft nicely worded documents. Putting conditions on IMF loans or the like is also probably ineffective. An impoverished country, with low rates of literacy, ruled by warlords, is not going to turn into some sort of version of Switzerland through any tactics or techniques known to humanity at this stage of the game.

"Constitutional design" is another area in which Ran Hirschl has expressed a healthy skepticism.[44] Constitutions, bills of rights, provisions for judicial review, along with other aspects of "constitutional design," are in themselves nothing more than words, pieces of paper, texts, and aspirations. And traditional "constitutional engineering" seems incapable of addressing the "core challenges" of the 21st century—like global warming—because these are "global in nature and require large-scale collective action and global collaboration."[45] Under some conditions, to be sure, good design does make at least *some* difference. The victorious powers imposed constitutional design on West Germany and Japan, at the end of the second World War. Many people doubted that this kind of legal vaccination against autocracy would make a difference. Both of these countries surely count as success stories—both are vibrant, effective democracies. But of course many factors entered into this development.

Hirschl's point is most valid on the issue of *design*. That there is a human rights movement, that it has widespread *popular* support, and perhaps even wider *elite* support, is another matter altogether. There are effective and efficient constitutional *systems* in the world; they do not depend, for the most part, on the exact wording of their constitutions, or whether there is a virile system of judicial review. Judicial review surely helps. But ultimately, these constitutional systems depend on their publics, their norms and habits, their beliefs, their trust in their institutions; in short, on civil society.

RIGHTS CONSCIOUSNESS

I have been describing what I consider to be a major trend in recent history. Major, and in some ways overwhelming. Old people can remember a time in which most of the world was under dictatorial rule. Most of Africa was ruled by British, French, or Portuguese empires. In the 1930's, Germany, Italy, and Spain were fascist dictatorships or worse. Joseph Stalin held Russia in his paranoid and murderous grip. Japan was a military dictatorship. Whatever China was, it was not a thriving democracy. There were few if any democracies in Asia, or even in Latin America. It is within living memory that most of Europe became solidly and (we hope) permanently democratic. It is even more recent that Chile, Argentina, and Uruguay returned to the democratic fold. Democracy is a recent growth in South Korea and Taiwan. Democracy in Hungary, Estonia, or the Czech Republic had to wait until the Soviet Union collapsed. Quite a few other countries seem to making progress—sometimes quite slowly—in the direction of democracy. South Africa is solidly democratic; and so are a few other African countries.

It is tempting to think that democracy and human rights will inevitably become universal. But what has happened so far is the product of concrete historical conditions and situations—economic, political, social, even technological. Situations and social forces can and do change all the time, sometimes quite rapidly. It is foolish to make predictions about the future. In a London barbershop, a middle-aged, intelligent woman from Bulgaria, as she cut my hair, lamented the fall of the Communist regime. She was no Marxist; and she seemed to lack any real ideology. She just mourned the Bulgaria she once knew—a Bulgaria which (she said) guaranteed her a job and health care of a sort; where the crime rate was low, and people were friendly to each other. Of course, she was painting Communist Bulgaria in rosy colors; and looking at the Bulgaria of today with a jaundiced eye. Perhaps her views are not at all typical. But people change their minds and their opinions. Life is in constant motion. There is no such thing as the end of history. There is no final resting-place for societies. All we know about the future is that we know very little about it. New forms of government, new forms of society will un-doubtedly emerge—at some point. They may be radically different from what we know today. I will return to this subject in the concluding chapter.

Legal culture—one of the main themes of this book—can be defined as people's ideas, attitudes, opinions, and expectations about law and legal structures.[46] Specifically, this book is about contemporary legal culture—the culture of our times. But this will not be the culture of times to come. A whirlwind of technological change shaped many aspects of our world. We are at the threshold of new times—humanity is always at a threshold—and what will come to be in 50 or 100 years is as unpredictable as the computer revolu-tion a hundred years ago. Science fiction imagined individual flying machines (we are still waiting) and visits from distant planets and the like; but even the most daring did not dream about powers of instant communication any child with a laptop has at his fingertips. The age of human rights can end as rapidly as it began. I hope not; but one cannot be sure.

Already, not everybody accepts the premises of the human rights move-ment. A lot depends on the particular society. "Individualism" of the kind stressed here is a matter of more or less. And it too varies culturally. A study in Germany, of native-born Germans, and of Turkish Kurds and Lebanese, showed that the native-born Germans ranked higher on a scale of indiv-idualism than the others—which is not surprising.[47] One would guess that the Germans themselves would rank lower on such a scale than, say, Americans; but it is hard to be sure. A recent survey asked people whether they agreed with the statement that "success in life" is "determined by forces outside our control." 60% of the Americans disagreed, and 59% of the Canadians; but these countries were definitely outliers. 47% of the British, 69% of the Ger-mans, and 79% of the people of India *agreed* with the statement.[48] "Indiv-idualism" and this sense of powerlessness can certainly coexist; but somewhat uneasily.

And when we speak about a culture of human rights, it is certainly legitimate to ask, how deeply has such a culture penetrated into society. Survey research gives some answers; it suggests that the human rights culture is at present quite strong. A study of Turkish university students, for example, found a high level of support for basic human rights.[49] The questions were pretty abstract; and a cynic might argue that Turkish students were giving answers they knew were expected of them. But even this would be of some significance. And other surveys have suggested similar findings. Should governments "make an effort to prevent discrimination against women?" 96% in Mexico said yes; 93% in Indonesia—higher than the 82% in the United States, and the 88% in France.[50] On the right to practice "any religion," there was more of a split between non-Muslim countries and the more conservative Muslim ones: 76% yes in Mexico, 67% yes in the United States, 59% yes in Great Britain, but only 31% in Egypt.[51]

Whether people know much about how the system works, about what institutions exist to enforce human rights, and how they operate or should operate in practice, is another question. In 1995, Gibson and Caldeira published a study of attitudes in Europe toward the European Court of Justice. Only a few people (4.5%) claimed to be "very aware" of the Court. In Portugal, Spain, and Italy, almost half of the sample actually had never heard of the Court before they were interviewed.[52] Conceivably, this is less true today. The European Court of Human Rights probably gets more publicity, and perhaps a greater degree of awareness; but surely most Europeans would have trouble explaining the difference between the two courts. Yet both of these courts are busy and active; and have no trouble filling their dockets; on the contrary, their work overload is one of their biggest problems. The tribunals at work with regard to Yugoslavia, Rwanda, and Cambodia, and the new International Criminal Court might conceivably be better known, too—undoubtedly so in the affected countries.

No doubt most people know what freedom of speech means, more or less; and they understand the freedom to travel (especially when a regime tries to restrict it); and they are aware of freedom of religion, and it is not hard for them to grasp some sort of anti-discrimination principle. Social learning is an important factor in the process. People hear about "rights," in school, in the press, and from their peers. Some people act on these rights. It is probably true that a small class of people, an elite class of people most likely, within a given community, is likely to be more rights-conscious than the rest; and is the most willing and able to do something to enforce or realize their basic rights. The same is probably true of the less basic rights; or of the less basic interpretations of basic rights. This small class of people includes activists whose cases swell the dockets of the various constitutional courts, and also the dockets of the transnational courts; or more likely, the NGO's that represent these people. But even if this group is small, it is surely larger than it was in the past; and this is a significant fact in its own right.

3
A Small Dose of History

As we pointed out, ideas of fundamental rights, and the particular rights that are so defined, vary over time, and from culture to culture. The human rights movement has had a complex history. Has it been a long history? In one sense, very long; but I will argue that from about the late 1940's on, this history took a new and dramatic turn. Of course, it is always possible to trace almost anything to the ancient Greeks; or, if this is too much of a leap, then to the intellectuals who created the field of international law during the Renaissance, men like Hugo Grotius. In Asia, it is also always possible to trace everything to Confucius or Buddha. As the book of Ecclesiastes put it, there is nothing new under the sun. And surely this is true—in a way. But in a more important sense, it is profoundly wrong. Almost every day there is something entirely and uniquely new, under the sun, the moon, the stars, and on the face of the planet.

I will forego Grotius then, along with Magna Charta and other alleged milestones in the history of human rights. It is somewhat harder to ignore the landmarks of the more recent past, thinkers like Kant or John Locke; and particularly events and writings of the late 18th century, the period of the French and American revolutions.[53] One landmark in the history of human rights, undoubtedly, was the "Declaration of the Rights of Man and the Citizen," of August 1789, issued in revolutionary France. The preamble talks about "natural, inalienable, and sacred rights." The rights themselves are set out in the form of 17 brief articles. The first of these declares that "Men are born free and remain free and equal in rights." Law, according to Article 6, is "the expression of the general will... It must be the same for all, whether it protects or punishes." Everyone is "presumed innocent until he has been pronounced guilty" (Article 9). Under Article 10, no one is to be disturbed "on account of his opinions, even religious," unless they "upset... public order"; and by Article 11, it is declared that "every citizen can...freely speak, write, and print," though subject to "responsibility for...abuse of this freedom." Property (Article 17) was declared to be a "sacred" and "inviolable right." If taken for public use, there must be "a just...indemnity."

The American Revolution had its own founding document, the Declaration of Independence, some years before the French Revolution. The Declaration, of July 4, 1776, began by declaring some "truths to be self-evident." All men "are created equal," and "endowed by their Creator with certain unalienable rights, that among these are Life, Liberty, and the pursuit of Happiness." But of course this could not have been meant literally. Women did not vote or hold political office; and nobody intended otherwise.

Moreover, there were African slaves in every one of the colonies. Nor, for that matter, did women vote in France, despite the sonorous language of the Declaration of the Rights of Man.

Still, these Declarations were important cultural milestones. Some scholars argue that events of the 19th century—independence movements in Latin America, the revolution in Haiti, the struggles of workers against their bosses—are directly relevant to the growth of a human rights movement.[54] One might also point to the campaign against slavery and the slave trade. Interestingly, this was an *international* campaign—a campaign that crossed borders; and that involved people in, say, England, who tried to force the hand of other countries which were still trafficking in human flesh. Indeed, in the 19th century, the British entered into treaties with a number of other countries, calling for the creation of international courts to deal with issues arising out of the ban on the slave trade.[55] These courts came into existence, and functioned in a number of places: Freetown, Sierra Leone; Havana, Rio de Janeiro, and Suriname. These were active courts. At Sierra Leone, no less than 484 ships were condemned for carrying slaves.[56] The literature has strangely and unduly neglected these courts; they can, in fact, be considered important precursors of modern international tribunals. And, as Professor Jenny Martinez has pointed out, they change the "narrative" of the history of international human rights law. This is because, unlike Nuremberg and the other international tribunals, the story of these courts is one that "places a much greater emphasis on nonstate actors," that is, the slave traders on the one hand, and the "civil society leaders of the abolitionist movements" on the other.[57]

The campaign against the slave trade—and the abolitionist movement in the United States—are indeed significant. But they have to be understood in context. Wiktor Osiatynski has argued that the campaign against the slave trade was based on "humanitarianism," rather than any idea of universal freedom and rights.[58] Culturally, then, according to his view, the ethos that lay behind the anti-slavery movement, in general, was vastly different from the ethos of the modern human rights movement. It was more like campaigns against child labor, or sweat shops—based on pity for human suffering, and rich empathy, rather than an ideology of equal rights for all. This may be a bit of an exaggeration. The campaign against slavery perhaps did rest on two pillars: humanitarian sympathy; but also a sense that slavery violated the basic rights of the slave. Nonetheless, those who passionately opposed the slave trade, and thought that slavery violated some sort of natural law, did not necessarily feel that (black) slaves were or ought to be socially and legally equal to whites.

In the United States and England, in the 19th century, the "rights of man" were clearly understood to include freedom of speech, and freedom of religion. But what these phrases *meant* was quite different from what they mean today. A Catholic could not sit in Parliament, in England, until 1829. Many European countries had established churches and state religions.

Freedom of speech did not extend to "sedition," or to anything felt to be obscene. Rules against blasphemy were only slowly given up. Still, the 19th century did not burn heretics at the stake. As for freedom of speech, it meant primarily freedom to argue about politics; freedom to criticize the government, for example (though within limits). In the United States, state constitutions supposedly protected freedom of speech; but this did not prevent slave states from passing laws banning abolitionist propaganda. The southern states felt they had a right—a duty, perhaps—to prevent any literature that might foment rebellion among slaves, or threaten the institution of slavery.

Governments also believed they had the right and the duty to outlaw pornography, and keep obscene books and pictures off the market. The Comstock Act of the 1870's made it a crime to send pornography through the mail in the United States; and any information about birth control or abortion was also taboo.[59] The great Oxford Dictionary, scientific to the core, simply could not bring itself to include two very common four-letter words. Every English speaking man and no doubt most women knew these words; but they were banned from the august pages of the dictionary. (The second edition restored these words to their proper place.) Movies were censored in the early 20th century, in many American cities; and in other countries as well, for example, in Germany. The British stage was subject to vigorous censorship; and important literary works—Bernard Shaw's play, "Mrs. Warren's Profession," for one—could not be shown in public. In all this censorship, there was a strong streak of class-consciousness: fear that dirty literature could and would corrupt the masses. There are still traces of such an attitude in Europe. But it disappeared almost totally in the United States (and largely so elsewhere).[60] Society today is much more permissive; and forms of expression (about sex, for example) that were forbidden in the past are now under the sheltering wing of the concept of freedom of speech. "Freedom of speech" now covers a lot more ground than simply getting rid of taboos against such serious literary works as *Lady Chatterley's Lover* or Joyce's *Ulysses*. If Jefferson or John Locke or John Milton would be shocked by Joyce and D. H. Lawrence; these men in turn might be shocked to see what is allowed in print, or shown in the movies in the 21st century. There is a sharp cleavage between classic definitions of freedom of speech and the working definition today. This vast increase in tolerance for sexual material is not accidental. It is part of more basic changes in society—the move to expressive individualism, for example, and personal freedom of choice.

Religious freedom has also undergone its own dramatic evolution. In the 19th century, there was religious freedom in England and the United States; and nobody could be punished for failure to join established or mainstream churches; or any church at all. All known and popular religions were tolerated. Tolerated, of course, is not the same as accepted. Citizens of the United States had full freedom of religion; and minority religions had the right to exist, to build houses of worship, and to thrive. There were limits, to be sure—Mormon polygamy was too much for the majority to swallow. Yet despite American tolerance toward religions—enshrined in constitutions—one cannot imagine a 19th century President sending greetings to his fellow-citizens on the occasion of Jewish, Buddhist, or Moslem holidays. The Protestant Bible was read in many public schools. The Catholics established their own private school system, partly because they found the public schools too Protestant for their taste. In chapter 4, I return to the subject of contemporary religion.

The state was quite anxious to protect property rights in the 19th century.[61] Until later in the century, only property owners could vote in some of the American states. Property rights were felt to be the very core of a free society. The Supreme Court, in the late 19th century and into the next century, sometimes read the Constitution as if, in some sense, it was a charter of laissez-faire capitalism, as if its main purpose was to protect corporations and the rights of private property. The high-water mark in many ways was the notorious *Lochner* case (1905).[62] A New York state statute regulated sanitary conditions in bakeries and, among other things, set a limit on the number of hours bakers could work. The Supreme Court struck down the statute, as a violation of the federal constitution. Some state courts went even further in voiding social legislation.

To be sure, the legal situation was quite complicated. Laissez-faire was never absolute. Most social legislation escaped the fate of the law in *Lochner*. Still, in an important sense property was king in the 19th century.[63] Though never without rebellious subjects. The late 19th century was a turbulent period in Europe and North America, a period of labor strife, strikes, boycotts, and court struggles over the rights of labor. Generally, in the Western world, the Industrial Revolution unsettled time-honored social arrangements. Masses of landless workers moved from the countryside, to work long hours in factories and mines. Their jobs and their lives were precarious. Capital and labor were at each others' throats. In countries like England and the United States, adult men all had or had gained the vote, rich and poor alike, but this did not mean that the state bent to the will of the working class majority. Not immediately, at any rate. Political and social gains were a long time coming. And the welfare state, the triumph of social democracy, is largely the product of the 20th century.

By the end of the 20th century, to be sure, every rich developed country had its own form or dialect of the welfare state. Some aspects of the welfare state are so old, and so ingrained, that people do not usually think of them in terms of the welfare state: free public education, very notably. Others are more variable (health care, for example). There were (and are) big differences between, say, the welfare systems of Sweden and Japan, or between France and the United States. But old age pensions, unemployment insurance, and some kind of support for the poor and the disabled exist more or less in every country, though in somewhat different forms. Everybody has access to free medical care in Great Britain and in Canada, and in certain European countries; in the United States, medical care is provided by the state mainly for the elderly (people over 65) and for the indigent; and attempts to institute a program of national or universal health insurance have so far failed; the latest attempt—President Obama's health care plan, bitterly opposed by the Republican party—hangs in the balance at the time of this writing. The United States, in general, is rather less of a welfare state than the European democracies; though it too has come a long way since the 19th century.

In general, everywhere *political* rights came first, and to a degree, freedom of religion; and a loosening of the reins that governed the market. Much later were personality rights (privacy); and also later (and in some sense not yet) the so-called social rights—housing, health care, the right to a job. Of course, state-sponsored housing, health care, and employment are not rarities. But aside from education, and the dole, only recently, and in a very limited sense, have the social rights become, or tended to become, "human rights" in the constitutional sense, as we will see.

20TH CENTURY: THE FUNDAMENTAL TEXTS

In the 20th century, at the end of the first World War, a League of Nations was formed—without the participation of the United States, to be sure. The Charter of this organization dealt mainly with war and peace. Article 22, however, concerned the colonies that had been stripped from the war's losers, notably Germany and the Ottoman Empire.[64] People in these colonies were, supposedly, "not yet able to stand by themselves under the strenuous conditions of the modern world." Consequently, instead of independence, these colonies were handed over to various "advanced nations" under a League of Nations "mandate." The Mandatory powers were instructed to guarantee "freedom of conscience and religion, subject only to the maintenance of public order and morals," even with regard to colonies in central Africa, which were considered less advanced than some of the others.[65]

The League of Nations was a failure. Probably no organization, with or without the United States, could have been a success at that time. The League did not and could not prevent the rise of fascism in Italy. It could not keep Francisco Franco from coming to power in Spain, or, most important of all, block Adolf Hitler from taking control of Germany and launching a second World War in 1939—a war which was unusually bloody, savage, protracted, and disastrous. In 1941, President Franklin Delano Roosevelt, and the British Prime Minister, Winston Churchill, met and agreed on a set of principles; this has come to be known as the Atlantic Charter. Very notably, one of these principles was a commitment to peace, and an "assurance that all the men in all the lands may live out their lives in freedom from fear and want."[66]

Roosevelt dreamt of a new international body, the United Nations, to replace the dead League of Nations, and to succeed where the league had failed. The "big three" (United States, Great Britain, and the Soviet Union), meeting at Yalta, in February, 1945, as the war was winding down, agreed to create this organization. On June 26, 1945, 51 nations signed the United Nations charter in San Francisco. Since that time, the membership has grown dramatically; it now stands at 192. The United Nations Charter is mainly concerned with the structure of the organization; and the first and most prominent function of the UN was to "maintain international peace and security" (Chapter 1, Article 1, section 1). But the Charter also asserts, as one purpose (section 3 of the same Article) "promoting and encouraging respect for human rights and for fundamental freedoms for all, without distinction as to race, sex, language, or religion."

The United Nations Charter, despite this phrase, had little more to say about human rights. In 1948, however, the UN turned its attention to this subject, and promulgated a Universal Declaration of Human Rights.[67] In many ways, this was a remarkable document—ahead of its time, and quite forward-looking. The drafting process was long and painful—the Cold War had begun, and international tensions ran high. In the end, the Declaration was endorsed by almost all of the members (the Soviet Union, some of its satellites, and Saudi Arabia abstained). The preamble of the Declaration began by stating that "recognition of the inherent dignity and inalienable rights of all members of the human family is the foundation of freedom, justice, and peace in the world." According to the first article, "all human beings" are "born free and equal in dignity and rights." The second article provided that all people were "entitled to all the rights and freedoms" in the Declaration, regardless of "race, colour, sex, language, religion, political or other opinion, national or social origin, property, birth or other status." The Declaration also outlawed torture and slavery, expressed its opposition to "arbitrary arrest, detention, or exile," and contained a number of provisions designed to guarantee fair trials; in general (Article 7), everyone was to be "equal before the law and...entitled...to equal protection of the law." The Declaration listed many other rights—freedom of movement, the right to marry and have a family (but marriage "shall be entered into only with the free and full consent of the intending spouses"), the right to own property, the right to freedom of expression. The Declaration also included some of the so-called social rights, notably the right to an "adequate" standard of living, including "food, clothing, housing and medical care and necessary social services" (Article 25). Everyone had a "right to education," which "should be free, at least in the elementary and funda-mental stages" (Article 26). And education, according to the same article, was to be "directed to the full development of the human personality."[68] The UDHR, in short, balanced political and civil rights, with the so-called "social rights."

The Declaration was a remarkable document. But it was bold and remarkable, in part, because nobody was required to take it seriously. There was (and is) no real enforcement mechanism. Plans for an actual treaty to provide such a mechanism, and for some court or some agency which could deal with violations, never came to fruition—at least not at that time. As Paul Lauren has put it, any attempt to insert verbs of action, like "protect" or "guarantee" or "implement" or "ensure" human rights, "died an unceremonious death in committee."[69] The Soviets, of course, had no interest in enforcement; but neither did the United States.[70] In the end, there was only the Declaration: a statement of ideals.

But the ideals were not unimportant; and the text is revealing. The Declaration expressed what we have described as the fundamental premise of the human rights movement: equality of every last human soul. It spoke the language of expressive individualism. The "full development of the human personality" is not something which, centuries ago, would have struck someone in Europe, or Asia, or Africa, or anywhere, as a primary goal for human beings. The Declaration presented, in Mary Ann Glendon's words, a "vision of freedom as linked to social security...grounded in respect for equal human dignity, and guarded by the rule of law." It affirmed that its "rights belong to everyone," and thus it "aimed to put an end to the idea that a nation's treatment of its own citizens or subjects was immune from outside scrutiny."[71]

This Declaration was followed up by two more important international documents, both promulgated by the United Nations in 1976, after long delays and complex maneuvering. One was an "International Covenant on Economic, Social, and Cultural Rights." It too in its preamble spoke of the "inherent dignity of the human person," and the "equal and inalienable rights of all members of the human family." This "covenant," as the name suggests, included the so-called "social rights." Everyone should have the right to work, and to enjoy "social security, including social insurance." The Covenant called the family the "natural and fundamental group unit of society." Marriages should be consensual. Working mothers should get paid leave. There should also be rights to health benefits, and education.

The same year, the United Nations also produced an "International Covenant on Civil and Political Rights." The preamble was very similar to the preamble to the Covenant on Economic, Social, and Cultural Rights. The first article mentioned the right of "all peoples" to "self-determination." There were provisions against discrimination. States who signed the Covenant undertook "to ensure the equal right of men and women to the enjoyment of all civil and political rights set forth in the...Covenant." Every human being has "the inherent right to life," and this right was to be "protected by law." No one was to be "arbitrarily deprived of his life." Slavery was outlawed. Prisoners were to be "treated with humanity and with respect for [their]...inherent dignity." It was the duty of the law to protect against invasions of privacy and attacks on "honour and reputation." Another article of the Covenant dealt with freedom of thought, conscience and religion. The Covenant has been described as an "expanded hard-law version" of the 1948 Universal Declaration of Human Rights. The first "Optional Protocol" set up a system that allows individuals to complain to the Human Rights Committee that the Covenant has been violated. Quite a few countries have signed on to the Protocol. The United States has not. In many countries—of course not including the United States—the ICCPR has been absorbed or adopted into domestic law; and in some states it ranks as a legal source on a par with the country's constitution—or even higher (in Spain, for example).[72]

Important, too, are various specialized conventions and treaties. In 1965, the UN adopted a Convention on the Elimination of All Forms of Racial Discrimination; and in 1981, a Convention on the Elimination of all Forms of Discrimination against Women (CEDAW). CEDAW embodied the "principle of the equality of men and women" and called on all the states who signed CEDAW to end gender discrimination; and to take "all appropriate measures... to ensure the full development and advancement of women" (Articles 2 and 3). Article 5 called on countries to "modify...social and cultural patterns of conduct of men and women," in order to get rid of prejudice, and "all other practices which are based on the idea of the inferiority or the superiority of either of the sexes or on stereotyped roles for men and women." Later clauses were more specific: women were to have equal voting rights, equal pay at work, and, the same right as men to "freely...choose a spouse and to enter into marriage only with their free and full consent" (Art. 16). Most countries in the world have signed and ratified CEDAW (the United States has not); but some of them (particularly Moslem countries) have expressed "reservations" to various articles.[73]

CEDAW was followed by a Convention on the Rights of the Child, which was adopted by the General Assembly in 1989. This document repeated many of the points made in the other human rights conventions. The preamble "recognizes" that the child needs a "family environment, in an atmosphere of happiness, love and understanding" in order to achieve the "full and harmonious development of his or her personality." The child "should be fully prepared to live an individual life in society." Under Article 16, no child was to be "subject to arbitrary or unlawful interference with his or her privacy, family, home or correspondence, nor to unlawful attacks on his or her honour and reputation." The Convention included many clauses that dealt with positive duties of governments—states, for example, were supposed to take measures to "diminish...child mortality," combat disease, and provide "adequate nutritious foods and clean drinking-water" (Article 24); in general, every child was to have a right "to a standard of living adequate for the child's physical, mental, spiritual, moral and social development" (Article 27). In general, the Convention reflects the basic norms and ethos of the human rights movement: equality and expressive individualism. Article 29 states, for example, that the "education of the child" is to be directed to "the development of the child's personality, talents and mental and physical abilities to their fullest potential."

The march of international conventions continued. There is a Convention against Torture and Other Cruel, Inhuman or Degrading Treatment or Punishment, and an anti-genocide convention. In 1993, a "World Conference on Human Rights" was held.[74] The participants adopted the "Vienna Declaration and Programme of Action." The Vienna Declaration reaffirmed that human rights and "fundamental freedoms" are the "birthright of all human beings; their protection and promotion is the first responsibility of

Governments." This document contained a lot of familiar material from the other texts: democracy, women's rights (and the rights of the "girl-child"); no racial discrimination; rights of indigenous people. But it also contained other provisions: it called on "all States" to cooperate on the problem of "the dumping of toxic and dangerous products and waste"; it stressed the rights of "disabled persons, including their active participation in all aspects of society"; and called for efforts to "help alleviate the external debt burden of developing countries." The whole document breathes the air of the modern human rights movement. It constantly stresses universality; the rights it mentions belong to absolutely everyone. And it presupposes a form of expressive individualism. Thus, echoing the convention on children's rights, it declares that the child needs a protected family environment "for the full and harmonious development of his or her personality." In 2006, the UN adopted a Convention on the Rights of Persons with Disabilities. Its purpose was to promote and ensure "the full and equal enjoyment of all human rights" by persons with disabilities, and "to promote respect for their inherent dignity" (Article 1). Another section mentions "individual autonomy including the freedom to make one's own choices." States were supposed to "take appropriate measures" to ensure "access...to the physical environment," and to transportation and other facilities (among other things).

The United Nations has had a Human Rights Commission since 1947 (now called the Human Rights Council); and in 1993, a resolution of the General Assembly created the post of High Commissioner for Human Rights. Whether these documents and institutions, or any of them, have had any actual impact on the behavior of any country is another question entirely. It goes without saying that CEDAW, for example, has not revolutionized law and society in the Middle East. With regard to women's rights, the reality remains the same in Saudi Arabia, whether the country signs, does not sign, or signs with reservations. Women in Saudi Arabia have no voice in policy; and cannot even get a driver's license. Dictatorships, wars, genocide have all occurred in various parts of the world, despite all the high-sounding language, the noble Conventions, high and low commissions, and the heroic efforts on the part of organizations like Amnesty and Human Rights Watch.

Granted. Does it follow, then, that we should write off these documents, charters, and treaties? Should we dismiss them as useless; just more pieces of paper without real-world consequences? History is littered with the wreckage of laws, constitutions, and treaties that were violated, sneered at, ignored, stepped on, manipulated. Is it possible that the documents have had some influence on human affairs, or the conduct of statecraft? Some would say they have "symbolic" significance. Here too a hefty dose of skepticism is in order. When we are hard put to find real, concrete, behavioral influences, we often fall back on the argument that some text or declaration has "symbolic" importance. But "symbolic" importance often means no importance at all. A symbol that does nothing but symbolize soon loses whatever power it had as a symbol.

What is the value—if there is value—in expressing ideals, goals to strive for, hopes for the future, statements of what is right and what is wrong? I have no answer to this question. But the documents are interesting, less because they caused something to happen that would not have happened without them, than because they themselves reflect something happening in the world, something of enormous significance; something which caused *them* to come to life. They were, in other words, themselves effects of social norms, habits, and ideas, that became over time more and more powerful. Modernity in all its forms; the modern economy; expressive individualism: these norms, as they developed, wrote the script so to speak.

On the issue of concrete influence: here implementation is the key. There is, basically, little or no implementation of the various treaties and documents. As we have seen, dictatorships sign on to many of them, without a hint of embarrassment. Afghanistan, of all places, has ratified CEDAW, and without reservations. The Constitution of Afghanistan provides (Article 22) that the "citizens of Afghanistan—whether man or woman—have equal rights and duties before the law"; and "discrimination...among the citizens" is "prohibited." That would be news to the women of Afghanistan. But since most of them are illiterate, and many of them are virtual prisoners of their husbands, the news is unlikely to reach its audience. As Michael Ignatieff put it, the states that signed the Universal Declaration "never actually believed that it would constrain their behavior. After all, it lacked any enforcement mechanism." The drafters were under no illusions about this fact. But they were willing to accept a "mere declaration," because they hoped and believed it might "raise human rights consciousness."[75] How it was supposed to do this is unclear. After all, the texts were not exactly best sellers. It is more logical, then, as we suggested, to see the situation the other way around. The development of human rights norms within modern societies led to, stimulated, and molded the texts of these declarations. And insofar as law and society come closer to the ideals expressed, it is because of changes in society, and the massive power of political, cultural, and social developments, rather than the influence of the documents themselves.

Moreover, some countries (like the United States) which on the whole respect rights of their own citizens, turned out to be worse than uninterested in implementing the noble ideas of the declarations. National security—or what is assumed to be national security—has always been an enemy of human rights. In the name of national security, the United States put Japanese Americans who lived on the West Coast into camps in the Western desert—a gross violation of the rights of these citizens, for which the country later apologized. Canada, with even less reason, removed the Japanese (most of them Canadian citizens) from British Columbia, many of them also to internment camps. Both countries later apologized and paid reparations. During the Cold War, the United States aided, abetted, and approved of horrendous regimes, even murderous regimes like Guatemala under Rios Montt, and Pinochet's Chile, so long as they killed people in the name of a crusade against communism and the Soviet Union. President after president denounced Cuba for violating human rights, and instituted and maintain a stern embargo against trade with Cuba. Guatemala and Pinochet's Chile, on the other hand, were our friends. This was worse than a double standard. But the United States was not alone. The Soviet Union was also an offender; and of course, unlike the United States, it did not shy away from murdering masses of its own citizens. The Arab countries were only too eager to denounce Israel for violating the human rights of Palestinians, but of course any criticism of their own human rights records (uniformly poor) was resented and repelled, as a violation of their sacred sovereignty, or contrary to their rich cultural traditions. And, according to one study, respect for human rights was at best a trivial factor in national decisions to grant foreign aid, and to whom, and in what amounts.[76]

It is easy—perhaps too easy—to become cynical and pessimistic about the future of human rights. After the Soviet Union collapsed, nobody could take the threat of world seriously anymore; but Islamic terrorism conveniently entered the ring and provided a major excuse for harsh measures that erode civil rights. It is hard to argue that suicide bombers are the same sort of threat as a massive nuclear power like the Soviet Union. On the other hand, terrorism is random, insidious, and the danger is everywhere; it is more like the *Invasion of the Body Snatchers* than the invasion of an army.

But despite the various "national security" incursions, human rights consciousness has grown steadily over the years. It has, for example, stimulated the formation of a multitude of organizations (NGO's) which take up the battle for human rights. Amnesty International is one of the most prominent of these NGO's.[77] Its cause is political prisoners, and its main weapon is publicity. Amnesty International tries to call attention to "prisoners of conscience," wherever they might be. Its members, in chapters of Amnesty all over the world, flood the offending country with letters of protest. Sovereignty is no defense against the indignation these letters express. Amnesty and its members clearly reject the divine right of governments; its members clearly believe that it is *not* purely an internal matter to torture a member of the opposition, or that it is nobody's business if the state seizes a dissident and puts him in a windowless cell. To Amnesty, rights of conscience are global, and sovereignty has to take a back seat.

Amnesty's tactics do make a difference—at least sometimes. Publicity is often the last thing that dictators want. Indeed, it is a kind of tribute to Amnesty—though certainly not the type of tribute they would like—that governments in the 1970's began to change their tactics. They hit on the devilish scheme of simply making their critics disappear. If a regime arrested some dissident, and threw him in jail, they risked exposing themselves to a torrent of protesting letters. Better simply to arrange to have someone vanish off the face of the earth, often after sinister looking men appeared at night and carted him off. The government would then deny that they had anything to do with the matter. No, the man was not in custody at all. He had "simply vanished."[78]

There are other active human rights organizations—Human Rights Watch, for example. Other NGO's focus on this or that particular cause—women's rights, or political freedom in general. According to one estimate, there were 33 human rights international NGO's in 1953; and 168 in 1993.[79] In virtually every country there are NGO's struggling for some kind of improvement in human rights. They can, and do, cite the various charters, declarations, and manifestos. Or they make use of constitutions and other documents of fundamental (national) rights. It is not easy to tell whether these groups, and their tactics, accomplish very much. Their tactics vary—lobbying, mobilization of public opinion, advertising campaigns, litigation.

Hard evidence of impact is not easy to assemble. Impact is often difficult to measure. Closer to home, we can look at the civil rights movement in the United States, and ask what impact its litigation strategy had. Or, for example, what impact did *Brown v. Board of Education* have on segregation or desegregation?[80] Not much, according to some scholars.[81] It certainly did not create the civil rights movement, which began much earlier. Perhaps it helped that movement grow stronger. The *Brown* decision banned segregation in the public schools; and based that ban on the 14th Amendment to the United States Constitution. It was followed by a series of cases which made clear that segregation was unlawful everywhere, not just in the schools. Civil rights leaders were able to cite these cases, which strengthened the argument on their side, and encouraged their troops. The movement was able to claim a *right* to racial equality, a constitutional right, a fundamental right; guaranteed by the highest and most sacred law of the land. This claim, quite possibly, could have raised the consciousness of some African-Americans, north and south. It may have stimulated them to more militant action. It may have had an impact on quite a few white people as well. But much of this is sheer speculation.

Sally Merry has studied the campaign against gender violence in various countries. Elite women often act as leaders in the movement to do something to end the battering of women. The battered women themselves, especially in traditional communities, often feel helpless and powerless (not without reason). As a result, they tend to be politically inert—passive, fatalistic. But elite women have embraced ideas of basic human rights; and these ideas then "percolat[e]...into local communities." Activists "translate the global language into locally relevant terms." They encourage battered women "to think of themselves as having human rights"; they help to "build rights consciousness."[82] For these local women, what began as the simple and natural hope to escape beatings and assaults ends up as an awareness of fundamental rights. Very similar chains of causality can be documented, no doubt, for other rights movements in many countries. Among the countries Merry studied was Fiji. The movement to end domestic violence in Fiji "was inspired by international movements and the expansion of women's human rights." Local women leaders formed a Women's Crisis Center, and a Women's Rights Movement. These movements worked to change the laws of Fiji, as well as to counsel and help women who were victims or potential victims of violence.[83]

Each country, of course, has its own history, its own human rights trajectory. But there are features common to whole clusters of nations. A constitution and a constitutional court. NGO's devoted to advancing civil liberties. Increased rights consciousness. Plural equality. Movements that have global affiliations. Transnational networks. Everywhere, human rights activists will cite and refer to the various treaties, declarations and manifestoes; and to their own national charters. The ideas of these activists seem infectious. They fall on fertile soil; and they grow. Beyond a doubt, a human rights *consciousness* is an aspect of modern culture, and the human rights movement is both a cause and an effect.

In more or less democratic countries, too, institutions are in place that are supposed to make sure that human rights laws are not just empty words. In many of these countries, constitutions and bills of rights actually mean something, actually have power—something which was not always true of 19th century constitutions. In some countries, the regular courts have the power to enforce constitutional rights, with a Supreme Court on top; this is the U.S. pattern. A more and more common arrangement is to provide for a special constitutional court, which can exercise judicial review. So, for example, the Constitution of the Czech Republic (1992) provides for a Constitutional Court, which can "annul statutes...in conflict with the constitutional order" (Article 87(1)); the Constitutional Court of Portugal can do the same (Article 277). The German example has been particularly influential. Its influence on the Spanish Constitution has led, in turn, to the popularity of this particular device in Latin America.[84]

In short, judicial review is now flowering in places where the soil was once very inhospitable. The United Kingdom was once exceedingly barren terrain. The UK has never had a written constitution. The official doctrine is parliamentary supremacy. In theory, Parliament could pass a law calling for the murder of everyone over the age of 75; and no British court could say no. Of course, Parliament never passed any such law, or anything remotely similar. But, in any event, there was no such thing as judicial review; and Parliament did, in fact, have more leeway than (say) the American Congress. Today, however, Great Britain has a sort-of back-door constitution—the European Convention on Human Rights. And this gives it a sort-of constitutional court, the European Court of Human Rights, which I will discuss below. The Netherlands, too, has no such thing as a constitutional court, and has never had judicial review. This country, too, is subject to the European Convention and the ECHR. And both of these countries are members of the European Union, which has its own court, to which they are subject.

Canada, also, never had a written Constitution. Now, however, it has an "entrenched" Bill of Rights, which the courts can (and do) enforce. New Zealand, another country with a traditional "distrust of American-style judicial review," enacted a Bill of Rights in 1990. This was in some ways an ordinary statute; and made no provision for judicial review;[85] but the law did state that the "rights and freedoms" in the statute were "subject only to such reasonable limits prescribed by law as can be demonstrably justified in a free and democratic society" (Part l, section 5). In addition, courts were required to give laws "a meaning which is consistent with the rights and freedoms" mentioned, and "that meaning shall be preferred to any other meaning" (Part 1, section 6).[86] Finally, Israel, which also lacks a written constitution, now in a sense has one, through decisions of its high courts, either by means of creative "interpretation" of the country's declaration of independence, or through references to basic principles of democratic societies, or simply drawn from thin air.

Judicial review, to be sure, is feeble or non-existent in autocratic countries. Whatever a constitution or the like might say, one cannot imagine a court in Myanmar or North Korea defying the regime or striking down some act of the exalted leaders, on the grounds that they violate the constitution or are inconsistent with human rights law. Yet even in Pakistan, hardly a model of modern democracy, attacks by Musharraf, the military dictator, on the Supreme Court, led to a crisis, protest movements among Pakistani lawyers, and probably hastened the end of that particular regime. All of this reinforces a general point: the modern culture of human rights has considerable power. All but the most closed-in, repressive, and tyrannical states have to pay at least lip service to human rights.

REGIONAL DOCUMENTS OF HUMAN RIGHTS

The United Nations, from early on, has had a judicial body, the International Court of Justice, often called the World Court. This court deals only with international affairs, in the sense that only nations can invoke its jurisdiction (and then only if they agree to submit to the Court). The court has, therefore, little or nothing to do with charters of human rights. It does not exactly have a crowded docket. When it acts, however, the court does seem somewhat sensitive to human rights issues. In the *Corfu Channel* case, the very first case decided by the Court, Great Britain sued the People's Republic of Albania. In 1946, two British destroyers, passing through the straits of Corfu, in what they considered international waters, were damaged by mines; forty-five British officers and sailors were killed. Great Britain won the case; and the court awarded damages, which Albania simply refused to pay.[87] Some scholars think there is at least a chance the International Court of Justice might develop into a body of some importance in enforcing international human rights.[88] The ICJ has, indeed, handled some significant cases: for example, a case arising out of the Srbenica massacre in Bosnia.[89] It was also asked to give an advisory opinion on whether Israel had a legal right to build a separation barrier between parts of Israel proper and the occupied territories. An opinion of this kind inevitably involves issues of the human rights of individuals.[90] Enforcement of the judgments of the ICJ is another question. The United States feels free to ignore the court's decisions; and it has done so.[91]

Not all of the documents on fundamental human rights lack enforcement power. There are important regional institutions that have a certain amount of bite. Probably the most effective is the European Court of Human Rights, which enforces the European Convention on Human Rights.

The ECHR is an organ of the Council of Europe, which was originally formed in 1949 by a group of ten countries, all of them in western Europe. The purpose of the Council was to achieve "a greater unity between its members," in order to realize "the ideals and principles which are their common heritage," and facilitate "economic and social progress." The goals were democracy, the rule of law, and respect for human rights.[92]

The Council formulated a Convention on human rights, which was promulgated in 1953. It has been amended and added to with a series of "protocols." The Convention refers specifically to the Universal Declaration of Human Rights of the United Nations. Not much in the text is particularly new or surprising. Many provisions deal with the right to a fair trial; and the right to personal liberty. Article 8 states that everyone "has the right to respect for his private and family life, his home and his correspondence." Article 9 provides for "freedom of thought, conscience and religion," Article 10 for "freedom of expression"; Article 12 for the "right to marry and to found a family." Under Article 14, the "rights and freedoms" expressed in the Convention were to be "secured without discrimination on any ground such as sex, race, colour, language, religion, political or other opinion, [or] national or social origin."

More and more countries, big and little, signed on to this institution over the years, from Andorra to Russia; and by the early 21st century, it had become "truly pan-European, covering 47 States and more than 800 million people."[93] From 1959 on, there has been a European Court of Human Rights. The countries that signed could, however, decide for themselves whether or not they would accept the work of the Court; and whether or not they would make the Convention part of their own domestic law. Over time, more and more countries "received" the Convention, that is, they enacted legislation which gave the Convention some sort of legal force within their country. This happened relatively early in Germany, but many countries, even some of the original signers, were more hesitant about taking this step. Norway made the move in 1994, Sweden in 1995, the United Kingdom only in 2000, the Irish Republic, in 2003. In 1998, Protocol 11 changed the existing rule; from then on, a country that ratified the convention had to accept the jurisdiction of the Court.

In its early years, the Court had relatively little business. The European Commission on Human Rights heard cases, and would then refer them to the Court. The system was changed in 1998. The Commission was done away with. Cases could be brought directly to the Court. The number of cases "exploded"; in 1989, there were 1,445 applications to the court, and 25 judgments; in 2001, there were 13,842 applications, and 889 judgments; and the Court began to feel in crisis, because the sheer numbers of applications were almost overwhelming.[94] The situation got steadily worse. In 2007, the Court had 41,700 applications, and disposed of 1,503 judgments. Originally, the ECHR, it was felt, would hear mainly complaints between countries; but the present-day, restructured court hears almost none of such cases. Rather, it has become a court deluged with individual applications; there were "over 50 times the annual average for the first 30 years."[95] But the numbers do not tell the whole story. The Court, which sits in Strasbourg, has become more and more powerful over time, and its decisions have become more sweeping and more creative. Today, the Court is the "unrivalled master of the Convention," and it uses its power to "construct European fundamental rights in a prospective and progressive way."[96] National systems are "increasingly porous to the influence of the ECHR and the case law of its Court"; so that it can be said that the countries of Europe "no longer embody insular, autonomous, self-defined legal systems."[97]

The ECHR is a court whose judges come from common law countries, civil law countries, and former Socialist countries. One might wonder how successful these judges are in working together. One study of the Court, by Nina-Louisa Arold, analyzed cases on privacy and family law, freedom of religion, and freedom of expression—subjects that were "expected to be sensitive to differences in backgrounds and traditions." But no such differences emerged. Arold concluded that the Court had developed a common legal culture that "successfully overrides the (legal) differences between its member states." There is a high degree of "consensus in the decisions" which points to a "convergence of views."[98] This common culture overrides the line between civil and common law, between old and new democracies, between former members of the Soviet bloc and western Europe. The most important reason for this convergence, I would imagine, is common allegiance to the norms of the modern human rights movement. The judges may have different training and backgrounds; but the very fact that they were appointed to this particular court distinguishes them from most judges in their society. Also, there is a body of case law by now, which molds the work of the court; there is also a "climate of collegiality," and new judges are "exposed to strong peer group pressure." All of this goes to create the common culture of the court.[99]

In a way, then, the Convention is a kind of constitution, or at least a Bill of Rights. And the ECHR is a kind of constitutional court (though not exactly: it cannot declare laws void, or tell legislatures what they have to do). And, indeed, the right of individual application threatens to drown the court in work. But this problem—and it is a serious problem—is also a sign of how deeply the court is accepted by the public; and how deeply the human rights culture has penetrated at least into elite consciousness in Europe.

At the same time, and in the same period, country after country has gone the constitutional route. The relationship between the Convention, the Court, and the domestic laws of the various countries is technical and complicated. It can also vary somewhat from country to country. Originally, the Court had basically no power to supervise, enforce, or implement its rulings. Under Article 46 of the Convention, member states are supposed to follow the rulings of the Court; but there is no easy way for this to happen. Yet, in practice, almost everywhere, the influence of the Court and its decisions is growing. Its impact and its influence do depend a good deal on the individual countries. Russia and Turkey pose tougher issues than, say, Finland or the Czech Republic.

The passage of the Human Rights Act in Great Britain, in 1998, for example, reflected a desire to accommodate the decisions of the European Court of Human Rights. Great Britain has, historically, resisted judicial review, which it treated as a kind of legal heresy. Parliament is supposed to be supreme. But then along came the ECHR. British subjects could and did try their luck with this court; and often successfully. It was this "increasingly steady stream of cases" in Strasbourg that "more than any other fact, prompted the enactment of the HRA."[100] The law basically committed the British to the European Convention on Human Rights, and directed that any court which faced an issue "in connection with a Convention right" had to take into account any "judgment, decision, declaration or advisory opinion of the European Court of Human Rights." Moreover, legislation was to be "read and given effect in a way which is compatible with the Convention rights," as far as possible. And, in general, it was declared to be "unlawful" for a "public authority to act in a way which is incompatible with a Convention right."[101] Technically, the Human Rights Act does not confer the power of judicial review on British courts. They have only power to tell Parliament that some law or enactment does not conform to the European Convention on Human Rights. The Human Rights Act thus embodies a "subtle compromise," in that Parliament has "the ultimate power as to whether to comply with such a declaration."[102] But of course it is expected that Parliament will, in fact, comply; and if it does not, British subjects can always betake themselves to Strasbourg.[103] And the European Court of Human Rights, as we said, is most definitely an activist court. Many of its decisions are as bold and surprising as any decision of the United States Supreme Court, or the German Constitutional Court, or the high courts of India or South Africa.[104]

Over time, too, a second powerful court of human rights has developed in Europe. This is the European Court of Justice. It is an organ of the European Union. The Court was first established in 1952, at a time when the future EU was simply the European Coal and Steel Community. The permanent home of the ECJ is in Luxembourg. The EU is, of course, much smaller than the Council of Europe—Russia and Turkey, to name two important states, are not members of the EU; nor are Switzerland and Norway, to take two other examples. The European Union was originally basically a rather complex type of economic union; but it has grown way beyond coal and steel into something much different, though exactly what is not easy to say. It is not really a political union, or a federation; and it is certainly not a cultural union. It sets up a giant free trade area, and all sorts of economic regulations flow out of Brussels. But there are Union rules that can hardly be considered economic. Only democracies, countries that respect human rights, can enter this club. No member is allowed to use the death penalty; and abolition of the death penalty is a condition for joining.

Originally, the ECJ decided the sort of issues one would expect from the judicial organ of a free trade area—issues such as whether one country could discriminate against cheese produced in another member country, and the like. The ECJ has evolved over the years into a much more powerful court; and it has become also, in effect, a court of human rights. It did not simply invent a code of human rights. It built on various sources; but now this role has been formally strengthened. In 2000, the EU adopted a Charter of Fundamental Rights of the European Union. The Charter rests on "indivisible, universal values of human dignity, freedom, equality and solidarity"; further, it is "based on the principles of democracy and the rule of law." The very first article announced that "Human dignity is inviolable. It must be respected and protected." The Charter expresses many of the usual fundamental rights: freedom of thought, freedom of religion, freedom of expression. Everyone has the right to "engage in work," to "conduct a business," and to own property. Everyone is "equal before the law"; all forms of discrimination are banned; equality between men and women "must be ensured in all areas." At present, the legal status of the Charter is somewhat indefinite. It is not exactly "law," since it has never been ratified or become part of the fundamental law of the EU. It is however more or less recognized as valid if not absolutely binding; and the ECJ pays it considerable respect.

There are thus two "parallel" systems of human rights or fundamental freedoms in Europe, enforced by two separate courts, which behave differently in various technical ways; but are, I believe, committed basically to the same set of values and follow quite similar norms.[105] They are hardly competitors or rivals. Convergence here results from the usual source of convergence: the two Courts are part of the same social, moral, and normative universe, and inhabit the same corner of the modern world. But exactly how the work of the ECJ relates to the work of the ECHR—to what extent they overlap; to what extent they follow somewhat different norms—is a difficult and involved subject.

In *Carpenter v. Secretary of State for the Home Department* (2002),[106] the ECJ considered the case of one Mary Carpenter, who was appealing a deportation order. Ms Carpenter was a native of the Philippines. She entered the UK as a visitor in 1994, and overstayed her leave to enter. In 1996, she married Peter Carpenter, a British subject. She argued that her husband's business required him to travel about the EU; and she helped with his children while he was gone, so that deporting her would restrict her husband's rights under EU law. The ECJ was sympathetic. EU law "has recognized the importance of ensuring the protection of the family life of nationals of the Member States in order to eliminate obstacles to the exercise of...fundamental freedoms." Separating the Carpenters would be "detrimental to their family life and, therefore, to the conditions under which Mr. Carpenter exercises a fundamental freedom." The Court upheld, in short, Mary Carpenter's right to stay in England—and its own power to interpret and enforce these "fundamental freedoms."

Other regional organizations exist, which "drew inspiration from the human rights provisions of the United National Charter," and UDHR.[107] These regional systems are by no means as powerful and active in enforcing human rights as some might like. The basic reason is not hard to guess. The European countries are for the most part smoothly running democracies. There are exceptions, of course—it would be hard to put Russia or Turkey in the same category as Finland or Denmark. And, indeed, Russia and Turkey produced way more than their share of complaints before the ECHR. On the whole, however, the people of Europe *expect* democracy; and, more and more, they expect constitutional courts and judicial review. For the EU, allegiance to human rights is built into the very fabric of the organization. The same considerations, alas, are not as true—or, in some cases, not true at all—in other regions of the world.

There is, for example, an African Union.[108] There is also an African Charter on Human and Peoples' Rights, adopted in 1981. Nearly all African countries have signed on. The Charter is, in most regards, not very different from other such charters. It does, however, emphasize "duties" to a greater degree than most of the others, including a duty to serve the "national community," to "preserve and strengthen social and national solidarity," and to "preserve and strengthen African cultural values" (Article 29). There was an African Commission with some powers with regard to human rights; and in 1998, the Union decided to set up an African Court of Human and Peoples' Rights. It began its actual life in 2004. Another organ of the African Union was an African Court of Justice and Human Rights. These two courts are now to be merged into a single African Court of Justice and Human Rights. It is too soon to say what kind of impact this court is likely to have. Some skepticism is in order. Most of the members of the African Union hardly qualify as democracies, and some are dictatorships plain and simple. One might mention, however, the "Community Court of Justice of the Economic Community of West African States (Ecowas)." In 2008, Hadijatou Mani sued the government of Niger, for "failing to implement its own laws that criminalised slavery in 2003," and having "failed to protect her from being sold into a life of servitude and sexual slavery."[109]

Whether cases like this can and will lead to more vigorous enforcement of human rights in Africa is an open question. One is also entitled to be skeptical about the human rights credentials of the League of Arab States. The League has adopted an Arab Charter of Human Rights. If this has had any effect on the likes of Syria or Algeria, it is not visible to the naked eye.

The Organization of American States occupies a kind of middle ground. Most of the members of the OAS today are more or less democratic. But when the OAS was founded, this was hardly the case; and the history of Latin American democracies over the last two or so generations is not, shall we say, exactly linear. The road to democracy has been full of tragic zigzags and detours. At one time, not that long ago, military dictatorships were in power in Chile, Argentina, Brazil, and Uruguay. There was also one party rule in Mexico, death squads and paramilitary groups in Guatemala, and of course Communist rule in Cuba, very long lasting—and, more recently, such unclassifiable examples as Nicaragua or Venezuela. The situation, however, is in general better and brighter today. There may, therefore, be a future for the judicial organ of the OAS, the Inter-American Court of Human Rights. This Court has been in existence since 1978. It has seven judges, and it sits in San Jose, Costa Rica.

Up to this point, it has not been as effective as one might like. But things began to change with the spread of democracy in Latin America. The Court decided, in 1989, that Honduras had to pay damages to the wife and relatives of Angel Manfredo Velasquez-Rodriguez, who had been arrested without warrant, tortured, and then made to disappear. The money was actually paid to the family in the 1990's. In 1998, in *Blake v. Guatemala*,[110] it was shown that Nicholas Blake had been abducted and murdered in Guatemala. His body was not found until years after he was taken away and killed. His relatives brought an action against Guatemala; and the court decided that Guatemala had, indeed, violated provisions of the American Convention on Human Rights; and had also violated, "to the detriment of the relatives of Mr. Nicholas Chapman Blake, the right to humane treatment." Guatemala was therefore "obliged" to pay compensation to Blake's relatives, and to "use all the means at its disposal to investigate the acts denounced and punish those responsible for the disappearance and death of Mr. Nicholas Chapman Blake." Of course, the case could not bring Blake back to life. And, while the situation in Guatemala had definitely improved, this was only after a long and bloody period with governments that violated in the most brutal and hideous way the rights (and lives) of indigenous people, labor leaders, and anybody the government considered left-wing.

This points to what Helfer and Slaughter have called a "sad paradox." The international and supranational courts are "most effective in the states that arguably need them least: those whose officials commit relatively few, minor, and discrete human rights violations."[111] Or those where a despotic regime has been replaced by a democratic one. Still, the regional courts, as Helen Stacy has argued, do have some "unique institutional advantages for resolving human rights conflicts." They are closer to their people, better able to judge the needs of their people—better able, too, to assess the constraints on local governments."[112] They may ultimately be better able to cope with the tensions between the human rights movement, with its universalistic claims, and local cultures and traditions, with their more local and particular claims.

INTERNATIONAL CRIMINAL LAW

The Nuremberg trials were an important step on the road to some sort of international consciousness of human rights. The United States, Great Britain, France, and the Soviet Union put some of the leading Nazis on trial. They were accused of waging aggressive war, and of committing crimes against humanity. The Nazi regime was certainly guilty of enormous crimes, crimes of unspeakable brutality. It had butchered millions of Jews, Gypsies, Slavs, not to mention any Germans who dared speak out against the Nazi government. There was, at the time, some criticism of the Nuremberg trials. They were condemned as just a form of "victor's justice." Moreover, it was ironic, not to say hypocritical, to have judges from the Soviet Union, another wildly murderous regime, sitting in judgment. The Nazi crimes were, however, truly, crimes against *humanity*: they were hardly "illegal" in the eyes of the constituted government of Nazi Germany, indeed they were state policy.

The Nuremberg trials were the most famous of these proceedings after the second World War. But thousands of lesser Nazis and Nazi collaborators were also tried, either in Germany or in countries the Germans had occupied. The Norwegians put on trial Vidkun Quisling, the Nazi's puppet leader in Norway—the term "quisling" indeed came to mean traitor or collaborator—and executed Quisling for his crimes. There was also a special trial of Nazi doctors, who had performed cruel and often fatal experiments on Jews, Gypsies, prisoners of all sorts, and on twins. The war in the Pacific produced its own crop of war trials. The most notable of these was the International Military Tribunal for the Far East (most people refer to this as the "Tokyo War Crimes Trial"), which sat in 1946, and held for judgment Japanese leaders who were charged with war crimes. There were also many trials conducted by the British; some by the Australians; others by the Chinese, and the governments of other Asian countries that had been conquered and occupied by the Japanese. In some of these trials defendants were convicted of capital offenses and put to death.

The end of the second World War, unfortunately, did not mark the end of "crimes against humanity." The slaughter of the innocents continued: in Rwanda, in Cambodia, in Bosnia, in Darfur. Savage armies in West Africa committed terrible atrocities—cutting off people's hands, raping women, recruiting children as soldiers, massacring helpless villagers. Uganda suffered under the bloody and tyrannical rule of Idi Amin. More recently, the so-called Lord's Resistance Army in Uganda has been guilty of horrible crimes; and in Darfur, in the Sudan, countless innocents have been killed or driven from their homes. There is a United Nations declaration against genocide; but it does not seem to act as much of a deterrent. Yet today there is at least a chance that men and women who are responsible for these awful crimes can be brought to some sort of justice. The General Assembly of the United Nations convened a conference in Rome, in 1998; and the countries gathered there entered into a treaty establishing an International Criminal Court. When 60 countries had ratified the statute in 2002, it went into effect. Most countries have now signed on; the hold-outs include China and the United States. The Court sits in The Hague; it has investigated a number of crimes against humanity, and taken action in a few. In October, 2005, the Court announced that it had issued arrest warrants against the leaders of the Lord's Resistance Army.[13] In 2009, it issued a warrant for the arrest of the President of the Sudan, Omar al-Bashir, accusing him of crimes against humanity, in connection with the tragic events in Darfur.[14] Bashir ignored the warrant—this was only to be expected—and retaliated by ordering a number of humanitarian organizations to leave the Sudan. The decision "opened a fierce debate over whether it will help pressure Bashir...or possibly spark consequences that will make a solution more difficult."[15] The international tribunals will be discussed in more detail in chapter 10.

THE GENESIS OF HUMAN RIGHTS

So far, we have noted the rise of a human rights culture. It has been influenced, no doubt, by the various declarations and conventions of the United Nations, of Europe, and elsewhere. There are also concrete institutions—domestic and international courts, international organizations, NGO's—which have the job, or the goal, of furthering the cause of human rights. And we have argued that we are in the presence of a genuine *movement*, with deep roots in the social order, especially in the developed world. I talk—as I must—about legal institutions, and how they have changed over time; and about institutional change and development. But more fundamentally, I am talking about changes in human consciousness.

It is no simple task to try to explain *why* a human rights culture has arisen. What is it about the world we live in, that has acted as a midwife to the movement, and nurtured it once it came into being? Some scholars have tried to explain the movement in terms of something profoundly and inherently human. People all have to die; all of us can feel suffering and pain; all of us are vulnerable in one way or another; and all of us also have the capacity to feel sympathy or empathy for other people.[16] Is it possible the human rights idea is grounded in these profoundly human facts? But I—and other people—find these explanations unconvincing. As Diane Elson points out, if "sympathy were freely available in adequate quantities, it is hard to see why we would need [formal] human rights."[17] And you do not have to be a cynic to notice that people have been slaughtering each other for thousands of years; and that there seems no obvious end to the slaughter. Empathy hardly seems to prevent genocide. And though, yes, we are all poor suffering and vulnerable human beings (some more than others) this too does not seem to stay the blood-soaked hands of oppressors. All too often it is precisely the most vulnerable who are most at risk of losing their rights, or not getting them in the first place. A more likely assumption, as Michael Ignatieff puts it, is that human rights are a "systematic attempt to correct and counteract the natural tendencies we discovered in ourselves as human beings."[118]

It seems impossible, then, to ground modern rights-consciousness in something universally human. Rights-consciousness seems obviously grounded in history. Lynn Hunt has tried to base the movement on human empathy and psychology, yet in a sophisticated and historical way. Her account is based on the rise of "new cultural experiences" from the 18th century on—she finds evidence in the novels of the period; and in the movement against torture. She argues, in fact that "reading accounts of torture or epistolary novels had physical effects that translated into brain changes and came back out as new concepts about the organization of social and political life." The new experiences led to "empathy," which "in turn made possible new social and political concepts (human rights)."[119] It is an intriguing hypothesis, which she grounds in deep historical study. Too deep, perhaps. To me, it seems clear that the growth of human rights and the consciousness of human rights, in the last 60 or 70 years, differ radically from anything in the the thoughts and habits of the 18th and 19th centuries. In recent years, the human rights movement burst out of its cocoon. The question is, why? Granted, the past casts a long shadow. But a full explanation, it seems to me, has to focus on more recent yesterdays than Hunt's.

There is an enormous literature on the "universality" of human rights.[120] At one level, clearly it is wrong to claim that human rights—or any of them—are inherent, timeless, and universal, just as it seems clearly wrong to base them on something in the human genome. If these rights were truly inherent and timeless, why did we have to wait so many long dreary years, so many centuries and epochs, before they exploded in our midst—and even then, hardly universally? On the contrary, although all societies, probably, have had some idea of rights, and certainly codes of law go far back in history, along with some notions we can treat as more or less equivalent to the rule of law, nonetheless, the rights movement today, and the general catalog of rights, seem specifically and peculiarly a product of quite modern and even contemporary society.

Human rights are surely not universal in some philosophical or absolute sense, or in an anthropological sense, and certainly they are not universal in any historical sense. They can, however, be universal in the sense that there is a social norm, an idea, a concept in millions of minds, which *treats* them as universal, thinks of them as universal, labels them as universal. Masses of people *in our contemporary world sincerely* believe in a menu of human rights, and that belief probably includes some notion of universality—that is, that these rights belong or should belong to everybody on earth. This social norm seems to be fairly general among people in developed societies. It also seems to be spreading rapidly to millions of people in other countries—people who live a middle-class life in such countries; but also more and more quite ordinary people.

We are looking, then, for an explanation of something quite basic to modernity. No doubt the human rights movement, and human rights norms, stem from a multitude of sources. But to me it seems that modern *individualism*, and, especially, *expressive* individualism must be a critical factor. It is beyond the scope of this book (and beyond my powers) to go deeply into the complex question of what makes the modern world what it is, what makes it distinctive and unprecedented; and it is even not possible to discuss the various forms that modern personalities take. But the strong pull of individualism on people in the rich, developed countries (if not elsewhere) strikes me as an obvious fact. The typical man or woman today, in France or New Zealand or even in Japan, has a feeling of individuality, or uniqueness; he or she feels more separate, more disconnected to some mass or clan or tribe than people in older or different times; perhaps disconnected even from the family, at least the extended family. To quote Cosmo Howard: because of "changes wrought by social modernization in the twentieth century," people's lives "have been extracted from the bonds of family tradition, and social collectives"; people have been given "greater control of and responsibility for their own lives."[121] Each of us is unique, distinct; we each have our own genome, our own fingerprints, and our own human potential. This leads to the idea that "each human being is a subject who is entitled to participate in the decisions that govern his or her life."[122]

Paradoxically, perhaps, the realization that we are each of us unique and different leads to a demand that we should all be equal, all be treated the same, all given the same chances in life. The *political* result of modern individualism is the demand for democracy, equality before the law, and (in a sense) equality of opportunity. Perhaps it was only men, at first, who felt this way strongly; but now it is women, too, at least in most democratic countries. And similarly for minorities, ethnic groups, and also the so-called sexual minorities; and old people; and illegitimate children; and handicapped people; in short almost everybody. And there seems little doubt that the human rights movement, and the emphasis in modern society on human rights, flows directly from this tilt toward individualism—to be more precise, what has been called expressive individualism. Expressive individualism, as defined by Robert Bellah, is that form of individualism which "holds that each person has a unique core of feeling and intuition that should unfold or be expressed if individuality is to be realized." The "meaning of life," is "to become one's own person, almost to give birth to oneself."[123]

To be sure, individualism as such is not a new idea. It probably makes little sense to talk about individualism among the Andaman Islanders, or the ancient Hittites; and perhaps among people in medieval Sweden as well. The 19th century is a different story. But, as Michael Les Benedict has put it, although Victorians were "individualists in the sense that they considered each person to be a free moral agent," they were "not individualists in the modern sense. They did not concede to each person the right to live freely according to his or her own moral code."[124] The individualism of the 19th century was an individualism of markets and economic life; it also extended to some aspects of political and religious life.

Modern individualism is clearly different and goes much further. It is the individualism of the "personal best"; of "do your own thing." And where did this come from? Not easy to say, of course. One way to look for an answer is to search out intellectual history; to scan the works of great thinkers and philosophers, and examine the trend of their thoughts, their influence on each other, and the like. But I prefer to think of these thinkers and their ideas as effects, rather than causes. They systematize, they deepen, they explore ideas and develop them; they certainly influence each other; perhaps their ideas trickle down to a more general public (perhaps not); but the general shape of their ideas, the assumptions that animate them, come ultimately from the social milieu, rather than the other way around.

Ruling ideas and concepts are products of society. What is taken for granted today was unthinkable yesterday—but will also seem completely ridiculous in centuries to come. Geniuses of the 17th century, who wrote about moral philosophy or ethics, had no concept of the kind of equality which any fool today considers quite natural. What made almost all men—and women— blind for centuries to the very idea of women's rights? How come great philosophers truly believed in the divine right of kings? Which beliefs of today will seem absurd in two hundred years? For all we know, that might include some of the most axiomatic of the human rights concepts.

In any event, any account of modern culture has to pay attention to what it is that makes modern society distinctive. And this includes the industrial revolution, the rise of capitalism, and that other revolution, the scientific and technological revolution. Exactly how these relate to legal culture is never obvious. But it seems almost axiomatic to me that legal culture is not autonomous; that it is molded by the general culture, and by the general structure of society. If legal culture emphasizes the naked individual, it is not because of its own traditions, but because of what is going on in the society surrounding it.

Capitalism lays heavy stress on producing and consuming. And advertising is a striking and ubiquitous feature of any capitalist economy. Advertising is everywhere, on the air, in the press, on the internet, and on billboards, park benches, in buses, any place it can be squeezed in. Advertising feeds on and helps create a profoundly *individual* personality. The message of advertising— regardless of the product—is always addressed to the individual. You can become richer, better, stronger, sexier, if you buy such and such a product; or do such and such a thing. It does not matter whether you are asked to buy toothpaste, join the navy, or vote for a certain politician. The message goes out to each listener or viewer, one by one. Even advertisements for traditional values and ways of life—advertisement sponsored by the Latter Day Saints or the Catholic Church—cannot avoid this aspect of modern life. And, indeed, advertising and the consumer society are in fact deadly enemies of traditional values and traditional ways of life.

The point is not that advertising *creates* individualism; but it feeds on it, it presupposes it. It presupposes consumers with choices and with some money to spend. *Leisure* also plays a critical role in modern society. The average person in, say, the Netherlands or Australia is no longer scrambling for sheer survival. Life can be hard, and not just for the poor. People have to struggle to achieve their goals. Nevertheless, there is vacation time for most people, there are Sundays and Saturdays and holidays, and typically a 40 hour week; not to mention retirement at a relatively early age (and many years of life after that, thanks to modern medicine.). People no longer have to work until they drop. Millions of people have some money, over and above what they need to keep body and soul together. Beyond the five-day work week, and the eight-hour day, and the eleven-month job, there is all that free time; and that free time gets filled up with sports, hobbies, shopping, fixing up the house. During vacation time, people can travel, and millions of them do; they can go to the beach or the mountains or visit historic cities. People also can and do join all sorts of organizations, and pursue all sorts of interests, religious, social, intellectual, or just plain fun. Of course, there is a tremendous amount of unpaid work within the family; and many families have to double up on jobs to keep their heads above water. But this still means, collectively, millions of hours of leisure, filled in with hobbies, and (above all) with forms of entertainment—TV, concerts, movies, video games. Even shopping and fixing up the house are, for many people, a form of amusement. In many countries, entertainment (in the broadest sense) is perhaps the single biggest industry. And leisure means the opportunity to develop oneself, to realize and fulfill one's uniqueness. And this, too, obliquely, leads to a sense of entitlement, a sense of fundamental right. The connection between wealth, democracy, and individualism is well established: "As growing socioeconomic resources broaden the range of activities that people can choose, self-expression values broaden the range of activities to which they aspire." And as "self-expression values" rise, people demand "the institutions that allow them to act according to their own choice,"[125] and this means institutions that foster human rights.

Individualism is thus a key concept for me. And individual choice. The uniqueness of each of us. Crafting our own lives, as much as we can, along the lines that we choose. Yet people often say we live in an age of conformity: that people are like sheep, that they travel in herds, slaves to fashion, and the like. The sociologist David Riesman, in his famous book *The Lonely Crowd* (1950), claimed that people of his day had become "other-directed," that is, they conformed to the norms of their peer; they ran with the herd.[126] This was in contrast to an earlier period, when people were "inner-directed," where they followed norms implanted in them during childhood—norms of hard work, virtue, and so on.

Riesman's argument certainly has the ring of truth; and even more so today. Fashions spread with the speed of light. Suddenly, everybody is wearing tight blue jeans; then, just as suddenly, baggy blue jeans. Email and the internet spread jokes, fashions, ideas, comments, with the speed of light. The mysterious and invisible power of the peer group dictates what most people wear, eat, think, and do. But whether or not Riesman is right about a shift from "inner-direction" to "other-direction," and whether he is right about the rampant conformity of modern life, conformity, paradoxically, implies freedom of choice. The modern man or woman—or boy or girl—no matter how much they run with the herd, at least gets to choose which herd to run with. They conform; but first comes the (conscious or unconscious) decision on *what* to conform to. Nobody talks about "conformity" in describing a tribal society in the middle of the Amazon jungle. "Conformity" in that society is taken for granted. Nobody in the tribe "chooses" to be what he or she is, except within very narrow ranges. Thus, oddly enough, "conformity" in modern society is an aspect of modern individualism, precisely because it is much more a matter of choice than it would have been in olden times, or even in the 19th century. "Other-directed" people can be "other-directed" in so many ways. They can follow a guru, they can be groupies, they can be members of parties, clubs, societies, they can dress like movie stars or tennis players; they can decide to be vegetarians or vegans; and so on and so forth. To be "individual" is not the same as to be creative and original. Riesman's "other-directed" people fit quite comfortably in societies dominated by expressive individualism.

Free choice involves yet another paradox. A wide area of choice seems to be a reality in modern societies. Sir Henry Maine, in the 19th century, described the evolution of law as a movement from status to contract. And contract means choice. Families no longer arrange marriages, for example, in modern developed societies. Men and women choose each other. They marry for love (and divorce for unlove). Children of carpenters do not become carpenters unless they want to. Parents who expect their children to be doctors discover they have instead produced rock musicians or computer geeks. A young Italian picks himself up and becomes a waiter in London. A child of devout Roman Catholics becomes a Buddhist, and travels to India for spiritual guidance.

Modern individualism, as a belief, a norm, an idea rattling around in peoples' heads, emphasizes individual choice, and puts it at the very core of peoples' lives. But modern social science teaches us that choice, in important ways, is an illusion. We think we choose, but social forces, odorless, colorless, and tasteless, dictate many of our choices. We are like puppets unaware of the strings on our arms, legs, and head; unaware, too, of the puppet-master who is pulling the strings. I buy a pair of shoes in a shoe store. I choose the shoe (and whether to buy it at all); I choose the color, the style. But for the most part I forget or ignore the fact that only a narrow range of shoes is available. My choices are constrained in crucial ways. The same is true for the foods I eat, the programs I watch on television, and of so many other aspects of life. I do, as it were, choose what I want from the menu; but I do not choose the menu itself. And customs, norms, traditions, fashions that act below the level of my consciousness all influence even my choices among those things that *are* on the menu. All this is well known and obvious to social scientists. But ordinary people are not anthropologists or sociologists; and they go through life without taking these constraints into account.

That does not mean, of course, that choice is totally an illusion; it most certainly is not. A middle-class family in Switzerland, in the early 21st century, has a range of options that medieval serfs never dreamt of; and even go far beyond what was available to the Swiss of the 19th century. Choice may be more extensive in some societies, less so in others; it may be valued differently by different groups, even within one society.[127] And there may be rigid boundaries to these options; but within the boundaries, the menu is rich and complex. The power of tradition, the power of the extended family—these have declined dramatically. Young people in modern developed societies enjoy an unprecedented degree of mobility and independence. They spend more time on their own before they get married; they are less isolated; their personal relations often represent a sharp break with what was once considered normal or acceptable. For example, millions of young people in developed countries live together without getting married; they enter freely into sexual relationships, and leave them just as freely. Some of these relationships are between two men, or two women.[128]

But the changes—I have to repeat—are *relative* not absolute changes. And of course we are not just free-floating individuals. We are social animals. We cannot thrive in isolation. We travel in packs. And we do have families, we have friends and neighbors, we have close and not-so-close ties to other people, we have group affiliations. But all of these noticeably less than before; and less binding; and less fixed for us in advance. The choices are greater, broader than ever. And the urge to achieve one's "personal best," whatever that may be, is also greater, broader than before.

Rights of various kinds seem particularly *necessary* for the modern individual, precisely because of that very individualism. More and more people are alone, uprooted, adrift. Individualism has its rewards, but also its risks and its downside. Life "loses its self-evident quality." There is another side of the coin—individualism is not only "autonomy, emancipation. . .freedom and self-liberation." It is also anomie; and the ever-present risk of downfall and failure.[129] And in the event of failure, the individual cannot count so much on family, friends, and the primary group. The individual must fall back on society—including the menu of human rights. Human rights thus occupy a double position in modern society—in the first place, expressive individualism *implies* equality and the right to be what we choose; this is a liberating factor. Rights, however, are also a protective factor—a safety net. There is the right to try walking a tight-rope; and a right to take care of your needs if you fall.

Of course the exact form modern individualism takes varies from society to society. In the United States, young people who are (say) 25 years old, especially young men, are unlikely to live with their parents. In fact, if years go by, and an unmarried man still lives with his mother and father, people are apt to ask: what's the matter with him? Young adults are expected to fly out of the nest, and make their own lives. This reflects a particular dialect of the culture of individualism. A French movie of 2001, *Tanguy*, dealt with the (comic) situation of an adult son, who lives at home, and whose parents desperately want him to move out. An American movie of 2006, *Failure to Launch*, had the same theme: Tripp, who is in his thirties, lives with his parents, who are extremely eager to get rid of him. They hire a woman to help out (of course the two of them fall in love). One wonders what people in Italy or Greece or Spain would make of these movies. In those countries, a young unmarried man would most likely keep on living with mother and dad; and an unmarried woman would be even more likely. In Spain, as of 1994, 79% of the men who were in their 20's and unmarried lived at home; the figure for the United Kingdom was 36%, for France, 41%.[130] Italy and Greece and Spain certainly share most aspects of modern culture and modern individualism, but the precise form of their dialect of modernity is not the same as in Sweden, the United States or the United Kingdom.

I used the term "dialect" advisedly. "Dialect" had no hard-edged and precise definition in linguistics. People commonly use it to describe speech forms which are different but not that different from some general norm. Nobody could doubt that there are cultural dialects. It does seem, however, that modern cultures, generally speaking, are moving toward convergence. This is most obvious in the rich, developed countries. Japanese culture to be sure is hardly identical with the culture of Spain or Israel or the United States. There are many and interesting differences; still, these differences must be seen against a backdrop of increasing convergence.

Classic (and modern) economic thought presupposes a certain theory of individual behavior. This theory, in many ways, connects with the individualism discussed here, historically and intellectually. But unlike some economists, I do not assume that the way people behave flows from anything so fundamental as "human nature." I am to be sure making assumptions about what people think and believe, and how they behave. And the "people" in question are the masses of people, mostly middle-class, in rich and developed societies, for the most part. There is no assumption that people are always or even mostly rational, or that they tend to maximize their self-interest. Sometimes they do and sometimes they do not. But they do feel strongly that they have certain rights, or ought to have them; and these rights flow from deeply held ideas, among them the notion that each of us is a unique individual, endowed somehow with the right to develop as we wish, and to choose that way of life which we prefer.

There is no doubt, too, that the human rights movement is not only global in itself; it is inextricably connected to globalization. A healthy debate is going on, whether globalization is good for human rights, or bad for it. The negative side rests on the usual critiques of globalization—some people view with alarm the global power of multinational corporations, for one thing; and they are dismayed by the "McDonaldization" of culture. But the plus side also has a strong case. Rhoda E. Howard-Hassmann, in a provocative essay, calls globalization the "second great transformation," and points out some of the consequences for human rights: to begin with, the "entire world is now constrained—to a greater or lesser extent—by the international human rights regime, a set of norms and laws which most countries have formally said they respect." I suspect that the "international human rights regime" is not *that* much of a constraint; but, as she points out, globalization "speeds up" access of people "to the very idea of rights" in every part of the world. The "evolution of a global communications network"—email and the internet, especially—bring this about. And the communications network "in turn enables the formation of global social movements in favor of human rights." Human rights movements "have benefitted from the ease of travel and communications."[131]

That this factor has had an enormous influence on the human rights movement seems undeniable. Paul Gordon Lauren has put it very eloquently: Technology, he says, has "created dangerous weapons." This is certainly true: dictators of today have at their fingertips powers of repression, and weapons of mass destruction, that older dictators never had at their disposal. The new technology is also a threat to privacy. But, on the other hand, it also poses a mortal threat to "egregious violators of human rights," who "thrived on darkness, on distance, on ignorance and superstition, on silence, and on their capacity to hide and deny information." Their enemies are cell phones, fax machines, computers, scanners and cameras—these can "override government media control....break down ignorance and disbelief, turn silence into debate," and spread the word. The world knows immediately when a girl in Pakistan "is punished by gang rape," when a Nigerian woman is sentenced to be stoned, when a father disappears "at the hands of Columbian security forces," or a "prisoner of conscience is tortured in Iraq."[132] Whether there will be remedies or responses is another question. But without the technology the human rights movement would be unable to mobilize for action.

4
On Modern Religion

In the world's constitutions, freedom of religion is generally listed as a basic right of citizens. Probably every declaration of human rights, every charter of human rights, every national and provincial bill of rights, will include freedom of religion. The right to worship as a person sees fit. The right (equally important) *not* to worship. An end to established churches, or at least an end to established churches with any real power over citizens. The United States is formally committed to the separation of church and state. The Bill of Rights has been so interpreted. There is, technically, an established church in Great Britain. But this seems to have little or no meaning these days. The idea that Elizabeth II is the formal head of a church establishment must strike people as archaic, and slightly absurd. In some other European countries, there is a "state" or "national" church (this is true of Sweden); but again, this has no practical meaning; people in Sweden can choose whatever religion or non-religion they want.

Freedom of religion embodies a deep-seated paradox. Many religions teach that they are the truth faith, and they alone—Catholicism and Islam, among others. Theologically, there are nuances and shadings to this idea; but there is little doubt about the core. Any such doctrine coexists most uneasily with freedom of religion. Logically, a person can believe his faith is the one true faith; and yet be tolerant of other religions. This person might be sorry that others are chasing false gods; she might worry about the future of their souls; but end up thinking, well, it's their affair. Psychologically this is not always possible. In a conservative Muslim country—Saudi Arabia is a good example—freedom of religion does not exist; and apostasy is a capital crime. The Saudi interpretation of Islam does not accept the idea that a Muslim has the right to change religions.[133] Orthodox Jews in Jerusalem sometimes throw stones at people who drive cars on the Sabbath; and they would like the Israeli government to ban the sale of pork, among other things. The situation in developed countries, on the whole, is much more tolerant. Freedom to practice any religion, or none, and to change religions, is a well-established norm.

Over the last two centuries or so, the role of religion as a force in peoples' lives has gone into a certain amount of decline. Today, in quite a number of European and Asian countries religion is not a very significant factor. On the other hand, in recent years, deeply conservative, fundamentalist religions seem to be gaining in strength. They are certainly gaining in numbers. In Latin America, evangelical Protestant groups pose a real challenge to the traditional Catholic faith of the population. Islamic radicals are a force in the modern world—a much feared force, one might add. In Israel, ultra-orthodox Jews are increasing their share of the population, partly because they produce so many babies. Hindu fundamentalism is increasingly a factor to be reckoned with in India. So far, no developed country has a fundamentalist majority. Whether this will continue to be the case is impossible to say.

The resurgence of militant, ultra-conservative Islam frightens the developed world. Any movement that produces young people who blow themselves up, in conspicuous places, in the name of religion; or who hijack airplanes and crash them into buildings, cannot be ignored. Islamic radicalism would not worry the West, if the radicals stayed put in Islamic countries. But they sometimes leave these countries, to inflict the pains of jihad on the West. Moreover, most European countries today have sizeable, and growing, Muslim minorities. Assimilation to the dominant culture seems to proceed fairly slowly. A small but worrisome fringe group is willing to use violence in a kind of war against the West, in particular against the Western country in which they live, as pay-back for real and imagined crimes against the Islamic world.

In a way, fundamentalism seems like a throwback to the middle ages. After all, Christians burned heretics at the stake; they launched crusades to throw Muslims out of the Holy Land and set up Christian kingdoms. In Spain, in the 15th and 16th centuries, Jews and Moslems were forced to convert, leave, or face deadly consequences. Militant Islamic fundamentalists seem archaic and disturbing. That they reject the West, its secularism, and its immorality, is true but not important in itself. Deeply religious people have always been able to reject what is worldly, and turn inward. There are Buddhist monks and Catholic nuns who cloister themselves away from the big, bad world. There are ultra-Orthodox Jews in Israel who refuse to recognize the state of Israel (because the Messiah has not yet come) and who even refuse to speak Hebrew, which would sully the holy tongue. They live, more or less, in a world of their own. There are small groups in the United States, like the Old Order Amish, who reject electricity, the automobile, computers, and most of the trappings of modernity. But no member of the Old Order Amish ever blew himself up in protest against anything; and certainly no member ever tried to massacre random people in this wicked world; no cloistered nun ever went on a rampage and delivered sinners to Hell.

The fundamentalists do not simply reject the West, and modern society; they feel threatened by it, and impelled to resist. God's cause, they believe, demands a violent counter-movement, a jihad, a war against the infidels and all their works. In their methods—cell phones, bombs, video releases—they embrace the technology of the secular world, and try to turn it against its creators. These movements do not retreat; rather, they aim to conquer. As Shmuel Eisenstadt has pointed out, these groups, even though they "promulgate ostensibly anti-modern, or rather anti-Enlightenment themes," are very much part of the modern world; they are trying to "establish a new social order," with roots in revolutionary and "universalistic ideological tenets." They reject raw nationalism or crude ethnic identity.[134] They are distinctly global. They refuse to accept freedom of religion, and much of the modern menu of human rights. But these doctrines provide them with an opening, a platform, an opportunity. Religious tolerance and pluralism—their sworn enemies— gives them their chance to grow; certainly in the developed world.

The Peace of Augsburg (1555) established the principle, cuius regio, eius religio, that is, the religion of each German princeling would determine the religion of his subjects; subjects of a Protestant would be Protestant; if he was Catholic, they would be too. The Peace of Westphalia (1648) confirmed this arrangement. But not all countries and principalities were religiously uniform. Nor did the principle put an end to religious persecution and religious war. The principle of freedom of religion made slow but steady progress in Europe. Today it is firmly entrenched in all democratic societies; and it is a freedom, not at the level of the prince or the King or the government, but at the level of the individual.

In modern Europe, the influx of Muslims, mostly from North Africa, has produced a new situation. The Muslims are problematic, less because they are not Christians (neither are Jews and Buddhists), but because some of them are too zealous for European tastes; and because people in the host country are afraid that some Muslims will not and cannot assimilate, and that they may become enemies, even violent enemies of society. Of course, Europe has a long history of anti-Semitism; and Hitler's regime slaughtered millions of Europe's Jews. Anti-Semitism is not dead; but it has diminished greatly, and is not a major factor in the politics of European states. The Muslim populations, on the other hand, are very definitely seen as problematic. The controversy over Muslim girls and their headscarves in French schools is a symptom of a profound national unease. In England, too, Muslim dress has evoked discussion. Jack Straw, the former foreign secretary, spoke out against the "Islamic custom of wearing a full facial veil." He called this custom a "visible statement of separation and of difference."[135]

Americans might wonder what the fuss is all about. But the "seemingly silly debate about what women wear" hides, according to a Canadian observer, a more profound issue. Many if not most of the major world religions, she points out, "insist that women must be covered, that they must be modestly dressed." Men are generally speaking exempt from this requirement. The "debate about modesty . . . is a surrogate for a . . . debate about the equality of women."[136] There are many ways to interpret the custom of wearing veils, headscarves, and full body coverings. But the custom does accentuate a gender difference—and for most people it implies a subordinate position for women. Here then is a conflict between religious principles—if not religious rights— and one of the most fundamental tenets of the human rights movement.

Perhaps one reason why Europeans find their new Muslim neighbors so disturbing is because these Muslims are so very devout. In the European world, religion has lost much of its power, and its hold on society has become quite tenuous. Survey data find very low rates of church attendance in some

European countries—5% in Norway, 14% in the Czech Republic, 16% in Switzerland.[137] Other countries have higher rates; or at least tell this to the people conducting the surveys. In Ireland, church attendance is reported to be 84%; in Poland, 55%, in Italy 45%.

Still, the United States seems to be in a different category altogether, if not in actually church attendance, than in the powerful role religion plays in the lives of vast numbers of people. The World Values Survey, at the very end of the 20th century, included the question, "How important is God in your life?" In Japan, only 6.9% said "very important"; in Sweden, 9%; in the United States, 58.3%. In answer to the question, do you believe in God, just over half in Japan and Sweden said yes; in the United States, 95.6%. When asked, "are you a religious person?," in Japan 26.5% said yes; in Sweden, 38.9%; in the United States, 82.5%.[138] Millions of Americans claim an actual, personal religious experience.

The United States thus seems to be a real outlier, among rich, developed countries. But American religiosity has been, like fundamentalism in general, bent and molded by the conditions of contemporary life. It is an important fact that the United States is extremely diverse, religiously speaking. There is no true majority religion. Most Americans are Christians, and more Christians are Protestants rather than Catholics, but Protestantism is hardly a single religion. It varies enormously—from dignified and moderate people who sit quietly in the churches of old-line religions (when they bother to go), to excited and passionate worshipers, in store-front churches where services are loud and charismatic, where penitents cry out, and congregations speak in tongues; or in huge mega-churches dominated by fundamentalist but spellbinding preachers. And a recent study has shown the surprising fact that religious life in the United States is, in one sense, astonishingly unstable. People shift from one religion to another in amazing numbers. According to this study, released in February 2008, "roughly 44% of Americans now profess a religious affiliation that is different from the religion in which they were raised."[139] Millions of Americans, apparently, shop around for a religion, until they find one that suits their needs, as they see these needs. Probably millions more shop around for a church and a pastor or priest more to their liking, within their particular religion.

Americans are also extremely tolerant on matters of religion. They mostly seem to reject the idea of one true church; or the belief that most people are eternally damned, because they are infidels or heretics or religious sinners. America's religious diversity, I suspect, is one reason why this is the case. Members of a family living in a middle-class suburb might be devout Catholics; but their next-door neighbors could be Lutheran, or Jewish, or even Muslim. The mother might have a Mormon brother-in-law; their dentist might be a Baha'i or a Buddhist, and the neighbors down the street might have no religion at all. Ethnic enclaves in most big cities have at least partly broken down. There still are Chinatowns and Italian neighborhoods and Polish neighborhoods; but as Chinese, Italian, and Polish families earn some money (and assimilate), they move to some chosen place in the vast kingdom of suburbia. Neighborhood pluralism—ethnic and religious—is much more likely than in the 19th and early 20th centuries.

Religion, under these conditions, undergoes a profound process of redefinition. It is no longer simply a matter of tradition, of what your father and mother did, and how you were raised. It also becomes less a search for the absolute, for the Gospel truth; it is now much more a personal spiritual quest. You look for the religion that most satisfies *your* spiritual needs; the doctrines and practices that fit your personality and your wishes and desires. Americans do place a very high value on religion in general. Atheists are taboo (only a tiny percentage of Americans call themselves atheists—about 1.6%),[140] but Americans accept genuinely religious people of all forms and shapes, regardless what religion they follow. A fairly healthy proportion of the population—maybe one-fifth—is "unaffiliated." I am not sure what this means. I suspect that many of the "unaffiliated" consider themselves religious, or at least spiritual. They simply have not yet found a congenial place to invest their spiritual capital.

My point, then, in short, is that religion in America has become for many people simply another aspect of expressive individualism. This tendency is helped along, to be sure, by the sheer number of religions. In some respects, when there are so many religions, they compete with each other, shopping for souls; and perhaps when the supply of religions increases, then so does the demand—the competition tends to stimulate participation in religious life.[141] But this is surely less a factor than the exuberance of expressive individualism. Religion has become, much more than before, a matter of choice, as the startling figures on church-hopping and church-shopping demonstrate. Religion's job, then, is to fulfill personal needs, above all else.

Theology as such is not terribly important to Americans; they pay little attention to it. What is important is religion itself, or religiosity, or whatever satisfies a hunger for spirituality and personal fulfillment. Thus choice becomes a crucial factor. People pick and choose from a menu of dogmas. Millions of American Catholics go to mass, get married in church, baptize their children, and consider themselves fairly devout. But they also practice birth control. The church says no, but they say yes. The church forbids divorce, and couple who get a civil divorce (the only kind) may not remarry in church. Yet many Catholics do divorce and do remarry. The church also considers abortion a terrible sin; one of the worst. This is one Catholic dogma that does command a considerable following; nonetheless, large numbers of Catholics disobey, though no doubt quietly. In a sense, all American Catholics are really Protestants. But what is true of Catholics, is probably true of other religions as well. People feel free to choose religions, and within religions, to choose those customs, rules, laws, dogmas, and practices that satisfy them; and reject those which do not.

In most other developed Western countries, no doubt fewer people change religions, because fewer people are religious in the first place. But for those who do profess a religion, I suspect much the same dynamic is at work as the one that obtains in the United States. In those countries, too, freedom of choice exists within religious communities—in fact, if not in theory. By reputation, Poland is a faithful member of the Roman Catholic flock. In some ways, the evidence bears this out. Rates of church attendance are very high. But Poland is also a country with an exceptionally low birth-rate. Either Polish couples have stopped having sex; or they are not obeying the rules against contraception. The second alternative strikes most of us as a good deal more plausible. Italy has the lowest birth-rate in Europe, even though almost half the population goes to church, and even though Italy is the seat of the Roman Catholic church, and the church is a considerable force in Italian society.

One main theme of this book is the existence of a pervasive and convergent *culture* of human rights in all developed countries. There are striking similarities in all of them, in law, and in society: a trend toward gender equality, for example; anti-discrimination laws; constitutional development, with judicial review, to name a few examples. Of course, all of these take different forms in different societies; and move at different paces. But beneath the differences and particularities—important as these are—one finds a fundamental sameness. The argument about religion is essentially a guess that the same is true in matters of religion: devout America, and indifferent Norway, are sisters under the skin.

Most religions, in Western countries, are not only tolerated; they are treated with honor and respect. This is true for all of the older, more established religions. There are, to be sure, some religions that are beyond the pale. Europeans have a problem with the more radical branches of Islam, as we have seen. And certain small religions, labeled "cults" rather than religions, do not share in the general glow of tolerance. There is no firm definition of a cult. The concept of a "cult" is a little bit like the concept of a weed. A "weed" is not a botanical category; a weed is simply a plant that grows where nobody wants it. And a "cult" is basically a religion (usually a small one) which is the object of general or widespread disapproval; a religion which many people find threatening, or absurd, or downright dangerous. But if the "cult" lasts long enough, and becomes big enough, and rich enough, it ceases to be a cult. The Latter-Day Saints (better known as Mormons) were treated as a dangerous cult in the 19th century. They were the target of enormous prejudice and were persecuted to the point where they felt compelled to leave the eastern part of the United States, and resettle in what is now the state of Utah.[142] The Mormons were hated and feared; they were branded as immoral and intolerably theocratic. Immoral, because of the practice of polygamy, which evoked utter horror in the general population, and which the federal government tried vigorously to stamp out. Theocratic, because the church had tight economic control over its members. The church, in the face of the government's more and more stringent policies against polygamy, officially abandoned the practice in the late 19th century. The Mormons multiplied and were fruitful. Today, the Mormon church is rich and powerful. It is a growing religion; its missionaries are active all over the world. Quite a bit of prejudice against Mormons simmers beneath the surface. But few people would call the Mormon church a cult. It is too old, too powerful, and has too many members for that.

Even the "cults" can enjoy many of the benefits of freedom of religion. In a series of cases, starting in the 1940's, the Supreme Court of the United States confronted issues that arose from actions of members of Jehovah's Witnesses —and the counter-actions of those who considered it a dangerous cult. Most Americans found this religion obnoxious, insidious, non-patriotic. Members refused, for example, to salute the American flag. Generally speaking, the Supreme Court came down on the side of the Witnesses.[143] Freedom of religion in the classic sense is not a major issue in modern societies. Nobody in Europe or North America, and elsewhere, would seriously consider putting restrictions on most religious practices, or questioning the right of religions to seek converts. There are limits, of course: human or animal sacrifices would not be tolerated. But these are exceptions.

Makau Mutua has criticized, on ethical and political grounds, the big "messianic" religions (Christianity and Islam) for their work in Africa, and the effect their efforts have had on indigenous religion (and culture). The "messianic" religions, he argues, think they have a monopoly on truth; they "actively demonize, systematically discredit, and forcibly destroy" the indigenous religions that might have competed with them. Christianity and Islam diligently work to win over souls. These religions gained proselytes through force and coercion during the high and palmy days of colonial rule. In the process, they destroyed indigenous cultures; and brought about a "fundamental distortion of ethnic identities and history." Mutua admits that probably nothing can be done to repair the damage and "reclaim...the African past." But, in his opinion, the "human rights corpus should outlaw those forms of proselytization used in Africa."[144]

Mutua has a point, of course; the big "Messianic" religions had a powerful impact on African society, and have a lot to answer for. But the brute fact remains: Humpty Dumpty cannot be put together again. The cruel scythe of modernity has destroyed much more than indigenous religions. The cultural and economic forces that blew in from Europe were mightily destructive to indigenous cultures. Colonialism devastated ways of life, tastes in food and clothing, family structures and habits of living; it has wiped out languages; it has descended on ancient, stable cultures like the black death, and gutted them. Nothing is the same after the tsunami of modernity sweeps ashore. But forced conversions are a thing of the past. The big religions do not need to stoop to these tactics. The age of the missionaries is over. The religions still troll for souls in Africa. But many Africans have taken their religions and cultural practices to the slaughterhouse of their own accord. Modernity, good or bad, is an incredibly powerful force. You can call it "neo-imperialism," and with some justice. But whatever you call it, many of the trends away from the past seem irreversible. As the ancient Greek saying has it, no one can get into the same river twice; and the current has been flowing steadily, and powerfully, for more than a century.

5
Is There a Culture of Human Rights?

I have already suggested an answer to the question in the title of this chapter. I have assumed that there is such a culture, that it has grown sensationally; and that it is one of the dominant facts of modern life. What evidence is there to support these statements?

There is, to begin with, indirect evidence. The various declarations, treaties, and international covenants must attest to *something* in modern culture, beyond an urge to say nice things in print. Moreover, in the period since the second World War, the cult of constitutions has grown and spread with enormous speed and energy. Almost all of these constitutions, to the best of my knowledge, provide in some way for a constitutional court; and for some kind of judicial review. In country after country, then, we find statements of fundamental rights, usually given some kind of status which puts them above ordinary laws. And there are institutions—usually courts—that have power to enforce these rights, at least to some extent. In open and relatively democratic systems, big structural changes in the legal system necessarily rest ultimately on powerful social norms. Of course, not everybody shares these norms. They may be the norms of most people; or the norms at least of articulate elites. But they are, in either case, important and even dominant norms.

A second piece of evidence, of the same sort, is simply this: in country after country, we find, in the late 20th century at least, social movements of more or less strength, demanding gender equality, gay rights, an end to race discrimination, and so on; and these have had, in many ways, amazing success, in country after country. In the United States, voters elected a black President in 2008; and the President appointed a woman to be his Secretary of State—she was, indeed, the third woman to hold this very high position. A woman, Margaret Thatcher, has served as Prime Minister of Great Britain. At the time of this writing, Angela Merkel is Chancellor of the Federal Republic of Germany. Women have been heads of government in the Scandinavian countries. Mary Robinson was President of the Irish Republic. Women sit in parliaments all over the world. They are mayors, governors, members of city councils.

Other groups, other categories, once despised and oppressed, have gotten on the bandwagon of rights. Gay people can marry in Massachusetts, Connecticut, Vermont, and Iowa; in Canada, by virtue of a national law in 2005; and in the Netherlands and Spain. Such a development would once have been completely unthinkable. Gay marriage is still exceedingly controversial; but civil unions and anti-discrimination laws and ordinances testify to the fact that norms here have changed enormously. Native groups that were once dispossessed, shunted into reservations, and stripped of their powers, now win lawsuits and squeeze land grants out of majority populations. Illegitimate children are no longer despised and disinherited. India has tried to break the barrier of caste and end the stigma that blocked the progress of the untouchables. Women, people of color, gay people and other minorities have broken through a web of social barriers. They appear on ads on television, and as characters in movies. Yet the United States, for example, is a country where, within living memory, no black opera singer sang with the Metropolitan Opera in New York, and no black athlete played with a major league baseball team. In England, one now sees black barristers in the courts, Pakistani actors on the stage, and Chinese characters in television commercials. Similar changes have taken place in other Western countries. All of this is indirect—but powerful—evidence of a growing and general norm of human equality.

Is there evidence, also, from survey research, on the place of the human rights ethos in the culture of citizens? There is, though the research is not as wide and as rich as one would like; and some of it may be misleading. McCloskey and Brill, in their study *Dimensions of Tolerance*, reviewing some of the survey evidence for the United States, argue that support for civil rights and civil liberties is fairly thin in American society. Naturally, if you ask people, do you favor freedom of speech, they will never say no. But when you move from the abstract to the particular, "the level of support drops off sharply." Thus, only 18% of the people surveyed would allow an American Nazi to hold a public meeting in a town hall.[45] Millions of people in the United States and no doubt in other countries think the state has a right to ban pornography, or to keep atheists from teaching school, or to prevent openly gay men from acting as scoutmasters. McClosky and Brill leave the reader with the impression that Americans care very little about civil liberties.

A study in Great Britain asked people to say whether they liked or disliked each of ten groups, including Fascists, Irish nationalists, and Communists. The study then tried to measure tolerance toward a person's least-liked group: would you let members of that group teach in state schools? Or hold a public rally? Most people said no: over 80% would deny members of that group the right to teach in state schools, about two-thirds said no to the idea of a public rally. And over 60% thought it was acceptable for the state to tap the phones of members of their least-favored group.[46]

But these two studies have to be taken with a grain of salt. The rights of Nazis, or atheists, or gay scoutmasters, or Fascist teachers, are contested issues at the outer fringes of civil liberties. McCloskey and Brill feel they have discovered what one author has called a "failure to understand the foundational values of a liberal democratic political culture." But some of these issues are simply "contestable"; that is, people hold different values and opinions with regard to them.[47] Indeed, nothing in McCloskey and Brill suggests that Americans really reject what is essential in the menu of human rights. Nothing in the study shows that Americans want or would accept government censorship of the press, for example. And certainly, there is a very high tolerance of political debate and religious diversity; and wide agreement about the rights of women and (more and more) the rights of minorities, now even including sexual minorities. Many people who approve of laws against pornography, would disapprove of a plan for the government to censor movies or to ban books that criticized the government.

In a classic study during the time of the great depression of the 1930's, people in an American town were asked to give their reaction to a series of vignettes. During this terrible period, many coal mines in the region had closed down. Coal was so cheap these mines no longer made a profit. Some out-of-work miners began taking coal for themselves. Mostly, they used the coal to heat their houses. Other miners also sold some coal. Asked their views, most respondents who were members of the union saw nothing wrong with these practices. Most business leaders disapproved.[148]

Did the men and women who thought it was acceptable to take the coal, believe in the rule of law? They probably did. They almost certainly supported the general constitutional structure of their country. The study is very old; attitudes may or may not have changed. Peoples' ideas about the rule of law, and about human rights, are often quite specific to particular situations and particular issues. There is no doubt that sensitivity to some aspects of human rights—rights of minorities, for example—has increased greatly since the time the study.

None of the studies is strong evidence against the idea of a culture of fundamental human rights. This culture, of course, is not uniform throughout the world. James Gibson has studied the development of a "human rights culture" in South Africa. He found significant differences in attitudes, among white, Africans, and the "coloured," on various measures of support for the rule of law.[149] South Africa is a developing country; and most of the population is quite poor. Germans, who live in a rich country, when asked in 1977 whether certain rights were "basic human rights" or "state-granted privilege," strongly identified, as a "basic human right, the "freedom to travel within one's own country" (80.8%), "freedom from censorship" (78.8%), "freedom to practice religion" (88%), and, strikingly, "equal rights for racial and religious minorities" (84.5%).[150]

Survey research, of course, is a difficult and sometimes treacherous art. And interpretation is always an issue. There are, it appears, differences between mass opinion, and the opinions of leaders and elites. In the studies cited by McCloskey and Brill, for example, elites had a richer culture of human rights than the general public. Elites, and especially lawyers, were much more likely to be against censorship of pornography, or banning the American Nazi party, and so too on many other issues. Barnum and Sullivan found, in their British survey, that members of Parliament were markedly more tolerant than the general public.[151] A study of "masses and elites" in Israel, however, found that in "situations of high threat," for example, "the political elite" did not "differ much from the general public."[152] The study was undertaken for the specific purpose of testing an "elitist theory of democracy." Still, it is clear that educated and articulate people take the lead in furthering human rights. No doubt the leaders of the opposition come from the same strata of society—at least sometimes.

The literature, in short, tells us that many issues of human rights and civil liberties are highly contested. Much depends on circumstances and situations. People who feel threatened—by crime, by drug pushers, or by jihadists—are often willing to sacrifice some civil liberty at the altar of security. A survey taken after the 9/11 attack on the World Trade Center in New York found that almost half of the Americans surveyed (45%) were among those willing to do this. But they differed greatly on specific issues: only 23% approved of "warrantless searches on suspicion"; while 71% were willing to make it a crime to belong to a terrorist organization.[153]

I also suspect that people make another fundamental distinction: between themselves and their group (however they define it), and marginal, threatening, and deviant groups in society. These facts are important (and sometimes depressing); but they do not deny the existence of a *general* culture of human rights, a culture that has been growing, expanding, developing, in recent times. It simply underscores the fact that the boundary lines of the culture are indistinct, and in dispute.

There is an enormous literature, as we mentioned, about whether the core human rights are universal. Universal is a tall order; it does seem clear that there is a remarkable degree of convergence on some core issues and norms. Certainly in the rich, developed countries; much less so elsewhere. There is formal convergence—laws, rules, constitutions, court systems; freedom of speech; freedom to travel; norms about gender equality, anti-discrimination rules, and the like. Underlying these formal aspects must be a good deal of normative and social convergence. Of course, countries differ—nations "facing common problems will nevertheless yield different outcomes," because of different histories and experiences.[154] Polling data suggest that these national differences certainly do exist;[155] and no doubt there are important differences *within* countries. But the differences between opinions on matters of fundamental right, in the modern sector, certainly seem flatter and less profound than in the past. The roots of the rights culture lie in historical processes which affect the whole of the developed world (and perhaps beyond it as well). They lie also in technological changes which are global, and in economic and cultural aspects of modern society which transcend national borders. But if this is true of the origins of the rights culture, then the convergence hypothesis follows almost as a matter of deductive logic.

"Convergence" and "universal" are words about sameness. How does this fit in with a very salient aspect of the modern rights culture, the flowering of minority rights? With the rediscovery, and obsessive search, for "roots?" If human rights are "universal," how does this square with cultural relativity, or multiculturalism, and the rights of indigenous peoples? These are real issues, which we will take up in the following chapter. The basic argument will be that multiculturalism is in some ways deceptive; or, as one essay puts it, a façade.[156] We will now proceed to look at this façade.

6
Universal and Particular

The menu of fundamental rights has changed greatly over time; and varies from place to place. This much is obvious. But are there core values, which everybody would agreed on—if not in the past, then in the world we live in today?

This is the subject of vigorous debate. The fundamental documents, to be sure, all *say* that human rights are universal. The very title of the Univeral Declaration of Human Rights uses the word universal. And UDHR in its very first article proclaims that "all human beings" are "born free and equal in dignity and rights." This point has been endlessly repeated. Not everybody, however, is comfortable with the idea. One common objection is that the conventional package of rights, and the various declarations and covenants, are not universal at all, but specifically Western. And a Western menu of rights does not, or may not, fit some non-Western cultures.

Attacks on the idea of universality come from both left and right. On the left, Marxists (for example) have tended to criticize or reject "bourgeois freedoms." In the debates leading up to the UDHR, representatives from the Soviet Union and its allies argued for inclusion of "social rights," the right to a full stomach and medical care and a job; and at times came close to suggesting that there was some kind of fundamental contradiction between the two kinds of right. The argument, if it makes sense at all, has to imply that somehow "bourgeois freedoms" are inconsistent with a just society, a society with food, schools, doctors, and jobs for everybody. Or that they act as a screen and excuse for the most naked and ruthless forms of capitalism. Some of the Western countries, on the other hand, were hesitant about the so-called "social rights." Most states simply could not afford them. In the end, "social rights" did appear in the UDHR.

The Kenyan scholar Makau Mutua, whom we have already mentioned, argues that the human rights movement is a form of imperialism. Human rights, and the "relentless campaign to universalize them," are part of a long, historical process of "Western conceptual and cultural dominance.... At the heart of this continuum is a seemingly incurable virus: the impulse to universalize Eurocentric norms and values by repudiating, demonizing, and 'othering' that which is different and non-European."[157]

Another version of this argument, from Asia, could be labeled an attack from the right. It rests on the idea that Asian countries have traditions unlike Western traditions, traditions that are opposed to the individualism of the West. And the mainstream ethos of human rights does rest on at least *some* version of individualism. Takeyoshi Kawashima, for example, writing in 1968, tells us that in Japanese culture an individual "is not considered to be an independent entity." Instead, his interest is "absorbed in the interest of the collectivity to which he belongs"; the interest of the collectivity has "primary importance"; the "interest of the individual has merely a secondary importance." This world-view leaves "no place for the concept of 'human rights."[158] Chinese culture, we are told, also emphasizes community, duty, order and harmony, respect for the elderly, discipline, and a kind of big-Daddy state.[159] Saudi Arabia never agreed to UDHR; for Islam, "universalizing rights discourse implies a sovereign and discrete individual," and from the perspective of the Koran, this is "blasphemous."[160] Islamic countries adopted their own counterpoise to the UDHR, the Cairo Declaration of Human Rights in Islam (1990), which listed many familiar rights, but omitted others, and based itself on its reading of Shariah. Yet another version of the notion that the UDHR is too "Western" comes from the more authoritarian societies in the East— Singapore, for example. Spokesmen for these societies agree that imported concepts of human rights do not fit Eastern societies. Eastern societies are either not "ready" for democracy; or, more fundamentally, cannot go along with Western democracy; their cultures, in some presumably deep-seated and persistent ways, need strong leaders or at the very least some kind of collective solidarity.

It is hard to know what to make of all these arguments empirically. Statements about deep-seated traditions or cultures that cannot absorb the human rights program might fit some small tribal society lost in the jungles of the Amazon, about which I have frankly nothing much to say, but the arguments seem just plain wrong if we are talking about 21st century Japan, or South Korea, or Taiwan; and very likely Singapore. All of these, except Singapore, have become in recent years quite solid, working democracies, with vibrant consciousness of rights. Indeed, even in 1968, Kawashima, whose essay was cited above, admitted that Japanese ideas of "social obligation and right" were not "inborn or racially predestined to the Japanese." Indeed, the notion of "human rights" was "accepted universally" in Japan "when the political power which had suppressed its growth collapsed...in 1945."[161] As Neil Englehart, among others, has pointed out, the "Asian values" argument has usually been "advanced for political and ideological reasons," with "very little to do with the traditional mores of the population."[162] And some African politicians used "the shield of culture as a barrier to criticism of practices that violate the most fundamental human rights and that their own citizens want stopped."[163] The authoritarian government of Singapore pushed Confucianism in the schools; this allowed the ruling party to "essentialize their citizens as people who are obedient and devoted to the community."[164]

Arguments about "Asian values" advance a "fundamentally conservative vision of culture"; these arguments imply that, in society, there is a "fixed cultural essence," so that a change to the Western style of thinking would "require altering the basic personality structure of an entire population."[165] But cultures, in fact, are not as fixed and inflexible as this "Asian values" argument supposes. In fact, cultures are often quite fluid, and particularly so in the modern context. Change the context, and you change the culture. Perhaps not at once, but certainly in a generation or so. The grandchildren of illiterate peasants who came to the United States have become thoroughly American. Often their parents had already made the transition. The grandchildren of Japanese soldiers who were willing to die for the emperor watch sitcoms on television, play computer games, and listen to hip-hop music. They also take democracy for granted.

Some human rights advocates defend themselves by arguing that human rights are not particularly Western, because they rest on "early conceptions of human dignity" and the like which "could be found in diverse, ancient Western and non-Western civilizations."[166] These scholars look for, and find, parallels and origins in Confucius, or the Koran, and other ancient texts. Or they stress the "unity of humankind," which means that human rights are "not a Western hegemonic imposition," but rest on "conceptions of human dignity...in diverse, ancient Western and non-Western civilizations, religions and philosophies."[167] I frankly find this particular argument unconvincing; to me, the gap between the ideas of Confucius, or the Koran, and modern concepts of rights, is simply too enormous to bear the weight of this argument. But this does not mean that human rights are primarily "Western." The gap between what Plato advocated, or St. Thomas Aquinas, and modern liberal conceptions of human rights, is almost equally enormous. Historically speaking, the menu of modern rights was almost completely absent from the West until relatively recently. In medieval Europe, governments beheaded people who denounced the King and his government. Religious dissenters were hounded mercilessly, and sometimes slaughtered. Torture was a regular feature of criminal procedure. Women had few rights. There was an unbridgeable chasm between commoners and nobles; and the nobles had the lion's share of whatever society had to offer. All of this changed over the course of the centuries, but slowly, and ideologies and philosophies changed along with the changes in social structure. The industrial revolution, and the capitalist revolution, were the most significant agents of transformation; then, later, the growth of the welfare-regulatory state. Along with political reform came theories and practices of human rights—in France, in the United States, in Sweden, in Switzerland, and in the West in general.

But as these agents of transformation reached Japan, India, Thailand, or South Africa, the human rights movement took root in these countries too, though obviously not in the same way or at the same pace or in the same timeframe. But neither is the history of human rights exactly the same in Finland, Greece, Portugal, or New Zealand.

My feeling, then, is that the basic cluster of human rights is not "Western" at all; rather, it is modern; it is an aspect of contemporary (developed) society. To be sure, there is a strong correlation between "the West" and the human rights movement; the movement began in the West, and its ideas flow, in the main, from Western thinkers. But this is not crucial. The music of

Bach and Beethoven is also Western; but many of the best classical musicians today come from Korea, Japan, or China. And why not? It is no more out of place than the Western admiration for Chinese art. Moreover, in countries like Japan, or South Korea, or Taiwan, there is full freedom of speech and freedom of religion; there is freedom to travel, to choose an occupation, and to come and go as one pleases. It would be absurd to consider this some sort of cultural mismatch. In short, the human rights movement is no more "Western" than Beethoven, no more "Western" than the automobile and the computer (which also hail from the West), or antibiotics; and nobody would argue that modern technology and modern medicine are unsuited to Japan or indeed to any other non-Western country. Indeed, the Japanese seem better at making computers and automobiles than most "Western" countries.

There is no question that societies have differences, and important ones, in how they define fundamental rights; and what they consider fundamental in the first place. Just about every democratic country agrees that freedom of speech is quite basic. But in Germany it is a crime to deny the Holocaust, or to spout Nazi doctrine; the law in the United States is otherwise. Different countries define the right of privacy quite differently. Obviously, concrete historical, social, and cultural factors explain these differences, though not always easily.

Yet the basic similarities are very strong; and they imply a strong degree of *convergence*; a coming together; a parallel process, whose motor causes are the same for all of these countries. As Volker Schmidt put it, modernization theory implies that modernization is a "homogenising process," that modernizing societies tend to "become more similar over time."[168] Modernity, then, would be (as it were) a single language, divided into a number of closely related dialects. Not everybody agrees. Some scholars have put forward the notion of multiple modernities—the idea that modernity takes on a number of fundamentally different forms, each of which has its roots in radically different forms of society. The Western form is only one of these modernities. There would also be a Chinese or Confucian version, a Hindu version, an Islamic version. S. N. Eisenstadt, very prominently, has argued for a "multiplicity of continually evolving modernities."[169] And if there are fundamentally different languages of modernity (to continue the metaphor), then it follows that there would be also different languages of human rights.

Nobody would be so foolish as to argue that there is nothing to this idea. The question is simply this: which is more fundament, the differences, or the similarities? Are the differences like the differences, say, in the Spanish of Mexico and the Spanish of Spain; or like the difference between French and Chinese? If we had an imaginary scale, and put similarities on one side, and differences on the other, which one would outbalance the other? I realize that nobody can really answer this question. Nobody has such a measuring rod. There is no objective way to test what is and what is not "fundamental." Is Japanese culture today so distinctive, so different from modern Italian culture (say), that it amounts to a difference in kind, rather than a difference in degree?

My personal feeling is that the similarities easily outbalance the differences. True, differences are often more striking than similarities. Visitors and tourists who come to Japan from the United States, or from Europe are often struck by all sorts of sights, sounds, and customs, that seem strange and different. Yet the similarities are even more salient. The streets are filled with cars. Tall buildings look the same as tall buildings all over the world. You enter a building, you take an elevator, get off on one of the top floors, you go into the offices of an insurance company, and there you see men working at computers, dressed in business suits and ties, and women wearing dresses or blouses and skirts. One man is taking a drink from a water cooler. A woman is talking on a cell phone. You go back out on the street, and pass young people in blue jeans, some of them with dyed hair, listening to rock-and-roll music on their iPods. At night, you can have dinner at a sushi restaurant—just like back home—or you can have pizza or French cuisine. You can pass up the Kabuki theater and go to a concert hall, where a symphony orchestra is playing Mendelssohn and Brahms (and doing it very well). By far the most alienating aspect of Japanese life is language; everything else shows the deep imprint of convergence. Our visitor, however, probably takes the vast similarities for granted—all of the things I just mentioned, plus the fact that one can buy aspirin tablets and vitamin pills and Kleenex in drug stores (and condoms, for that matter), and that the people dress "Western" except for ceremonial occasions; in the big cities, there are convenience stores, vending machines, and branches of fast-food restaurants; people go to movies (many of them American); they listen to contemporary music (Beethoven for some, rock-and-roll for others). The Japanese have even developed a taste for cheese and bread; and young Japanese send text messages to each other, and decide to meet friends at McDonald's. Most aspects of Japanese life have come to resemble, or run parallel to, aspects of life in other wealthy, developed countries.

Of course, one cannot ignore the differences. But there are differences, too, in Italy or Argentina; and yet, on balance, the texture of modern life seems much the same. The Japanese "sarariman" gets up in the morning, takes a shower, eats breakfast (either Japanese or Western style), takes a train or a car to his office, and at the office does office-like things, not unlike white-collar workers in other countries. Women are not equal to men; but they are more equal than they used to be. Even Japanese food is becoming less distinctive than it was. Not only are gaijin in many countries eating sushi; but the Japanese themselves now supplement sushi and sashimi with McDonald's and Kentucky Fried Chicken.

Which, then, are more "fundamental," in the case of Japan—the similarities or the differences? The work ethic, the way families are structured, attitudes toward authority: yes, these do seem very Japanese, and in sharp contrast to other Western countries. But the *trends* are toward "Western" ways, even in family life and gender relations (and away from traditional Japanese customs and habits). Cars, computers, elevators, and neckties may seem superficial; but they are the outer coat of changes that are, indeed, profound. They imply ways of living one's life, a rhythm of daily existence, that is essentially *modern* and hence more like the rhythm of life in Canada, than the rhythm of Japanese life in the age of the samurai, or in the period of court life described by Lady Murasaki.

The case for convergence, then, is very strong—convergence in technology, in institutions, and, more and more, in social relationships and in ways of thinking, behaving, and living.[170] At least this is true of the developed countries (and the elite strata in developing countries). Why, then, do the differences between societies seem so salient? For two reasons. First, because culture groups are often firmly convinced they are truly unique. In the United States, this is called "American exceptionalism." The Japanese seem to believe, quite fervently, that they are utterly distinctive; that they inhabit their own island universe. But the French, the Germans, the Italians are not far behind in such beliefs. The Russians talk about the Russian soul. People who think of themselves as unique quite naturally stress those things that (in their view) make them unique, the things that mark them off from other countries.

Secondly, as I have already suggested, in situations where A and B are *basically* the same, but not 100% the same, small differences tend to loom very large in the eyes of beholders. An Englishman notices an American or Australian accent immediately; a Spaniard notices the way a Mexican or a Chilean pronounces Spanish words. But the Englishman, the Australian, and the American are all speaking English. And the Mexican, the Spaniard, and the Chilean, are all speaking Castillian (that is, they are speaking standard Spanish). The core is the same; what differs are small matters on the periphery; whether you say carro or coche; whether you say lift or elevator, petrol or gas.

I might be wrong, but I do think that this point does not really contradict the thesis of "multiple modernities," which owes so much to the work of Eisenstadt. Eisenstadt believes that there is such a thing as "modernity"; its core idea is a "very strong emphasis on the autonomous participation of members of society in the constitution of the social and political order,"[171] This is certainly consistent with an argument based on plural equality and expressive individualism. The "multiple modernities" include an Islamic and a Confucian version.[172] But these seem to me to differ from the modernity we find in Portugal or New Zealand only insofar as they are not modern at all, or are anti-modern. Perhaps the crux is how one treats Japan, not China or Iran (though perhaps China is on the way). To me, Japan has left the realm of "multiple modernities," and joined the mainstream modernities. But of course, that is an arguable point.

As I have said, my argument applies mostly to the rich, industrial, developed countries; and to a certain degree, also to the educated and worldly elites in less-developed countries. It is among these people that one can speak about a culture of human rights. People in very traditional societies, or very traditional communities, may have a different consciousness of human rights. Or such a consciousness may be altogether lacking. The human rights movement preaches a code of universal values. But this code is part of the mental equipment of people in the developed world, for the most part. It is, however, a movement that is spreading rapidly, though never without some difficulty. As Sally Merry put it, human rights ideas are "embedded in cultural assumptions about the nature of the person, the community, and the state"; they "do not translate easily from one setting to another."[73]

Merry's research, for the most part, was in less-developed societies. Indeed, in these settings, human rights ideas—which are indeed "embedded" in cultural assumptions—are hard to "translate." They are hard to translate, too, in the various "modernities" that make up the world of "multiple modernities," if there is such a world. But these ideas are *not* hard to "translate" into the life of wealthy, developed societies, no matter what kind of history and traditions they have. To be sure, missionaries of human rights can, indeed, crash head-on with aspects of local culture. We will return to this issue in chapter 9, on cultural rights.

7
Women and Minorities

Probably nothing in the human rights movement, today, is as strong and as striking as the idea that men and women should be equal, should have equal rights, equal opportunities, and equal say in how society is run. If all persons are born equal, and have equal dignity, then this must be true of all races and ethnic groups, and it certainly must be true of both sexes. All of the conventions and charters of human rights have statements along these lines. So too of most, and probably all, of the modern constitutions. The dogma of the absolute equality of all human beings, or at least all law-abiding adults, is the fundamental premise of the human rights movement.

Women, after all, make up half of all humanity—they hold up half of the sky, as a Chinese proverb puts it. Yet women, historically, were never the equal of men, in rights, in social position, and in life-chances. This was true in society after society. It was certainly true of China, despite the nice proverb. Men ran society. Women were subservient to men. Long after men had the right to vote, and had wrested some power away from kings, nobles, and traditional elites, women were still supposed to inhabit a separate sphere. There was plenty of talk about the nobility of women's roles, how vital these roles were for society, how elevated the job of mothers and wives, how much society depended on women as the carriers of morality and soul. But in the United States in the mid-19th century—a country which foreign visitors like De Tocqueville, and Americans themselves, considered radically democratic— women had no real role in political life. They had certain basic rights; but no real political power. Married women, in particular, were subject to all sorts of disabilities. Their economic and legal identity was swallowed up by their husband's. Husband and wife, as Blackstone put it, were one flesh, "one person."[74] But it was the man who owned and managed the person and the flesh. A married woman had no right to buy or sell land, to enter into contracts, to make out a will. To be sure, there were ways around the rules of "coverture." But they were clumsy and expensive. Basically, they were available only for the upper class. In other western countries, the situation was somewhat similar. And, of course, in traditional societies, women and men each had a distinctive role, and the twain basically never met at all.

All this began to change in modern times, and particularly in the 19th century. One important step in the United States was the passage of married women's property laws. These laws removed some, and then all, of the disabilities of married women.[175] The earliest of these, from around 1840, were patchy and partial. But by the end of the century, married women generally speaking had full rights to own property, enter into contracts, and make out wills, the same as a man. It is not at all clear that the motive for making such laws was to emancipate women. More likely, these laws were meant to emancipate the land market; to unclog the wheels of trade. But they surely reflected *some* change in the way ordinary people thought about the rights, duties, powers, and abilities of women. There was also, in the 19th century, a woman's movement—small and slow at first. In England, a few pioneers, like Mary Shelley and John Stuart Mill, argued for the equality of the sexes. In the United States, a group of women and men met in Seneca Falls, New York, in 1848, under the leadership of Elizabeth Cady Stanton and Lucretia Mott, and issued a "Declaration of Sentiments," modeled somewhat on the Declaration of Independence, but with a difference—"all men and women are created equal," rather than "all men," for example. It also mentioned woman's "inalienable right to the elective franchise."[176] But the elective franchise was more elusive; it had to wait for the 20th century. The 19th Amendment to the United States Constitution provided that the right to vote "shall not be denied or abridged by the United States or by any State on account of sex." It went into effect in 1920.

The trend has been the same all over the Western world, although of course each country had its own peculiar history, its own political dynamic. The first country to grant women full voting rights was New Zealand, in 1893. Other pioneers were Australia (1902), and Finland. Denmark, Norway, and Iceland followed in 1915. In England, women over 30 were given the vote in 1918; in 1928, the age restriction was removed. Canada granted suffrage to women in 1920. Ecuador was the Latin American pioneer (1929); Thailand granted the right in 1932. But in France, women had to wait until 1944. Charles De Gaulle, who headed a Provisional Government, issued an "administration ordinance outlining plans for governing France," in April 1944, to go into effect when the country would be liberated from German occupation; the ordinance granted women the vote. Before this, suffrage bills had been passed by the Chamber of Deputies four times, starting in 1919; but the upper house killed each one of these.[177]

There were even slower countries. In Italy, women's suffrage came about only in 1946. Switzerland was a notable laggard. In this famously vibrant democracy, proposals to give women the vote were consistently voted down in the various cantons. On the federal level, women got the vote in 1971; and most of the cantons fell in line. But in the half-canton of Appenzell Ausserrhoden, women did not vote until 1989; and in Appenzell Innerrhoden—the last holdout—it took a decision of the Federal Supreme Court to give women suffrage rights at last; this was in 1990.[178] 1990 was also the year in which woman in Samoa got the vote; and in Kuwait, the year was 1995.[179] In Portugal, educated women were given voting rights in 1931 (men had to know only how to read and write); full equality had to wait until 1976. In South Africa, white women could vote in 1930, black women not until 1993. Women still do not vote in Qatar, Oman, Saudi Arabia, Brunei, and the United Arab Emirates (in some of these, to be sure, men do not vote either).[180]

The struggle for gender equality, of course, is much more than a matter of voting and holding office. For men and women to be truly equal—in society, in the family—a lot more is required; and this ideal has been achieved nowhere. In the United States, in the 20th century, an epic political battle raged, over a proposal to add an Equal Rights Amendment to the Constitution. The text provided, in words which echoed the 19th Amendment, that "Equality of rights under the law shall not be denied or abridged by the United States or by any State on account of sex." At one stage in the controversy, many progressives, men and women alike, felt the amendment was a mistake. Women, they argued, needed special protection, rather than equality. Nobody would make such an argument today. In 1972, Congress endorsed the ERA, and sent it to the states for ratification. Many states quickly agreed. But a powerful conservative backlash developed, led by Phyllis Schlafly, and the Amendment failed; not enough states ratified it to allow it to go into effect.[181] Schlafly and others argued that the ERA would force women into the Army as combat soldiers, that it would lead to the end of separate bathrooms, and that it would force women to work whether they wanted to or not. All this of course was nonsense; but conservatives in droves believed her. Schlafly won, and ERA lost. But it was a Pyrrhic victory. Women got to keep their separate bathrooms, and they also gained full legal equality—only not through the ERA.

The conflict over ERA had its parallels in other areas of American law. In *Muller v. Oregon* (1908),[182] a state law established maximum hours for women working in factories (ten hours a day). The United States Supreme Court upheld the law when it was challenged on constitutional grounds. Most (not all) women leaders hailed this as a great victory, a sign of progress. Today, the victory seems rather hollow; and the language of the opinion is (in today's terms) sexist enough to make most of us wince. The opinion stressed "woman's physical structure and the performance of maternal functions"; "healthy mothers," said the Court, were essential, because they produced "vigorous offspring." Women, in short, belonged in the home, not in the factory; but as long as they were actually in the factory, the state had a right—perhaps a duty—to protect them from physical wear and tear that would make them less good as mothers and potential mothers. At that time, women workers were also, on the whole, paid less than men. Progressives liked the decision, because it seemed pro-labor. Married women, in the early 20th century, no doubt preferred to stay home, and not slave away in factories—but only as long as husbands earned a decent wage.

What seems progressive in one period seems regressive in others. The spirit of *Muller v. Oregon* is miles away from the spirit of the great Civil Rights Act of 1964. This landmark statute outlawed discrimination in housing, education, public accommodations, and employment, on the basis of race, religion, nationality—and gender. Supposedly, inserting a ban on gender discrimination was something of an afterthought. The story is that Southern members of Congress, who wanted the bill defeated, engrafted on the text a ban on sex discrimination. They hoped this would scuttle the whole idea. If so, the tactic backfired. Seven years later, in 1971, the Supreme Court suddenly "discovered" that the Equal Protection Clause of the 14th Amendment— adopted in 1868, at a time when women did not vote or hold office—actually was meant to outlaw gender discrimination.[183] Since that time, the Supreme Court, and other federal courts, have built up an impressive body of case law on sex discrimination.[184] And an even more impressive body of law—rules, regulations, and cases—comes out of the Civil Rights Act, and the work of the Equal Employment Opportunity Commission (EEOC) which administers key aspects of that act.

Ironically—or maybe not so ironically—in many of the crucial cases, *men* rather than woman were the plaintiffs; and it was men, rather than women, who won the victories. In *Diaz v. Pan American World Airways* (1971),[185] the plaintiff, Celio Diaz, Jr., applied for a job as an airline flight attendant. He was turned down. The airline hired women, and women only, for this job. The airline argued that passengers preferred "female" stewardesses. A psychiatrist, speaking for Pan American, claimed that airplane cabins were enclosed, womb-like spaces; the "psychological needs" of the passengers were "better attended to by females." The court, however, refused to buy this rather far-fetched argument. Diaz won his case; and since then, men can and do apply for these jobs.

Arguably, if men get jobs as flight attendants, this means fewer jobs for women. But despite this, it was easy for feminists to applaud the decision. Similarly, in *Mississippi University for Women v. Hogan* (1982),[186] the plaintiff, Hogan, applied for admission to the University's School of Nursing. But Hogan was male; and the school took women only. The Supreme Court decided in favor of Hogan. The women-only policy violated the Constitution; it was discriminatory, and it tended to "perpetuate the stereotyped view of nursing as an exclusively woman's job."[187]

This is perhaps the crucial point about these cases. They are designed to break down stereotypes. They attack the idea of occupational ghettos. Why should doctors always be men, and women always nurses? Better to open up both professions. Medical schools are now full of women; and even though few men choose to be nurses, change might be on the way. Nursing programs are actively recruiting men (a program in Oregon used the slogan, "Are you Man Enough to be a Nurse?"). And if men can hand out tea and coffee on airlines, women can also patrol a beat, or sit in the cockpit of a jumbo jet and fly it across the ocean. This too is beginning to happen.

The decisions and statutes are, in many ways, as much effects as causes. Take for example the tremendous increase in women lawyers. Women began to demand the right to practice law in the 1870's. They met with bitter resistance. Myra Bradwell, of Illinois, was one of these pioneers. She was rebuffed by the state of Illinois; and when she appealed to the United States Supreme Court she lost again.[188] The "law of the Creator," according to Justice Joseph Bradley, decreed that the "paramount destiny and mission of women are to fulfill the noble and benign offices of wife and mother." A few bold pioneers in other states had better luck in the late 19th century. By 1900, the right of women to practice law was well established; and a number of law schools (though not some very notable schools, for example, Harvard) admitted women students. Still, few women took advantage of this opportunity. Why? Family pressures and social constraints held them back. It was only in the 1960's and 1970's that the situation began to change, and dramatically so. Today, in the United States, a quarter of all lawyers, and almost half of all law students, are women. The situation is similar in many other countries. French women struggled to gain the position of avocat; yet today, they represent nearly half of the avocats in France. In Germany, in 2006, 31% of the lawyers were women, and roughly the same proportion of judges.[189] In England, there were apparently no women solicitors until the 1920's, and in the late 1960's, they amounted to less than 3% of all solicitors. But by the end of the century, more than a third of all solicitors were women; and, as in other countries, since about half of all law students were women, the percentage was bound to go up.

The time-table for passage of anti-discrimination laws in many countries has followed a path somewhat like that of the United States, and in roughly the same period—the years after the end of the second World War. In France, government decrees from 1946 on demanded an end to pay discrimination; but failed to back up this pious hope with genuine sanctions. In the 1970's, however, true anti-discrimination laws were passed; and in 1983, a substantial and robust equal opportunity law.[190] In Canada, a human rights act was passed as early as 1962 in Ontario. Federal human rights legislation, which included a ban on sex discrimination, followed in the late 1970's. Sex discrimination in employment, education, and other areas was forbidden in a sweeping civil rights law passed in Germany in 2006.[191]

The real feminist revolution, of course, is a social revolution, and is, indeed, the source of the legal revolution. Real change—imperfect though it is—has come in regard to the social position of women, and, most fundamentally, on women's position in the family itself. Real change came when daughters redefined themselves as full human beings; and when fathers and mothers encouraged their daughters to become doctors, plumbers, accountants, lawyers, and police officers, instead of nurses and school-teachers, or just plain housewives. The feminist movement, then, at its core reflects the fundamental premise of the human rights movement: the legal equality of all human beings and, to the extent practical, the *social* equality as well. This, again, rests on an even more basic core, the modern versions of individualism; and, in particular, the emphasis on self-realization, and self-expression. The "emancipative social forces reflected in self-expression values" tend to liberate women, and to encourage movements in various societies to give women more power and rights.[192]

The feminist revolution has made a huge difference in society, but of course it has been only a partial success. There have been feminist movements in all Western countries. Each has its own peculiarities; but the movements reinforce and influence each other, and at core they are much the same. The trend of development has been uniformly in one direction: more women in business, in politics, in all walks of life. The Asian democracies are on the whole slower and more recalcitrant than the European democracies. But in theory and in formal law, Japanese or Taiwanese women have the same rights as men; and little by little theory is turning (more or less) into practice. Feminism has also reached third-world countries—it has impacted, obviously, the elite strata of society; but often it has gone deeper, too. Families in rural China still want sons, not daughters; but for the urban Chinese this is changing. Probably the most reluctant societies are the conservative Islamic countries. Even here there are some signs of mild rebellion on the part of at least some women.

The various declarations of rights, and the new constitutions, formally purport to make men and women equal before the law. For example, the German *Grundgesetz* provides: "Men and women have the same rights," and "No one should be either favored or disadvantaged on the basis of gender" (Article 3).[93] Many international treaties and charters express the ideal of gender equality. This includes the United Nations Charter of 1945, and, very notably, the Convention on the Elimination of All Forms of Discrimination against Women (CEDAW), of 1981. This document condemned "discrimination against women in all its forms." The states that signed it agreed "to pursue by all appropriate means and without delay a policy of eliminating discrimination" (Article 2). The Convention goes on to list, in some detail, what is (supposedly) required of the countries that signed on: this includes the right to vote "in all elections" on a par with men (Article 7); an end to discrimination in the job market (Article 11: the right to work is "an inalienable right of all human beings"); and in health care. Over 180 countries have signed on, including (of all places) Saudi Arabia and Afghanistan, not to mention North Korea; and while many of these countries have expressed "reservations," none of them seem to reject the idea of women's rights root and branch.

Gender equality, then, is accepted as a core constitutional principle; and a bedrock aspect of human rights. Turning theory into practice is another story. Men have been dominant in most societies since the dawn of time; and changes in the way men and women relate to each other, the attitudes they have, and the institutions that reinforce "patriarchy" are devilishly slow to change. But change *has* occurred, and in many ways more swiftly than most people might have imagined. And, as was true of the campaign against domestic violence, which Sally Merry has written about,[94] there is some evidence that the treaties and declarations do make a difference. At the very least, they start a debate and catalyze social movements for and about women. Beth Simmons has argued that this has been the case in Japan and in Colombia, where CEDAW has made at least some difference. Where women have "both the motive and the means to use international law to improve their rights chances, the CEDAW has proved to be a powerful tool in their hands."[95]

Of course in many countries—most countries? almost all countries?—the home and the family are still bastions and citadels of male supremacy. Even in developed countries, the details, and the limits, of gender equality are subject to considerable dispute. There is, for example, the issue of abortion. The American Supreme Court held, in the famous case of *Roe v. Wade*,[196] that the Constitution protected a woman's right to choose to end her pregnancy, particularly in the first months after conception. This has been, ever since, a highly controversial issue; the Supreme Court has waffled and wobbled, but *Roe v. Wade* has never been overruled.

The law in Germany has taken quite a different tack—constitutionally speaking, at any rate. In the 1970's, the German constitutional court struck down a law allowing abortion on demand in the first trimester; the court felt that the *Grundgesetz* gave the unborn the right to life, and the right to legal protection.[197] The Court did not close the door on laws which allowed abortion in some circumstances; and there was further litigation, and a great deal of legislative tinkering in the 1990's. The law ultimately allowed abortion, but provided for mandatory counseling; state health insurance would "pay for abortions that were 'legal' in the sense that they were carried out for reasons of rape, incest, or serious threat to the woman's life or health." This was an "uneasy compromise" that satisfied no one; but, unlike the American situation, "mobilization around the abortion issue has faded."[198]

The issue of sexual harassment provides another example of differences in approach. The courts in the United States consider sexual harassment a violation of rules against gender discrimination. But what exactly does sexual harassment consist of? American courts and agencies have found sexual harassment (and a "hostile work environment") in situations that would not qualify as such in other societies. Those opposed to the American approach sometimes even argue that "measures against sexual harassment" tend to "destroy national, natural, and healthy gender relations by stifling flirtation and eroticism at work." One even hears, in France, about a "Mediterranean culture of seduction" that somehow deserves to be protected.[199]

An interesting essay by Myra Marx Ferree points to the difference between European and American ways of framing the problem of gender inequality. Americans, she argues, use the "metaphor" of race in discussions of gender, more or less equating problems of gender and race. Europeans see gender inequality as *class* discrimination, rather than as social practice comparable to race discrimination. The distinction, she feels, has important consequences. If gender is like race, then gender politics tends not to focus quite so much on "the importance of group membership"; rather, the aim is to help individuals achieve their "full potential." Treating gender like class has both plusses and minuses. It helps mobilize women, along with other oppressed groups; but it also tends to downplay any special claims of women—claims to be different in some way from other victim groups.[200]

This distinction reminds us of the debate, within the women's movement, for and against gender "essentialism." Stripped of complexities, this is the question whether women are or are not "essentially" different from men. Obviously, there are biological differences: women get pregnant, give birth to children, and breast-feed them. They have less body hair and tend to be shorter than men. Men have bigger muscles, on average; they can impregnate women, but the rest of the nine month period is entirely her share of the process. So much is clear. But is there anything much beyond this? Claims that women are more nurturing and empathetic than men; or, on the other hand, that they are less intellectual or creative; or that they are morally superior; or that they cannot do math; or that they have less sexual appetite—are all of these only cultural, or (to put it another way) socially constructed? Do they all come out of a male-dominated social order, and serve the interests of patriarchy? In the old days, the usual answer to this question was clearly no. Women were both romanticized and denigrated (and sometimes demonized), but in any case, they were considered fundamentally different from men, inhabiting a different sphere, a different world, which was sometimes a haven, and sometimes a kind of social prison.[201]

Some feminists are themselves "essentialists," but the basic thrust of modern law—and the strong trend in modern society—is anti-essentialist. Or, to put it another way, law starts from the assumption that women can do anything men can do, and should be allowed to try; their talents and ambitions may also be the same as those of men. They should be allowed equal access to any opportunities. They should have free choice of occupations. They should be allowed to be police officers, symphony conductors, jet pilots, and anything else they wish, including heading high offices of state. The talents of at least some women lie in these directions.

What about the right to be a "sex-worker," or more bluntly put, a prostitute? Recent German law has said yes; bowing to the demands of prostitutes themselves, who formed a lobby. Women, under this law, may register as members of the profession, and may pay into pension and health insurance plans. This law, in a sense, gave status to what is often called "the oldest profession." As Rebecca Pates has pointed out, this was a response to the idea that "the provision of sexual services" flowed from "the right to self-determination," the right to decide "what to do with one's body." In Sweden, on the other hand, prostitution (as is common elsewhere) is against the law. The Swedish view is that prostitution has been "an aspect of male violence," and "a form of exploitation of women," which is "harmful not only to the individual prostituted woman...but also to society at large." Gender equality will "remain unattainable as long as men buy, sell and exploit women...by prostituting them."[202]

Both views can be defended on feminist grounds. The Swedish view is obviously in one sense more realistic: it looks at prostitution in its social context, and it does not like what it sees there. The German statute seems to suggest that women choose this line of business, rationally and coolly, just as they might choose to become a bank teller or a flight attendant. But prostitution might be a special case. Letting women choose to be airline pilots or police officers does not raise the same issues. The general trend in the law is to break down barriers that keep women out of certain occupations. This means granting women the same choices—and the same dignity—as men. Whether entering the "oldest profession" is just an example of choice is a complex issue, more complex than making room for women as dentists. Obviously, no state will decide to forbid women to stay home, watch the children, cook, and darn the husband's socks; but it is not realistic to pretend that when a woman does choose to be a Hausfrau, her decision is completely voluntary and unconstrained. Society, in context, imbues this choice with meanings; and the same is true of a woman's "choice" to sell her body for cash. Women (like men) are pushed in certain directions, often by forces they do not clearly grasp or understand.

Most occupational choices are less fraught with meaning and controversy than the choice of "sex-work." At the present stage of development, fewer women than men decide to be airline pilots or police officers. But policy demands that the doors not be locked against those who do make this decision. And some women *will* make this choice. Perhaps more and more as time goes by. Anti-essentialism is thus an important attitude, from a policy standpoint. This is so, whether women do behave the same as men, or not; whether they have the same talents and emotions or not; and whether they *ever* will behave the same as men. For policy reasons, then, the "American" attitude in Ferree's essay may be preferable to the "European" attitude. It is truer to the fundamental premise of the human rights movement, that is, the equality of all human beings, in law and in society; and to the underlying ethos of individualism that is at the core of the movement.

PLURAL EQUALITY

The civil rights movement in the United States was a prominent and striking social phenomenon of the late 20th century. The movement demanded equality, rights, and opportunities for African-Americans. Women demanded their rights as well. A small vanguard of feminists had been agitating for more than century; but in the period after the second World War, the movement became stronger — more comprehensive as well; and much more successful. Other minorities — Hispanics, for example, and the Native American peoples — advanced their own causes; and in addition, the elderly and the handicapped; and the so-called sexual minorities. Each of these groups achieved results that would have seemed both astonishing and impossible in earlier times.

Nor are these simply or even primarily American movements. Wherever there were racial minorities, we find civil rights movements or the equivalent. Very striking have been movements demanding rights for indigenous peoples—in Latin America, in Australia and Canada. The various movements influence and inspire each other. In Brazil, for example, the American civil rights movement raised the consciousness of Afro-Brazilians; and helped to counter the myth that there was no such thing as racial discrimination in Brazil. Every developed country has its women's movement; and some under-developed ones as well. The United States pioneered age discrimination laws; but these have now spread to Australia, Canada, and the European Union, in various forms. Australia, too, has a Disability Discrimination Act, passed in 1992, two years after Congress passed the Americans With Disabilities Act. The DDA aimed to "promote a recognition and acceptance...of the principle that persons with disabilities have the same fundamental rights as the rest of the community."²⁰³

What all of these have in common is an ideology I call plural equality. Plural equality is more than an attack on overt discrimination; it also challenges more subtle patterns of domination; and demands equality of legitimacy, dignity, respect. Minorities want not simply to be tolerated, but to be *recognized*—to be considered just as entitled to share in the polity as the majority, and to be considered just as worthy as the ruling race, gender, or language. The majority in the United States or France or the Czech Republic is white and Christian. Plural equality is the notion that other races and religions are equal to the majority in rights, dignity, and opportunities. Of course, this is an ideal, not a reality. Discrimination against African-Americans is not dead; the Romany people are persecuted in the Czech Republic; and it would be naïve to argue that anti-Semitism is only a bad memory; or that Moslems in France have the same life-chances as "real" Frenchmen. But the ideal is important, and not simply as an ideology. It has real political and social consequences.

We drew a distinction between tolerance and plural equality. In the 19th century, in the United States, in Great Britain, and in other European countries, non-Christian religions were certainly "tolerated." But Christianity (Protestantism in some countries, Catholicism in others) was the dominant religion, and the only religion which had real recognition. Nobody suffered religious persecution. There was no Inquisition, no auto da fé. Jews could build synagogues, Moslems could build mosques. But these other religions lived, as it were, as tenants in somebody else's house. The state recognized the Christian Sabbath not the Jewish or Muslim day of rest. Christmas and Easter were national holidays. In some parts of the United States, in the early 19th century, "blasphemy" was a crime. Laws existed which (potentially) punished people who reviled Christianity, not people who reviled Islam or Judaism, or, for that matter, paganism. England still had an established church. Nineteenth century England no longer murdered Catholics; and Catholics, indeed, ultimately gained the right to vote and sit in Parliament. "Dissenters" were free to build their chapels and worship as they chose. But again, all this was tolerance, not plural equality. A dominant majority graciously granted these rights; but everybody understood which people actually owned the house, and which ones did not; which ones were allowed to come and go as they pleased, but without any sense of true ownership.

Plural equality, if you take it to its "logical extreme," implies "that there *are* no minorities; there is no cultural and moral hegemony." After all, each person regardless of race, gender, and so on is a "unique individual"; no individual should suffer because of membership in a group, whether the group is racial or religious; or even if the group is deaf people or old people or women attracted to women instead of men.[204]

In a way, the central idea is what we might call mainstreaming. This term is used to describe the policy of putting children with disabilities (say) in the same classes as students who have no disabilities. Or it might describe the practice of fitting up buses with little elevators so that people in wheelchairs could ride them. Plural equality, in other words, goes way past the policy of outlawing overt discrimination. To be sure, that is the first step, so that a brilliant black baseball player with talent can play with the New York Yankees; and a black woman with a remarkable, beautiful voice can sing with the Metropolitan opera. But it means going beyond steps to remove formal obstacles; it also means "leveling the playing field." This might require books published in Braille, and ramps and elevators to permit the handicapped to enjoy public facilities. It might mean affirmative action to wipe out the legacy of past discrimination. And it might mean, above all, treating each of the groups in question as if they *were* part of the majority, and dealing with them on a plane of emotional and psychological equality.

Where does plural equality come from? It is the translation into social terms, and into real life, of the ideals expressed in all the charters and manifestoes and declarations: that everybody is or should be equal in dignity and in rights to everybody else. It is the contemporary ideology of individualism—an ideology not of philosophers, but of ordinary and not-so-ordinary people, or at least many of them—something they feel, something in the air they breathe, something that is meaningful to them, even though they might not be able to put it into words; or even be conscious of it. It is simply there, all around them, and they act on it, without knowing why they think as they do; and why they act as they do.

The sacred individual: yet the rights of racial and ethnic minorities seem, on the surface, to be group rights, not individual rights. But if you analyze them carefully, as we mentioned, one sees that they are really individual rights. A major goal of the feminist movement is to make sure that women have the same *individual* choices as men; and the only way to do this is to remove barriers, and do battle against stereotypes and prejudices. The same point can be made about racial policies, and policies on behalf of indigenous peoples and the so-called sexual minorities. For people in wheelchairs, as we said, plural equality might require tricking out buses with devices to lift the wheelchair. It means mainstreaming. But mainstreaming, in a way, is what all the new groups require. Mainstreaming means nothing more or less than trying to fulfill the dream of human equality, person by person, one step at a time.

8
Privacy and Dignity[205]

In the armory of human rights talk, it would be hard to find a more slippery concept than "privacy." The word has many meanings and many nuances. Daniel Solove has argued, rather convincingly, that there really is no common denominator among the various definitions; that it is hopeless to try to extract some sort of essence from the tohu-bohu of this vast and intractable literature. Many people have tried and failed dismally. Privacy simply has too many meanings, and is used in too many different ways, to be tied up into a single neat package.[206]

I will not add my name to Solove's list of failed attempts. Privacy does have many shifting meanings. "Privacy" in the American constitutional sense seems to mean the right to make fundamental life choices—choices about sex and marriage, choices about having or not having babies. "Privacy" also means the right to keep parts of your life free from snooping; it means controls on such things as government surveillance or wiretapping or warrantless searches —the classic right to treat your home as a castle. "Privacy" is also the right to send letters without some bureaucrat steaming it open and reading what you wrote. Closely related is the right to resist intrusion from paparazzi, scandal sheets, and nosey neighbors. This is the sense in the so-called "right of privacy" in tort law, which dates from the late 19th century, and has had a fitful career since then.

As is obvious, then, the "right of privacy" is a particularly muddled concept in the United States. Historically, there was always some protection for "privacy" in a classic sense. The Bill of Rights forbids unreasonable searches and seizures. State constitutions do the same. The heavy hand of the state had to be kept in check. "Privacy" in this sense (the word was not necessarily used) meant freedom from the power of the central government.

"Privacy" in one or more of its dimensions is mentioned in many of the fundamental texts about human rights. As always, interpretation is the rub. Article 12 of the Universal Declaration of Human Rights provides that "No one shall be subjected to arbitrary interference with his privacy, family, home or correspondence, nor to attacks upon his honour and reputation. Everyone has the right to the protection of the law against such interference or attacks." This suggests, among other things, the sanctity of the home, a time-honored right. The sanctity of letters and other correspondence is specifically mentioned. But "privacy" is not further defined. It is significant, though, that protection of privacy is coupled with protection of "honor" and "reputation." The concept remains vague: but the texts make clear that something called privacy is an aspect of human rights.

PRIVACY: THE AMERICAN STORY

It may be useful to describe, at least briefly, how American law and society has confronted issues of privacy. The Fourth Amendment, part of the Bill of Rights, expressed the right of people "to be secure in their persons, houses, papers, and effects, against unreasonable searches and seizures." A warrant was not to be issued except "upon probable cause, supported by Oath or affirmation," describing what was to be searched or seized. Dozens of federal and state decisions wrestled with the question of how far the protection extends. Obviously, new technology made the issue more complicated. Jefferson and Madison could not conceive of the brave new world of wiretapping and satellite pictures, not to mention Google Earth.

In 1928, in *Olmstead v. United States*,[207] the Supreme Court of the United States first faced the issue of wiretapping. Olmstead was a convicted bootlegger, during Prohibition. He was quite a big time operator. The government gathered evidence for its case by using a wiretap: small "wires...inserted along the ordinary telephone wires" from the houses of some of Olmstead's fellow-violators. Could the government use this evidence at trial? Was wiretapping an illegal search and seizure, forbidden by the Bill of Rights? A bare majority of the Court thought not. Nobody had invaded Olmstead's house. The tap was made "without trespass upon any property of the defendants.... The taps from house lines were made in the streets near the houses." The dissenters, on the other hand, felt the government had invaded Olmstead's privacy. The evidence, they argued, should have been excluded. The 1934 Federal Communications Act made it unlawful to "divulge or publish" communications, or to "intercept any communication and divulge or publish" the contents.[208] Many states had already outlawed wiretapping. In 1967, the Supreme Court specifically overruled the *Olmstead* case, in *Katz v. United States*.[209] Katz, the defendant, had been transmitting "wagering information by telephone from Los Angeles to Miami and Boston." The calls were made from a "public telephone booth." The government argued that these dastardly phone calls were not protected, since they were not made from Katz' home, but in a more or less public place. The Supreme Court reversed Katz' conviction. The Fourth Amendment, said the Court, in a phrase often quoted since then, "protects people, not places." The Fourth Amendment applies, then, to any place or situation where people have a "reasonable" expectation of privacy.

"Reasonable" is not exactly a precise and objective concept. It changes shape, color, and meaning over the years. What was a "reasonable" expectation of privacy in one period may seem unreasonable in another, and vice versa. Nobody today much objects, for example, to metal detectors that scan our bodies at the entrance to a courthouse, or in the security line at an airport. We take off our shoes in the security line, and if the buzzer rings, some employee of the Transportation Security Administrarion pats us down and feels around for whatever set off the machine. This is standard practice. Of course, years ago, this might have been considered quite objectionable—an invasion of bodily integrity. But no longer.

In 1989, in *Florida v. Riley*,[210] the police suspected that a certain Riley was growing marijuana in a greenhouse on his land. The sheriff flew over the property in a helicopter. Two roof panels were missing; thus the sheriff was able to peek inside the greenhouse. He thought he saw marijuana growing there. Did this helicopter excursion violate Riley's rights? Was this a search of his property (without a warrant)? A bare majority of the Supreme Court thought not. Riley had no reasonable expectation of privacy, under the circumstances.

Another close case was *Kyllo v. United States* (2001).[211] Here, instead of a helicopter, the authorities used a thermal imaging device on Danny Lee Kyllo—another man suspected of growing marijuana. This device could not actually "penetrate" a house, listen in to conversations, or detect whatever else was going on. But it could, and did, make a record of heat coming from the home. Kyllo's house was emitting a *lot* of heat. Growing marijuana indoors takes a lot of light and heat. The heat of the house confirmed the suspicion that Kyllo was growing marijuana indoors. The police then got a warrant, searched the house, and found the dreaded plants. This was another case decided by a closely-divided Supreme Court. Five justices sided with Kyllo. Thermal imaging was a kind of "search": the authorities should have gotten a warrant *before* they used the device.

This little corner of constitutional law continues to give the courts trouble. At the core of the problem is the onward march of technology. At one time, people *were* quite "private" at home. As soon as they closed the door and pulled down the shades, they were totally secure. Nobody, unless that person was hiding in the closet or under the bed, could spy on them at home. But this is less and less true. Who knows what technical marvels will follow on the heels of "thermal imaging"? The homely and old-fashioned camera has become very sophisticated; perhaps we are already able to see through walls. "Imaging" at airports is already a reality.

The rules about wiretapping and similar devices are complex and confusing. The reasons are clear. There is a kind of arms race between law-breakers and law-enforcers. The public is on both sides at once. The public wants criminals found out, caught, and punished. The public tends to be willing to buy security at the price of a loss of privacy, especially if it is somebody else's privacy. The so-called war on terror has made the issue more and more intense. Life since 2001 has been a constant state of orange alert. People will support any tactic or technology, if it can frustrate the people with bombs strapped to their bellies, or concealed in their shoes or their underwear. And yet, at the same time, people want a zone of privacy, a zone of immunity; they hate radar detectors; and, in Germany, even a proposed census was considered far too intrusive, in the form it was first proposed. The German Constitutional Court agreed; the census law violated fundamental rights, at least in part; and the result "was to reduce some 40 million questionnaire forms to a heap of worthless waste paper."[212]

PRIVACY: THE CONSTITUTIONAL DIMENSION

Perhaps the various meanings of privacy do have a kind of common denominator. Underlying many of them is the concept of choice—the right to decide what is and what is not a private decision, including the right to decide whether or not to have babies, and how many, and what kind of sex to have (of course with consenting adults). Or how much of oneself to strip naked, so to speak, and how much to keep closeted. Choice itself, of course, is a key concept in the world of expressive individualism. In any event, the critical life-choices just mentioned are, in the United States, constitutionally protected, and in the name of "privacy."

This constitutional "right of privacy," as the United States Supreme Court developed it, is a very different beast from the traditional Warren and Brandeis common-law right, discussed in the next section. It is not simply the right to be left alone, or to enjoy private life free from prying eyes; the life-choices are not necessarily secret at all. They can be shouted from the rooftops. Nonetheless, the Supreme Court has chosen to use that word to describe certain rights it protects from government interference.

The word "privacy" is not mentioned, of course, in the federal constitution. The issue of "privacy" as such was not discussed, as far as I know, in the late 18th century. The justices themselves eventually developed privacy as a constitutional concept. An early decision, in 1942, seemed (at least in hindsight) to foreshadow the later doctrine. The case, *Skinner v. Oklahoma*,[213] arose under a statute, once of a fairly common type, which gave the state the right to sterilize habitual criminals and people who were "feeble-minded." The Supreme Court struck down this law. Legally, the Court rested its opinion on the equal protection clause of the 14th amendment. Skinner had stolen chickens and committed armed robbery. This made him a candidate for sterilization—otherwise, however, if his crime had been (say) embezzlement. This distinction the Court found irrational and unsustainable. The opinion tapped into a growing revulsion against sterilization, which the Nazi regime had made even more deeply suspect. The Court's opinion did, however, at one point state that the "right to have offspring" was "basic." This point was an aside; but perhaps a prophetic one.

The real beginning of the right to privacy, in the constitutional sense, began with *Griswold v. Connecticut*, decided in 1965.[214] A Connecticut law essentially made it a crime to sell or use contraceptives. The Supreme Court struck down the statute. The main opinion, by the same Justice, Douglas, who wrote the opinion in *Skinner*, claimed that a "zone of privacy" (not visible to the naked eye) lurked somewhere hidden in the text of the Bill of Rights. In his words (often sneered at), the rights in the Bill of Rights "have penumbras, formed by emanations from those guarantees that help give them life and substance." Justice Goldberg, who wrote a concurring opinion, felt that the word "liberty" in the Constitution implied protection for personal rights, whether or not they were specifically mentioned, so long as they were "fundamental." The *Griswold* case may rest on jerry-built legal reasoning and shaky logic—the whole idea of "penumbras" and "emanations" is almost if not quite ridiculous—but socially the case has proven as powerful as the rock of Gibraltar. Some of the later cases—very notably the abortion decisions—are wildly controversial, and the right wing wants them overruled. But nobody (or almost nobody) calls for overruling *Griswold v. Connecticut.*

Seven years after *Griswold*, in *Eisenstadt v. Baird* (1972),[215] the Supreme Court justices went a step beyond *Griswold* and expanded the right to privacy which they had so recently discovered. Massachusetts had a law less sweeping than Connecticut's; contraceptives were not banned, but they were available, legally, only to married couples, and only doctors and pharmacists were entitled to distribute them. Baird, the defendant, gave a lecture on birth control at Boston University, and afterwards distributed Emko Vaginal Foam to a woman who had heard his lecture. The Supreme Court reversed his conviction. Justice Brennan talked about the right of the "individual," whether married or not, to be free from government intrusion into so fundamental a decision as "whether to bear or beget a child."

One year later came the notorious abortion case, *Roe v. Wade*.[216] Restrictions on abortion, the Court held, invaded a right to privacy—the decision to have or not have a child belonged, by rights, to women and their doctors. At least in the early months of pregnancy, no restriction on a woman's right to end her pregnancy was constitutionally acceptable.

How far did this right of privacy extend? In *Bowers v. Hardwick* (1986),[217] five justices refused to hold that the right of privacy protected same-sex relations between consenting adults. This even though the sex took place in defendant's own home. This turned out to be only a speed-bump on the road to an expanded right of privacy. In 2003, in *Lawrence v. Texas*,[218] the Supreme Court overruled *Bowers v. Hardwick*, and struck down a Texas statute which made homosexual behavior ("sodomy") a crime.

In some ways, the Court in this line of cases moved ahead of public opinion. But public opinion itself is not easy to measure; and it changes over time. The abortion decision is still a political lightning rod. Millions of people detest it, and would like to see it undone. Probably millions of people detest the gay rights movement, and disapprove of cases like *Lawrence v. Texas*. But the winds of change are sweeping across the country. Even before *Lawrence v. Texas*, the gay rights movement had made amazing progress. At the time of the decision, most states had already repealed their sodomy laws; only about a dozen or so were left. At this writing, some states, including Massachusetts and Iowa, have gone so far as to legalize gay marriage. Gays may also marry in Spain and the Netherlands. And a number of American states provide for civil unions or domestic partnerships, which are almost marriages packaged under different labels.

The Court may be out ahead of the general public; but it is not—and almost never is—*very* far ahead. The Court did in fact *invent* the right of privacy; that much is true. The Court here was doing what it often does—making new law—but thinly disguised as an interpretation of ancient texts. But even when making new law, the justices remain creatures of context. The constitutional right of privacy fits comfortably within the ethos of the human rights movement. In this regard, the United States has simply joined, without benefit of constitutional language, a world-wide constitutional movement. Whatever the United States Supreme Court has done has its parallels in other countries, either under the heading of privacy, human dignity, or some similar rubric.

Many of the new constitutions explicit recognize something called "privacy," either in so many words, or with some other name. The Constitution of Paraguay (1992) provides that "personal and family intimacy" ("la intimidad personal y familiar") is "inviolable"; the law will protect this "intimacy," as well as the dignity of the individual. (Art. 34). This Constitution also provides that everyone has the right to the "free expression of his personality, to creativity, and to the formation of his own identity and image" (Art. 25). The Korean Constitution provides for protection of the privacy of the home, and of communications (Art. 16 and 18).[219] The Estonian Constitution (Art. 2, sec. 26), speaks of the "inviolability of private and family life"; the state shall not, as a general rule, "interfere with the private or family life of any person."[220] Many provisions in these constitutions recognize a classic right—privacy of the home—but add nuances which reflect modern social norms, in particular, rights to "personality" and its development, which means, in essence, expressive individualism.

Even in the United States, some state constitutions, in recent times, have added clauses which recognize and make explicit a right to "privacy." These provisions are, on the whole, remarkably vague. This is only to be expected. Many seem to reflect a narrower and more literal idea of "privacy" than the one the Supreme Court recognizes. The Montana Constitution (Art. II, sec. 10) states that "The right of individual privacy is essential to the well-being of a free society and shall not be infringed without the showing of a compelling state interest." The Hawaii Constitution (Art. I, sec. 6) says much the same thing, and directs the legislature to "take effective steps to implement this right." The Florida Constitution (Art. I, sec. 23), has a somewhat different approach. It states that "Every natural person has the right to be let alone and free from government intrusion into the person's private life." The California Constitution specifically mentions the word privacy: The people's "inalienable" rights include "pursuing and obtaining safety, happiness, and privacy" (Art. 1, sec. 1). The word also appears in the Illinois Constitution. People have a right to be "secure in their persons, houses, papers and other possessions against unreasonable searches, seizures, invasions of privacy or interceptions of communications by eavesdropping devices or other means" (Art. 1, sec. 6).[221]

Some state courts have also been active in "discovering" privacy rights hidden in their constitutions. The Supreme Court, in *Bowers v. Hardwick*, upheld state sodomy laws, despite the new-minted right of privacy, as we have seen. But two state courts, Kentucky and Georgia, held exactly the opposite—based on their own constitutions. The Montana court reached the same result in 1997, under the privacy provision of the Montana constitution.[222] In each case, it was something of a stretch for these courts; and a skeptic might suggest that the Kentucky, Georgia, and Montana courts simply made the whole thing up. On the other hand, they were surely responding (unconsciously, perhaps) to the Zeitgeist. What is rather remarkable is that these courts were located in quite conservative states. The privacy decisions may be *legally* bold; socially, they were less so. The courts were marching in harmony with the norms of a large segment of the public—even, perhaps, a majority.

PERSONAL PRIVACY

Discussion of other aspects of "privacy" law in the United States conventionally begin with a classic article by Boston law partners Samuel Warren and Louis Brandeis, which appeared in the *Harvard Law Review* in 1890.[223] This was the age of so-called yellow journalism—the age of cheap, sensational newspapers, which catered to the tastes of the mass public. The two learned authors, men of high reputation, and members of the legal elite, were scandalized by the antics of the press, which went, they said, beyond the limits of "decency." Newspapers were broadcasting "idle gossip" to the world, even details of "sexual relations." Technology was also an enemy. A wonderful new invention, the Kodak or "candid" camera, now made it possible to take a person's picture without his permission, and even without his knowledge.[224] The common law, the authors argued, could and should protect the right of privacy, the right to be left alone, to right to be free from prying eyes and prying cameras. The tone of their argument was distinctly elitist. Their dominant concern was personal privacy for respectable, prominent people: people who might be hounded and besieged by gossip columnists and by what later came to be called paparazzi.

As we will see, for "public figures" (Warren and Brandeis surely were such figures), the right to privacy has eroded greatly. It collides with the sense that the public has a right to know all about such people. But ordinary people do value their privacy and their right to be left alone.

For most people privacy is a right; and it is connected to concepts of human dignity and worth. People feel they should have the right to control personal information, along with their pictures, and their behavior. The exact contours of this right rest on social judgments; and they change over time.

Parts of our lives are very private; and people want to keep them private, even though there is nothing shameful or wrong in what is done. Suppose, for example, someone rigged a hidden camera in a neighbor's bedroom, and took pictures of a married couple making love. There is nothing illegal or immoral about sex—indeed, the future of the species depends on it. Yet almost everybody would be outraged at this invasion of privacy.[225] Similarly, secret photographs showing people moving their bowels, although this is a very natural process. Or spy cams taking pictures of people in the shower. Most people would find a nude picture of themselves, taken secretly, quite intolerable; or even a picture of them in their underwear. But on the beach, the same people might wear a bathing suit that would have been considered indecent a century ago, and which nobody would have dared to wear in public. Norms are, obviously, changing. Nonetheless, we want to make our own decisions about what we show and when we show it. It is my right to decide, for example, whether or not to tell people I have diabetes. For this reason, perhaps, there has been a tremendous increase in sensitivity to medical privacy. "Privacy" in these personal senses has a powerful emotional pull.

The law struggles to protect these rights. A high—and growing—volume of reported cases turn on the right of privacy—in America, and in Europe as well. In California, dozens and dozens of cases invoke Article 1, section 1 of the California Constitution, which uses the magic word privacy. Courts have given the concept a broad definition. These are rights, not just against the government, but also against private individuals and companies. But how much protection, where, and when? The legal meaning of "privacy" is hard to pin down. A key (legal) doctrine gives protection in times and places where people have a "reasonable expectation" of privacy. Clearly, these places include our bathrooms, bedrooms, and showers. But where else? In *Vo v. City of Garden Grove* (2004),[226] the city, in Orange County, California, devised an ordinance to regulate cybercafés, where, they feared, gangs were hanging out. One provision of the ordinance required cybercafés to "install a video surveillance system," covering "all entrances and exit points and all interior spaces, excepting bathroom and private office areas." Was this an invasion of privacy? The court said no. The cameras were not intrusive; and the customers had no "reasonable expectation of privacy." The court mentioned "the near ubiquitous use of video surveillance in retail establishments, at automated bank teller machines, and at road intersections." If so, how could the customers in the cybercafé, who were used to such video cameras, claim a "reasonable expectation of privacy"?[227]

A good question. People do seem to accept surveillance cameras in banks, and metal detectors at the entrance to courthouses and other public buildings. But was this always the case? Probably not. The public has simply gotten used to these forms of surveillance, and accepts them. Our times are obsessed not only with crime, but also with fears of terrorist attacks. In the name of security, a good many things are permitted; and come to seem "reasonable," which would not have seemed reasonable before.

Note, too, that the ordinance made bathrooms and private office areas off limits to surveillance cameras. This was a policy choice. In an earlier California case (1998), the city of Newport Beach, acting under a local ordinance, closed down *The Mermaid*, an "adult entertainment establishment."[228] The owners brought suit; but the California Court of Appeal sided with the city. It did strike down some parts of the ordinance. One provision required such places to hire a "restroom attendant," to prevent people from performing "specified sexual activities." The court felt this went too far, but on grounds other than privacy. Whatever the "sensibilities" of the patrons, "there is no constitutional right to privacy in the restrooms of a place of public accommodation." Still, many people would probably find the idea of cameras or snoopers in a public restroom repellent, and a breach of *something*, whether or not they could identify what that something was. The concept of a "reasonable expectation of privacy" is necessarily a work in progress.

PRIVACY AND THE RIGHT TO KNOW

Privacy, as people understood it, implies a right to keep certain areas of life strictly private. Legally, the boundaries of the right have to be hammered out, case by case. The popular understanding of privacy flows from modern norms of choice and individualism, as we have argued. But these same norms support a right to government transparency and information about matters of public interest. These norms often come into conflict.

In Florida, a fourteen year old boy, Glenn Williams, died of an "apparent drug overdose."[229] The staff of the medical examiner performed an autopsy. Some policemen took still photographs of the proceeding; and another officer, "using a borrowed video camera, made an approximately hour long videotape of the autopsy." This officer, at his home, showed the tape to two other police officers, and also to another man, who had once been a police officer himself. A local newspaper broke the news about the viewing, and claimed it took place "in a party atmosphere," where people "joked and laughed" (the officers denied this, and said the atmosphere was "professional"). The mother and sister of the dead boy sued the city, claiming (among other things) invasion of privacy. Under Florida law, public records are available for public inspection, and the trial court held that the videotape was a public record. The appeal court reversed, but not on privacy grounds. In fact, the court felt that dead people have no privacy rights. [230] But many people would probably disagree with the court; they might think that a sacred right had been violated, a private grief held up to ridicule, or at least to prying eyes.

Neither Glenn Williams nor his mother and sister were "public figures" in the sense of the American President, or the Pope, or, for that matter, a famous rock star. On the other hand, what happened to him was to a degree newsworthy; to a degree it was a matter of public interest. One contested issue in privacy law is the question: who do the rules protect? Here law and society make a sharp distinction between ordinary people and "public figures." For public figures, the right to know looms very large. In the United States, practically speaking, even the sex life of a public figure, or the kind of underwear she buys and wears, seems to be fair game. The (assumed) right of the public to know everything about public life and public figures rests apparently (or ostensibly) on the grounds that this information is important in a democratic society.

Brandeis and Warren were worried, in their day, about gossip, the yellow press, and violations of the privacy rights of respectable members of the national elite. They would be even more worried today. This is the age of fan magazines, scandal sheets, and tabloids; the age of television, the internet, and surveillance cameras. The paparazzi are like flies buzzing about the world of the rich and famous; and they have zoom lenses and infinite patience and gall. And Warren and Brandeis would be sorely disappointed with the current state of American law. Their goal—a kind of cocoon of tort law protecting elites—is all but dead. The edifice of privacy, at least for public figures, has been largely dismantled by the courts. For those who *are* public figures, not much is left of privacy rights, at least in the United States. Perhaps there is a limit. We can ask whether the public has a right to know absolutely *everything* about the President, including his sex life; or every single steamy, sleazy detail of the lives and personal habits of movie stars. Perhaps not. Still, if you are rich, prominent, or important; if you step onto the public stage, so to speak, you can say goodbye to most if not all of your right of privacy.[231]

In the United States, an important line of Supreme Court cases, beginning with *New York Times v. Sullivan* (1964),[232] has a direct bearing on the issue. This case did not concern privacy at all, but rather defamation. As usual, the actual facts of the case help explain its outcome. This was, essentially, a civil rights case. Southern segregationists were trying yet another tactic in their battle to crush the civil rights movement. The vehicle they used was a libel case against the *New York Times*, which had run an ad sponsored by civil rights organizations. The ad criticized certain southern public officials; and it did in fact contain some minor errors of fact. These errors were enough to embolden an all-white southern jury to slap a heavy fine on the *Times*. The Supreme Court came to the rescue. It nullified the defamation case. The Constitution, said the Court, protects the right to criticize public officials. Even if the criticism is factually wrong, it is privileged, and cannot form the basis of an action for defamation—unless, that is, the criticism was a deliberate lie, or made in "reckless disregard" of the truth. Later the Court extended the rule, beyond the facts of *New York Times* and beyond public officials; all public *figures*, that is, basically everybody famous or noteworthy, shared this immunity.[233] The principle also applied to privacy cases—public figures, in other words, were entitled to less privacy protection than ordinary people, because information about their lives, loves, and behavior was in the public interest.

Clearly, the President, cabinet members, mayors and governors are public figures; but so too are movie stars, famous basketball players, and celebrities in general; not to mention business leaders, opera singers, authors of best-selling novels, and Nobel prize-winning scientists. A more difficult question involves so-called involuntary public figures. How much protection should there be, in the law of privacy and defamation, for ordinary people suddenly thrust into the limelight—people who win the lottery, or victims of a sensational crime or natural disaster, or people who *commit* a sensational crime, or people suffering from rare and fascinating diseases? There is no simple answer; and the law is still in flux.

Fundamentally, modern democratic societies have a duty to keep secrecy to a minimum. This follows from the very nature of democracy. The public has a right to know what the government is up to. Under the American Freedom of Information Act,[234] the public has access to acts, documents, papers, and files of public agencies. Most countries have something more or less similar— for example, the Right to Information Act of India, enacted in 2005. Naturally, there are limits: nobody has the right to demand the secrets of building a hydrogen bomb, or the names of undercover CIA agents working in China or Iran. But the right to know has become extremely broad; in members of the British commonwealth, many of the right-to-know laws replaced or sup- plemented older laws which were often called "Official Secrecy Acts." The change in name is significant. Today, "transparency" is a popular buzz-word. The work of government agencies should be by rights an open book. And if so, shouldn't the life and record of a candidate for Parliament or Congress be an open book as well? My right to know is therefore inconsistent with the privacy rights of the high and mighty; and with the privacy rights of anybody the public takes a legitimate interest in.

The right to choose, so fundamental in modern society,[235] and which includes the right to choose leaders, necessarily requires information. Choices made without full knowledge are aimless gropings in the dark. The right to know goes beyond the political and the public; it permeates private life as well. There is, for example, the idea of "informed consent" in medical affairs. This doctrine appeared in the 1950's, and is now generally accepted.[236] The doctor must tell the patient just about everything: what treatment is recom- mended, what treatment is not recommended, and why, what are the risks and the side effects, and so on. A doctor who falls short is considered just as negligent, just as culpable, as a doctor who botches an operation. The patient has a right to decide on her own course of treatment. And this right would be meaningless without total information.

In family affairs, recent changes in adoption law make it possible for adopted children, under certain circumstances, to find and identify their birth parents. This was once simply out of the question. No longer.[237] There are of course, good reasons why children might want to know something about their genetic history—this can be quite relevant medical information. But the real forces behind the movement seem much more visceral—nothing less than the right to know. And the right to know is linked to the right to choose—in this case, between birth parents and adoptive parents. The constitutional right of privacy, as we have seen, covers the right to choose, without state interference, whether to have children or not. For adopted children at least, there is a kind of right to have parents or not, and which ones.

PRIVACY AND THE CELEBRITY SOCIETY

A general right to know, with regard to Presidents, governors, and public officials, can rest on straight democratic theory. But why should there be a right to know everything about the private life of a rock-and-roll musician, or a football player, or a television star? What gives the average person the right to invade their privacy? There may be a case for a free flow of information about business, civic, and religious leaders, more or less parallel to the case with regard to political leaders. For the football player, the case seems much weaker. Yet he too is classified as a "public figure," and in the United States, there is precious little protection for his privacy rights. The American case may be extreme; but there is at least a tendency in this direction in other countries as well.

What is involved here, perhaps, is quite another feature of modern society. Modern societies, in general, are obsessed with and idolize celebrities. A celebrity is not simply a famous person. A celebrity is a famous and *familiar* person. The distinction between fame and celebrity is crucial. Kings, popes, and emperors, for example, have always been famous, but before modern times they were not celebrities. They were distant and mysterious figures, hardly ever seen by the masses. Their habits and ways of life were unknown except to a small and intimate circle. Popes for a long time never stirred from the Vatican. The Emperor of Japan and the Dalai Lama were even more remote. Today, popes are *celebrities*; they travel, they go out to the public; they are or can be media stars; the public knows what they look like, what they sound like, how they walk and talk. The Dalai Lama gives speeches before rapt Western audiences. In general, the media—especially television—act to break down the barrier between celebrities and the public. We see the celebrities so often that they become familiar. We get the illusion that we actually *know* them. And in a way we do. They, however, do not see or know *us*. The television screen acts as a kind of one-way mirror.[238]

The celebrity is a product of modern society. Celebrity status depends on the media. How many Americans ever *saw* Thomas Jefferson, or heard his voice? How many British subjects had seen or heard Queen Victoria? She was a face on postage stamps and coins, nothing more. But today's presidents and queens have most definitely become celebrities, just as the Pope has become a celebrity; and prime ministers within their own countries at least. These august personages might be (or seem) more familiar to us, perhaps, than the people who live next door. And we may know more (or think we know more) about them.

Technology, then, created the celebrity society—radio, movies, television, and now the internet. The world of the one-way mirror has "transformed politics. To a large extent image replaces ideology."[239] Technology reduces the social distance between the celebrity and the audience. There are still real barriers, of course; but they matter much less psychologically. In a celebrity society, people tend to think that they know everything there is to know about sports stars, political figures, religious figures, and others; and people also feel they have a right to know. This expectation, at least arguably, has an impact on the law of privacy; arguably, it is one reason why judges in the United States have blurred the line between public figures and the rest of us, and why they have stripped so much privacy protection from public figures.

One issue is definition: exactly who counts as a public figure? One old but well-known case is *Sidis v. F-R. Publishing Corp.*, decided in 1940.[240] William Sidis had been a child prodigy. He graduated from Harvard at the age of 16. In 1937, the *New Yorker* magazine ran a series of articles, "Where Are They Now?" For Sidis, the answer to the question was: pretty much nowhere. The one-time prodigy had done very little with his life. He toiled away as a clerk in utter obscurity. Sidis had been, as it were, a kind of rocket or shooting star, a flash of light that quickly sputtered and died. But he was a human being, with feelings; and Sidis was most unhappy with this article. He brought suit for invasion of privacy—in vain. The court mentioned the "public interest in obtaining information," though it is hard to see what that public interest consisted of. Essentially (though to a degree implicitly), the case held, first, that once a public figure, always a public figure; second, that anybody newsworthy is a public figure; and third, that anything that the public is interested in is something the public has a right to know. Almost by definition, if a magazine publishes a story about somebody, this must mean the public is or can be interested. Not every court, then or now, has gone as far as *Sidis*,[241] but the general trend is in this direction: defining "public figure" quite broadly; and, once that is done, construing the privacy rights of such people very narrowly.

In this regard, the privacy laws of Europe seem somewhat different, or, if you will, seem to lag somewhat behind the laws of the United States. These laws seem to give more privacy protection, even to public figures. All modern nations are celebrity societies, and European nations are no exception, judging by the tabloids and fan magazines one sees in every kiosk. But perhaps traditions of deference in some European cultures (and the culture of Japan) support differences in *legal* aspects of privacy law. In other words, European law may reflect a strong difference between the legal culture of the masses, and the legal culture of elites (especially legal elites—judges, very notably), compared to the United States. This, of course, can only be a guess.

In Germany, what in English would be called a public figure goes by the rather curious term "a person of contemporary history" ["Zeitgeschichte"]. The chancellor of Germany is obviously such a person, and many famous people also qualify; but there are gray areas. One of these is well illustrated in a case from 1973, decided by the German Constitutional Court. In the background was a sensational crime, an attack on a munitions depot. Four sleeping soldiers were killed, and the attackers stole weapons and munitions.[242]

The plaintiff was a man who had nothing to do with the actual killings. But he had helped the main perpetrators, and perhaps had had a sexual relationship with one of them. He was tried and convicted and sentenced to six years in prison. By 1973, he had served part of his sentence and was about to be released and sent home. Meanwhile, a television company had prepared a documentary, "The Murder of the Soldiers at Lebach," and planned to broadcast this film. An actor would play the part of the plaintiff; and the plaintiff's name would be repeatedly mentioned. The plaintiff wanted to keep this documentary off the air. Not that it was inaccurate; he made no claim that this was so. Accuracy was not the issue. Privacy and dignity were. The Constitutional Court agreed with the plaintiff. The documentary would interfere with his re-socialization. Freedom of expression was an extremely high constitutional value, and one which had to be balanced against the plaintiff's rights. But in the end, the balance tilted in favor of the plaintiff.[243] Such a result would be almost inconceivable in the United States.

A more recent, and even more extreme, example concerned Armin Meiwes, the German cannibal.[244] Meiwes had a sick craving for human flesh; and he contacted (through the internet) another even sicker soul, Bernd Brandes, who was actually willing to be eaten. The two got together, and after a bizarre ceremony, Meiwes did in fact kill and eat his victim. When, later on, this fact became known to the authorities, Meiwes was arrested and put on trial. Eventually, he was convicted of murder, and sentenced to life in prison.[245] His case, as you can imagine, was the stuff of lurid headlines all over the country. A movie company prepared a film obviously based on the case. It was called, in German, "Rohtenburg," a play on the name of the German town, Rotenburg, and the word "roh" meaning uncooked; the English title was "Butterfly: A Grimm Love Story." The movie was scheduled for release in Germany in 2006; but Meiwes went to court and asked the court to prevent any public showing. The film, he claimed, invaded his privacy rights. Surprisingly, he won—at least at the level of the first two courts where the case was tried. Only on appeal to the Bundesgerichtshof was Meiwes' claim rejected. This court reversed the lower courts; for one thing, the court felt, Meiwes himself had made public many details about his life and his crime. There was no right to "demand that he be portrayed publicly only in the way he would wish to be portrayed." Still, although Meiwes lost in the end, he had gotten quite far climbing up the pyramid of courts; and important tribunals had taken his argument quite seriously. In the United States, he would have had no case at all. His notorious crime, plastered all over the pages of tabloids and magazines, would have made him, unquestionably, a public figure.

The lower court decisions are interesting, too, in that they give off a definite odor of elitism. Indeed, they seem to echo some of the concerns of Warren and Brandeis. Armin Meiwes had certainly made himself some sort of public figure; but the proposed film (in these courts' view) served no particular purpose. It was a horror movie, and as such, did not rise above mere entertainment, and nasty entertainment at that. It served only to satisfy a kind of morbid and prurient curiosity on the part of the public.

These courts, then, were willing to grant *some* measure of privacy, even to a public figure; and they rejected the idea that anything the public is interested in, is in the public interest. In a Japanese case, a newspaper published a "scoop" about the daughter of a prominent politician. According to the newspaper, this woman had married over her parents' objections. She then moved to Los Angeles, where she later got a divorce. The woman, Miss Tanaka, tried to stop publication. Ultimately, she lost. An appeals court did agree that her marital adventures were private and no business of the public. But the court also felt that there was no great harm done to her reputation, and denied her claim on that basis.[246] Again, in the United States, it is hard to see that she would have had any case at all.

English law seems to be in a state of flux. The right of privacy, such as it is, rests not on statute law, but case law and European conventions. But English judges seem to harbor attitudes similar to the attitudes of some of the German judges. The recent affair of Max Mosley is a striking illustration. Mosley is the son of a notorious figure, Sir Oswald Mosley, the leader of Britain's fascist organization in the period of the second World War. The younger Mosley was the head of the Formula One racing organization, which runs the Grand Prix auto race among other things. Thus Mosley was a more or less well-known figure in his own right. A British tabloid "printed pictures and published videos of him indulging in a five-hour sadomasochistic sex session with prostitutes in a Chelsea apartment." Mosley sued for invasion of privacy, and in July, 2008, won 60,000 pounds—"the highest in recent legal history in a privacy action"—plus costs.[247] For the British judges, like the German judges, the morbid curiosity of the public was no reason in and of itself why this lurid tale should be exposed to view. No doubt the story of Mosley's sex life sold many, many newspapers. But there was "no public interest or other justification for the clandestine recording...or for the placing of the video extracts on the News of the World website." There were limits, then, in what the public has a right to know.

A recent case before the European Court of Human Rights (2004) involved Princess Caroline, a member of the royal family of Monaco.[248] The paparazzi had been plaguing the Princess, and she sued to prevent publication, in Germany, of some of the many photos they had taken of her and her family. There was nothing sensational about these photographs. They showed her on horseback, on a ski holiday, in a canoe with her daughter, shopping, playing tennis. In one series of photos, the Princess, at a Beach Club, dressed in a bathing suit and wrapped up in a towel, tripped and fell on her face.

The German Constitutional Court held that she was a public figure. Yes, she was entitled to respect for her private life; but outside the home, she had no right of privacy unless she was in a "secluded place—away from the public eye." Consequently, it declined to grant her relief. The European Court of Human Rights, however, disagreed. The Court felt that the Princess had a right to privacy, and the mere fact that she was in a public place did not destroy that right. It was going too far to insist that she be in an isolated, secluded spot. Besides, the photographs in question, if published, could not "be deemed to contribute to any debate of general interest to society." The sole purpose of such publication would be "to satisfy the curiosity of a particular readership." Note once more the elitist tone: public "curiosity" is not enough to justify invasion of privacy, in marked contrast to the general tenor of American case-law.

James Whitman has suggested that there are two separate cultures of privacy. They are based on two "different core sets of values." The European "core" is its "interest in personal dignity, threatened primarily by the mass media"; the American core is an interest in "liberty, threatened primarily by the government."[249] Many aspects of this thesis are attractive and even persuasive. But, first, the differences between the two cultures may be fairly narrow. Second, if I am right about celebrity culture, then the differences may be differences in internal legal culture (the culture of judges, to be precise), rather than differences in general legal culture. The public in Europe, as I said, seems just as obsessed with celebrities as the public on the other side of the Atlantic. That the paparazzi should be so eager to take photographs of the daily life of Princess Caroline certainly suggests as much. There was a *market* for these photographs. A German tabloid once published a picture of Prince Charles, the Prince of Wales, in the shower, under the screaming headline: "Charles Naked!" as if that were some sort of cosmic event. The British royal family grumbled, but decided (probably wisely) not to do anything further. How such a case would have fared in the courts is an interesting question. It is hard to see how Charles' rather ordinary body would be relevant to any important public issue. It would, however, sell many thousands of newspapers. The case-law suggests, then, that some fragments of an old culture of deference, an old elitism, might still survive in Europe, having found some sort of asylum in the rarefied world of the judges.

PRIVACY AND ITS DISCONTENTS

The privacy of ordinary citizens is a major issue today. It is also a specifically modern issue. In traditional societies, there is hardly any real privacy, and nobody expects anything different. There was even less privacy in pre-modern societies. In medieval Europe, the common people lived in tiny huts, together with their children, and no doubt pigs and chickens as well. In the great houses of the nobility, servants were everywhere, and even kings and queens lacked a kind of privacy that any middle-class person takes for granted today. Crowds of nobles watched Louis XIV of France get dressed, washed and shaved. The King for the most part lived a kind of gilded fish-bowl life.

Modern culture is sharply different. Middle class parents are sure their children need personal space in order to flourish. Ideally, each child should have its own room. And privacy does mean space: literally, and figuratively. It means a zone within which people can express themselves. A place where the state has no right to intrude. Perhaps a room where *parents* have no right to intrude. It is the right to be left alone; and the right to be alone. To be alone, even in a crowd of people. Privacy also implies the right to be anonymous in most situations. The celebrity of course has no anonymity. But ordinary people ordinarily do. They may have come to tolerate surveillance cameras, in public places; but they probably assume that the images are not stored permanently; and they become so inured to the cameras, that they even lose awareness of the spying eye of the state.

Expectations of privacy, then, are for the most part deeply ingrained in modern life. The expectation springs from the same root as the human rights movement in general. Privacy rights are the blood brother of modern individualism. The self requires space to grow in, and scope to choose; and this implies privacy, in both of Whitman's senses. Both the media and the state have to be kept at bay.

Yet, as expectations of privacy have grown, so have the threats to privacy. Here one must mention the incredible development of surveillance techniques, and the more and more widespread *use* of these techniques. Cameras and other such devices are weapons in the war on crime, and very much weapons in the war on terror. Probably the public accepts and even welcomes much of this kind of surveillance. Hardly anybody blinks an eye at cameras in banks, or inspection of luggage and handbags at airports. There are thousands of surveillance cameras on the streets of London, eyes that never sleep; in 2003, there were more than four million of these closed circuit television cameras. Seventy-five other cities in the UK have public surveillance systems. The city of Chicago, Illinois, has thousands of its own. The Mayor of Chicago defended the practice—"We're not," he said, "inside your home or your business," as if these were the only places when true privacy reigned. After all, he explained, the city "owns the sidewalks."[250]

The use of these cameras can be troubling. In an interesting case, *Peck v. United Kingdom* (2003), a decision of the ECHR,[251] the plaintiff, Peck, was a troubled soul, suffering from deep depression. In 1995, at night, he "walked alone down the high street towards a central junction in the centre of Brentwood with a kitchen knife in his hand and he attempted to commit suicide by cutting his wrists." The camera filmed him, the police were called, they detained Peck (saving his life), and got him into treatment. So far so good. But film, showing him walking in the street with the knife (the film did not show the attempted suicide), was released, and seen on TV, and noted in the press. This was done in such a way as to identify Peck to his friends. He brought a lawsuit against the local government which had released the tape, claiming an invasion of privacy. The English court turned him down.[252] He then appealed to the ECHR, which found in his favor, citing Article 8 of the European Convention, which gives everyone the "right to respect for his private and family life." The British government argued, of course, that this regrettable event "did not form part of his private life," as his "actions were already in the public domain." The Court disagreed. Filming was one thing; releasing the film was another. Article 8 had been violated; and they awarded Peck substantial damages.[253]

The case is a good example of the boldness and creativity of the ECHR. It also illustrates the way in which the European Convention works as a kind of bill of rights, and also as a constitutional document. It acts, as we pointed out, as a kind of supplementary constitution in many countries, and a sort-of constitution for countries without a written constitution (England and Holland are examples).[254]

The case also illustrates one of the facts—and dangers—of modern life. Arguably, privacy is in crisis. Some mutation of the privacy concept is a fundamental human right; or so people think. But privacy is also in a way an endangered species. Our names, messages, and images are matters of record. The check-out stand at the supermarket records what cans of soup and boxes of soap powder customers buy. Cameras sweep the streets we walk on, the buildings we visit, the trips we take. If we program our TV set to record our favorite talk show (and imagine, quite wrongly, that we are frustrating greedy advertisers), our actions make sure that this bit of information is noted, recorded and stored for future use, including use by advertisers.[255] Modern technology makes it possible for machines to see everything, record everything, store everything, and retrieve everything. Everything, of course, depends on how the technology is used. Technology can also take or destroy our precious anonymity; yet anonymity is an important aspect of our *sense* of privacy. The city may own the sidewalks of Chicago; and a man who walks down Michigan Boulevard is "in public"; but he does not expect to be filmed, or if he does, he expects the film to be soon erased and gone forever. Along with a right to anonymity, there is a (felt) right of evanescence: we want, and need, a situation in which most of what we say or do is gone with the wind.

It is too early to sound a note of doom. What most powerfully protects the privacy rights of ordinary people is the simple fact that nobody in high places is interested in what they do. But as soon as they enter some sort of vague sphere of public concern, even that barrier comes down. It is hard to find and impose some sort of legal and institutional balance between the private and the public. Many people are justifiably uneasy. Accordingly to a front page story in the *New York Times* in October, 2009, people in England had become "weary of surveillance in minor cases."[256] England was described as a country "where security cameras lurk at every corner," and "giant databases keep track of intimate personal details." Jenny Paton, a "40-year-old mother of three," was suspected of "falsifying her address to get her daughter into the neighborhood school." The local authorities began a massive surveillance operation. They turned up nothing. But what surprised a lot of people was that local governments have the power to use these surveillance operations for all sorts of purposes: "to catch people who fail to recycle, people who put their trash out too early...people whose dogs bark too loudly," or who "illegally operate taxicabs."[257] And the people who are being watched and investigated often have no idea that this process is underway. This gives local governments what is potentially an awesome power. Yet England is a free, democratic country—it seems—and proud of its democratic traditions.

Conceptions of human rights are never static. They are malleable, open to change, and influenced by all sorts of circumstances. This is a crucial point. There is, to the best of my knowledge, no big protest movement aimed at getting rid of the London cameras. These cameras, after all, are weapons in the never-ending war against evil-doers. "Wars" on crime, on drugs, on terrorists, give rise to measures hard to justify on other grounds. The latest, and perhaps most dangerous example, is the so-called "war on terror." Suicide bombers, especially the ones that attacked the World Trade Center in 2001, led to something close to social panic. And, very notably, an eruption of programs and laws in many countries. Many of these laws are quite draconian; sometimes they conflict with the usual understanding of the rule of law, not to mention concepts of privacy and dignity. The British, for their part, used rather extreme, even brutal, measures in fighting Irish Republican terrorists. Very few people complained. There was little outcry in the United States against many of the measures which the administration of George W. Bush hustled through Congress, or adopted by executive order. A few people suggested that maybe constitutional rights were, shall we say, somewhat stretched. But Congress hardly uttered a whimper of protest (at first). Rather, Congress acted in almost indecent haste to pass the "USA Patriot Act," shortly after the attack on the World Trade Center. This law greatly expanded the executive's powers to fight the new "war" on terror.

Many reasonable people defend all of these measures. The Constitution, as one (rather hateful) phrase put it, is not a suicide pact. Extreme times demand extreme measures—locking people up without trials, Guantánamo Bay and the equivalent, "renditions" and secret prisons, various kinds of searches and seizures, warrantless wiretapping, and perhaps even torture (especially if a bomb is ticking away, although this never actually happens). All this in blatant disregard of what would usually be considered constitutional rights, of people accused or suspected of dangerous or illegal acts. The laws also skew the shape of the government. They increase "executive power, both in absolute and relative terms"; they reduce the power of legislatures and courts.[258] This tendency is by no means confined to Britain and the United States. Measures in Germany have run parallel. Rolf Goessner speaks of "collateral damage" on the "home front." In the war on terror, he argues, the danger of terrorist attacks is enormously exaggerated; and the rule of law is a casualty. Some measures taken in Germany, in the name of security, almost amount to a reversal of the presumption of innocence.[259] The war on terror feeds on deep feelings of insecurity. The tendency of the mass media to emphasize what is sensational, titillating, and dangerous adds to the lethal brew. The state and its security organs are the ones who gain from this process.

Terrorism is only one type of crime. It creates an extraordinary climate of fear, perhaps because it is so random and unpredictable. A rising crime rate in general—or, to be more exact, a rising rate of violent crime—also creates a climate of fear. When gripped by this kind of panic, the public tends to demand drastic measures. And it becomes willing to tolerate some erosion of what people would normally consider their liberties. The loss of rights is greatest for people the mass public cares very little about: the poor, underdogs in general—not to mention the people who are actually committing crimes. Many European countries have managed to avoid this sort of panic; their systems are at least *relatively* humane; they work hard to keep prison rates low, to rehabilitate prisoners, and to treat prisoners with dignity. The United States, alas, is sharply different.[260] And certain countries that are "in transition" may have a special problem. The "transition" is usually from some kind of dictatorship to something more democratic. If crime rates rise—or seem to rise—this tends to evoke a dangerous sort of nostalgia, a longing for the past, for the good old days, when the authorities were adept at keeping the lid on in the country.[261]

But, as the British situation illustrates, letting this particular tiger out of its cage can be exceedingly dangerous. The weapons used against terror and violent crime turn out to have other uses too: snooping on ordinary people in their everyday ordinary lives; like Jenny Paton in her quiet corner of England. Almost everybody thinks that enforcing the law is generally speaking a good thing. That's what police and criminal justice and prisons are all about. But people have always assumed that enforcement will be imperfect. They would like more enforcement—against murderers, rapists, drug pushers. But what about people who drive faster than the speed limit? Or even people who drive while slightly tipsy? People behave on the assumption that most speeders will get away with their speeding. They themselves go faster than the speed limit, though mostly within reason. The same for mildly drunken drivers; they do not expect to get caught, and mostly they are right. People also assume that if they make a personal call or two at work nobody will know and nobody will care. Or if they take a few ball point pens home from the office. People feel, in other words, that there are loopholes and leeways in law as in life. What would a full enforcement state feel like? My guess is that it would feel impossibly oppressive. Yet technology makes a full enforcement state a distinct possibility. Whether we are at the brink of this kind of dystopia is another question.

9
Social, Economic, and Cultural Rights

SOCIAL AND ECONOMIC RIGHTS

There has been a great deal of discussion in the literature of so-called social and economic rights, rights to such things as medical care, food, jobs.[262] Many writers on human rights have drawn a distinction between negative and positive rights. The "negative" rights, or "freedoms," are rules that tell governments what they must not do—they must not, for example, abridge the freedom of speech or of the press, or adopt measures that impair freedom of religion. Anti-discrimination laws fall into this category, too. The "positive" rights are the social rights. They call on the government to *do* something— provide some social good, like housing or education or the like.

These are, it seems to me, unfortunate terms: there is nothing "negative" about the right to have a fair trial, or the right of free speech. It takes a lot of state action, and sometimes a lot of money and effort, to equalize the way men and women are treated. It takes money and effort to level the playing field in employment for blind people or people in wheelchairs. But, as usual, logic has little or nothing to do with the issue. The "negative" rights, in general, came first, historically speaking. They may be expensive; but they are also a lot cheaper than some of the "positive" rights. One "positive" right, however (the right to free education, at least at the primary school level) is both old and expensive. What is more crucial, of course, is what elites and publics think about which rights are "fundamental" or "inherent" and the like. Many of the core "negative" rights (freedom of speech, for example) have moved pretty much beyond serious controversy, at least in democratic societies. The idea of a "right" to food or housing has not made this move—at least not yet. The right to an education, on the other hand, definitely has. And so, too, of the right to health care: huge majorities in most countries (perhaps even in the United States) think government should be "responsible" for meeting health care needs.[263]

The older constitutions—the United States Constitution is just about the oldest still in force—typically said nothing at all about social rights. But many of the newer ones do. The South African Constitution is one of the most widely discussed; it has many clauses on "social rights." A right to education is not particularly surprising. But the South African Constitution also speaks about "access to adequate housing" (section 26), a right to "health care services," to "sufficient food and water," and to "social security" (section 27).

Section 7 of the Bill of Rights imposes on the state the duty to "respect, protect, promote and fulfill" the listed rights. The Colombian Constitution of 1991 instructs the state to guarantee social security, as well as food subsidies for the poor (Art. 46); another article (49) speaks of access to health care for all; still another (51) on a right to appropriate housing. There is even a provision recognizing the right of all persons to recreation and sports; these are part of the educational system, and are to be publicly supported ("constituyen gasto público social," Art. 52). Amendments to the Indonesian Constitution provide that 20% of the state budget, at a minimum, must be spent on education; the state also has a duty to take care of the poor, to "develop a system of social security and empower the underprivileged," and to "provide public services including medical facilities."[264] The Croatian Constitution provides a "right to assistance" for the "basic needs" of the "weak, helpless and other unprovided-for citizens" (Art. 3, section 57); the "right to health care" is "guaranteed" to every citizen (section 58); moreover, everyone has a "right to a healthy life" and a "healthy environment" (section 69). And in 1986, the General Assembly of the United Nations adopted a "Declaration on the Right to Development." The "right to development," according to this document, is an "inalienable human right"; everybody is "entitled to participate in...economic, social, cultural and political development." There are clauses about peace, the elimination of racism and so on; but also (Art. 8) "equality of opportunity" with regard to "access to basic resources, education, health services, food, housing, employment and the fair distribution of income."[265]

As usual, the Declaration has no teeth. Governments are told what to do, but there is no way to make sure they follow these commands. The same is basically true of the various constitutional provisions on social rights. Curiously, many of these lists are to be found in the constitutions of poor or developing countries, rather than in the constitutions of richer countries, which could afford them. Not everybody, of course, agrees that these "social rights" are fundamental. Conservative opinion, in many countries, would, for example, reject the notion that the state should provide "health care services"; or housing, or pensions, let alone good food and drinking water for everyone. Governments, they feel, are tyrannical and inefficient by nature. Socialized services are also a threat to individual responsibility, a precious commodity. The market does things well; government does not. Such matters as health care and housing should be left to the free market, as much as possible. The debate over health care reform in the United States has shown the current political strength of this point of view, at least in that country.

Of course, many people agree about the virtues, in general, of a free market system, but still think a free market needs a lot of help, to say the least; and that when markets fail, the state should step in; the state should help out the poor and unfortunate, and should provide some kind of social safety net. The debate rages on and on, and seems to go in circles. In many countries, much of the debate seems purely academic. The welfare state is probably here to stay. It is genuinely popular. Even in the United States, Social Security and Medicare are sacred and (so far) untouchable. Nonetheless, we can certainly ask whether it is helpful (or necessary) to make housing or medical care constitutional rights. The question is, what is gained or lost, by inserting the welfare state into the constitution? And what do these provisions tell us about concepts of fundamental rights?

If we look at the issue of social rights historically, the lines of evolution are reasonably clear. The trend is unmistakable, despite various zigs and zags. In the last century and a half or so, responsibility has shifted gradually, from individuals, and from free markets, to some sort of collective responsibility, and to a bigger role for governments. All of the developed countries can be described as welfare-regulatory states. The free market is very much alive (and quite a few state functions have been "privatized"), but the state also controls and circumscribes the market system. This has been, of course, a slow, gradual, and piecemeal process. A right to free primary education, for example, comes along earlier than the right to free medical care. Or old age pensions. The changes, of course, do not take place in a vacuum. Old age pensions make little sense in an agricultural society. They become an issue when people work in stores, factories, and mines; and when the extended family decays under the conditions of modern urban life. Pensions and other welfare provisions take the place of norms that made adult children chiefly responsible for the care and feeding of the old folks. More significant, perhaps, is the fact that many societies feel they are rich enough to pay for these services. Whatever their legal position, once firmly in place, they come to be seen as rights, rather than privileges.

The case of the United States demonstrates what should be obvious— that there are political and cultural differences between societies. In an interesting survey (done in 1977, and therefore somewhat dated), people in various countries were asked whether the main emphasis in "human rights" should be on "political rights, like personal liberty and freedom of speech"; or whether the emphasis "should be on economic rights, like adequate food and shelter." In Germany, 51% chose political rights, 25% economic rights; 24% were undecided. In France it was exactly the reverse: 53% for economic rights, 23.9% for political rights (22.9% undecided).[266] Today, most European countries take for granted universal health insurance or (in some cases) a medical plan run by the state. The United States is an outlier; a health care plan was (barely) adopted under the Obama administration, and faces, at this writing, an uncertain fate in the courts and in political life. Powerful economic forces have opposed "socialized medicine," or whatever they define as such, and have been implacable foes of "Obamacare." But such forces as insurance companies, pharmaceutical companies, and big business in general would not have so much heft if they did not tap into deep cultural and ideological roots. Sandra Levitsky studied American support groups for family caregivers in Los Angeles. These were men and women struggling with the hard and thankless job of taking care of, say, old and demented relatives. Levitsky's people did not think they were entitled to help from the government; they had a strong "normative commitment" to the idea that "families should bear primary responsibility for long-term care on their own."[267]

This leads to a question: is there something paradoxical in the movement toward social rights in developed countries? Is this inconsistent with expressive individualism? How does it fit the rise of plural equality, which means, basically, giving everybody the right to *be* individuals? What is the relationship of the welfare state to the norms—not of political philosophers, but of ordinary people—in the developed world (primarily), their thought patterns, behaviors, and customs?

Are people simply inconsistent? Do they think they want freedom, autonomy, and the right to choose; but at the same time, they want what a paternal government can give them—security and benefits? Millions of Americans repeat the mantra that government is the problem, not the solution. They are constantly ragging about high taxes and government meddling in the economy. Yet they certainly want free education, and they love programs like Social Security and Medicare, not to mention other "social" rights (like the police and the armed forces). Europeans, perhaps, are less inconsistent; but not entirely so.

But inconsistent ideas, like ideas in general, are a social phenomenon. We have to explain how and why people are inconsistent. Or one can argue that there is no real inconsistency here. Individual autonomy *depends* on law, on government. As many writers have pointed out, "freedom" is not just an "absence of interference with rights." It also includes the "genuine ability to exercise those rights."[268] People who are illiterate and starving cannot do much with their package of human rights. As Berthold Brecht put it, in the *Three Penny Opera*, "Erst kommt das Fressen, dann kommt die Moral." A full belly, in other words, comes before anything else. Brecht had a point. Many people have pointed out that "negative" rights like freedom of speech *imply* "positive" rights—the so-called social rights. If society—and the state—must do nothing that impairs autonomy and dignity, then health, education, and a social safety net are absolute musts.

In fact, every developed country has elaborate welfare laws, although they differ in scope and in details. Some of these countries list some of the rights in the constitution. But whether these rights are *felt* as rights does not, of course, depend on what kind of legal status they have. It depends on what the public expects. And the public, in places like France or Sweden, expects a great deal. Indeed, as I have already pointed out, states like India and South Africa, which are most explicit about expressing social rights in constitutions, are the *least* likely to be able to do much about these rights. The educated public, in those countries, must be well aware of this fact.

Countries like Sweden—and the United States—are also what we might call societies of second chances. Not only do they provide a social safety net, they also take steps to prevent people from falling too far too fast. This is the literal meaning of a safety net. It is also what motivates an ideology of second chances. When a delinquent grows up, and mends his ways, his juvenile record is expunged. Particularly in the United States, the educational system has been constructed in such a way as to provide many opportunities to make up for past failure. Students who did miserably in high school can mend their ways in a community college, and eventually go on to higher and higher education. In European countries, this was historically less true; by late adolescence, you were stamped as working-class or not, and it was hard to escape the status you were labeled with. But here too the systems are changing, and there is more social mobility than was historically the case.

Even the world of business and finance is full of second chances. We no longer put debtors in jail. A basic aim of bankruptcy law is a second chance for debtors. Perhaps it would be more accurate to call this a basic *result*. A social and economic safety net not only feels like simple justice; it is also, arguably, important for society. Just as a safety net can encourage tight-rope walkers, because it takes away one horrendous risk, so too can an economic safety net encourage risk-taking and entrepreneurship. Opening a restaurant or a clothing store is risky business. So too of trying to market your own little invention. People might be more likely to innovate, or take risks in business, if the cost of failure is not debtor's prison or a lifetime of struggle to pay back hopeless amounts of debt. Nobody *wants* to go bankrupt; but it is better than many of the alternatives.

Human Rights and Human Nature

This book has laid great stress on modern forms of individualism. Whether I or you or anybody else *likes* modern individualism is not the issue. If I am right about what modal personalities today are like, then *people* are individualists, and whether philosophers or political theorists think this is good or bad is in an important sense irrelevant. A tremendous literature critiques this or that aspect of the human rights movement. Words like "hegemony" and "neo-imperialism" dot the literature like raisins in a cake. There is also a rich literature which criticizes, on ethical grounds, any movement which focuses on individual rights. The "language of rights" cannot "give moral substance to the claim that people ought to be, for example, properly fed and housed…. [S]imply to state that human beings have 'rights' to food, shelter, medical care, and even 'development,' says very little about who or what must act to ensure that this occurs." What is needed, then, is to move "our thoughts" away from "rights," toward "notions of caring and responsibility."[269] How one would accomplish this is a mystery to me.

On the other side are ideologues, who think that human beings are and always will be rational maximizers; that people are simply incapable, for the most part, of doing anything except looking out for Number One. Human nature is surely more flexible and pliable than most economists imagine. When we talk about human nature, we have to remember that homo sapiens is a *social* animal. Men and women generally live in families; they are also part of groups and clans and communities. People are inveterate joiners and belongers. In developed societies, there is a drastic reduction in clans, tribes, and extended families. Indeed, millions of people live alone. Many of them even like it. But for many of these people, a solitary life is just a prelude to getting married and settling down; or, for the widows and widowers who live alone, a postlude. The family in modern societies has been twisted and reshaped and battered almost beyond recognition, but it survives, perhaps in different forms. Some of these forms seem strange to traditional people—gay marriages (with or without children), for example. But the family, in some version, is surely here to stay. It can be redefined and reshaped, but it cannot die. Ties between children and parents will always be strong. Babies need to be cared for. In fact, society cannot go on without family ties.

In short, economic man is a caricature. It may be a valuable one, but it is still a caricature. Modern society *created* economic man, as a concept, and (in some degree) as a reality; but economic man is not "human nature"; it is not genetically programmed into people, the way life as a lonely hunter is built into the genes of the leopard. Humans are not like fish, where females drop eggs in the ocean, and males drop sperm, and for the most part swim away. In the year 3000, homo economicus, for all we know, might be as extinct as Neanderthal man. Or not. This is something we simply cannot know.

The future of social rights does not depend on changes in human character. In the developed world, some social rights have been totally accepted—the right to a free education, for example. Societies wrangle over higher education, should it be free, should it be open to more or less students; on the elementary school level, there are arguments about the form education should take, and the role of private schools. But almost nobody argues that the state should get out of the business entirely. Rather, it is taken as a solemn obligation to spend tax money to teach children to read and write and do math. This is true whether or not there is a formal constitutional "right" to education. Similarly, the right to basic health care is solidly imbedded in the laws and in the consciousness, by now, in Canada, or France, or Israel.[270] People, not surprisingly, really want these "social rights"; and as soon as a society is rich enough to give it to them, they have the habit of demanding these rights. The struggle for social rights is not a struggle between neo-liberal, capitalist societies and the rest of the world. To put it this way ignores the fact that rich, neo-liberal capitalist societies are precisely the societies that *grant* these rights. The public wants it this way. Neo-liberal societies may hand over garbage collection to private entrepreneurs, or auction off the state telephone company and the national airline. They may try hard to foster markets and competition, but always within limits. Poor countries, on the other hand, can talk about social rights, and amend their constitutions; but where will the money come from? Beggars can try to divide up a few crusts of bread, if this is all they have; but they cannot go much further.

Social Rights: Ideal and Reality

This, in fact, is the most potent objection to social rights: they cannot be implemented. You can put these words into a statute or a constitution, but words never fed anybody or gave them a roof overhead. A country cannot wave a wand, or wave dense legal pages of text, and give families decent and affordable homes, or jobs for everybody who wants to work.

Even rich countries fall short. Free education is, as we said, almost universal in some form; and (in most countries) basic health care. In some countries, the government has built a stock of housing for people who cannot afford market rents—council housing in England, for example. Singapore has provided housing for most of its population. Decades of agitation, discussion, and strong social movements, followed by and crowned by legislation and tax provision, produced the welfare state. It developed, in other words, largely without constitutional help.[271] By now, people may feel the same way about the right to education or medical care as they do about freedom of the press or of religion, depending on the country. Obviously, a right to housing does not build houses; and a right to work does not make jobs. Do constitutional clauses on social rights have any real impact? In a few countries, they have opened the door to lawsuits—to demands that the state make good on its (constitutional) promises. One can even talk, by now, of a "social rights jurisprudence."[272] South Africa and India are among the countries that have contributed to this "jurisprudence."[273] One South African case, from 2002, invoked Section 27 of the Constitution, which gives everyone the right to "health care services," and 28(1), which gives children the right to "basic health care services." The plaintiff wanted to force the government to "plan and implement an effective...programme for the prevention of mother-to-child transmission of HIV."[274] The Court admitted that the AIDS pandemic posed "daunting problems" to the government, and recognized "huge demands" for "access to education, land, housing, health care, food, water and social security." These "socio-economic rights" were "entrenched in the Constitution." It was "an extraordinarily difficult task" to respond to the complaint, but it was nonetheless "an obligation imposed on the State by the Constitution." Accordingly, the Court issued orders for dealing with the AIDS issue. Some of these orders were quite specific—for example, removal of restrictions on the use of a drug, Nevirapine, and an order to take steps to make the drug readily available.

The Indian Constitution, in Article 39, directs the state to take action to secure "the right to an adequate means of livelihood," and calls for distribution of national resources which would "subserve the common good"; measures should be taken to prevent "the concentration of wealth and means of production." The high courts have, indeed, occasionally faced cases on how to transform these general directives into positive law. They have, for example, insisted on better care for the mentally ill, even going so far as to demand that the government come up with the necessary cash. In another case, in 2001, the

Indian Supreme Court announced a right to food, which it deduced from the general right to life. The Court commented that "Plenty of food is available, but distribution...amongst the very poor...is scarce and non-existent." The Court issued orders to remedy the situation, even a scheme "requiring mid-day meals at schools.... Not just a supply of food but a proper cooked meal."[275]

In another case, the Supreme Court of India solemnly declared that the right to life, which was guaranteed by the Indian Constitution, implied a right to a livelihood as well. This case, decided in 1985, concerned squatters in Mumbai; these squatters had been living on the streets, "in the midst of filth and squalor."[276] The Chief Justice began his opinion with a vivid description of the awful conditions of life on the streets of Mumbai: "Rabid dogs in search of stinking meat and cats in search of hungry rats keep them company.... [N]o conveniences are available to them.... The...women pick lice from each other's hair. The boys beg." The people on the streets "ask for a judgment that they cannot be evicted from their squalid shelters without being offered alternative accommodations." And they claim that "the right to life is illusory" unless the state protects their search for ways to earn a living. The squatters were, after all, among the throngs that flocked to cities like Mumbai, where they hoped to find at least a "bare subsistence."

The Court went on to hold that the right to life does indeed include the right to work. "To work means to eat and it also means to live." The "right to live and the right to work are integrated and interdependent." Thus, the "very right to life" of a person who lost his job because he had been evicted had been "put in jeopardy." But, after these eloquent words, the Court's actual decision comes as something of an anti-climax. The Court agreed with one key argument of the city government: nobody has a right to obstruct the streets, or to encroach on "footpaths, pavements," and other public places—gardens or playgrounds, for example. The city has a right to clear the streets and these other places, and to evict the people who are living there. The Court saw no "short term or marginal solution to the question of squatter colonies." The government had a duty to do something for these unfortunate people. And, in the long run, the country needed "thoroughgoing land reform, re-grouping and distribution of resources to the...bottom half of the population."

In a law review article—and in the light of decisions like those in India—Sigrun Skogly asked: "Is There a Right Not to Be Poor?"[277] Of course, literally, the answer has to be no; but (so the argument goes) there is a case at least for "guiding principles on poverty and human rights." Poverty is "not only about lack of material well-being, but also an expression of the deprivation of human dignity."[278] Poor people do not simply lack food, shelter, medical care and the like; they cannot, because they are so poor, develop themselves to the fullest. And this, of course, violates the fundamental premise of the human rights movement.

Yet what would a right not to be poor mean, practically speaking? Implementation is all. Do decisions of the Indian Supreme Court make a difference? Obviously, courts cannot run a country. Courts lack the money, power, and organization to follow through. The Supreme Court of India may push a little here and there. may force local and national governments to make minor changes; and such decisions might make *some* difference in India. But courts cannot (and should not?) "attempt the impossible."[279] Sometimes, to be sure, attempting the impossible does do a little: it pushes toward accomplishing a few things which are, in fact, definitely possible.

The South African Constitutional Court is another court that, from time to time, takes social rights seriously. In one case, some 900 people had been squatting, in modest huts, on vacant land that was privately owned. They faced eviction. In defense, the squatters cited the constitutional right to housing. The Constitutional Court agreed that the clause did mean something; it required the government to undertake some sort of reasonable housing program. But the Court "refrained from ordering concrete measures," and a journalist, who visited the area four years later, reported that "the living conditions of the community were as inhuman as they were at the time of the judgment."[280] Obviously, in South Africa as in India, no court opinion will make jobs, houses, and a better standard of living appear as if by magic. Whether the case-law has any impact at all is an empirical question. Arguably, courts (and society) have a duty to "optimize" these social rights "so far as legally and factually possible." Complete realization of these rights "may be delayed by factual impediments such as the lack of resources" (an under-statement if there ever was one); but some do hope that perhaps in the fullness of time, the situation will improve and social rights can be implemented in reality.[281]

But when will that be? Rich countries and poor countries have different answers to the question. For poor countries, the great day is probably very far off. For rich countries, the day comes when the public demands it. It is a question of norms as well as politics. The public in the rich countries feels entitled to free speech, free education, and free medical care (in most of them); but not free access to a job. That might yet happen someday. Is it more likely to happen if the demand takes the form of a claim of right? That is, if a guaranteed job is considered a fundamental right, rather than something interest groups demand and want but is not considered a fundamental right, is success more likely? The precise *legal* form is probably irrelevant. What is crucial is the consciousness of right. When and if this occurs, societies that can afford it will move toward realizing that right.

But even in the rich countries, there are practical as well as ideological obstacles. In a global economy, the obstacles may be greater than ever. In today's world, companies shift factories at will, from high-wage to low-wage countries. They can outsource almost everything except haircuts and appendectomies. Millions of manufacturing jobs have disappeared in the United States, Europe, and Japan. The welfare state depended, in the past, on good factory jobs paying good wages. Hundreds of thousands of these jobs have disappeared. Demography, too, is making trouble. People retire early, have few babies, and live a long time. Germany, Italy, Hungary, Japan—all of these countries are losing population. This puts enormous pressure on pensions. Not enough young workers pay into the system to support hordes of retired, older people. Especially if people retire at 60 and live until 90. There are ways to mitigate the problem—immigration is one; another is getting rid of mandatory retirement (the United States and Australia, for example, have done this). But these either create new problems, or are resisted politically, or have too small an effect. And when the welfare state is in trouble—when it has to scramble to keep up already existing social rights—people may be less likely to demand even more of these rights, whether or not they are listed in the constitution. And if they do demand these rights, the government will be hard pressed to give them what they want.

CULTURAL RIGHTS

Another fairly new group of rights—or new to be recognized at least—are the so-called cultural rights. In 1992, the United Nations adopted yet another declaration, this time on "the Rights of Persons Belonging to National or Ethnic, Religious and Linguistic Minorities." Governments are required to protect "national or ethnic, cultural, religious and linguistic identity of minorities" and have a duty to "encourage conditions for the promotion of that identity" (Art. 1).[282] Cultural rights technically are not the same as minority rights; but in practice, we can treat these as synonymous. Dutch language and culture is in no danger in the Netherlands; but Frisian language and culture is.

Minority and cultural rights are, thus, "recognized" by international bodies, and are the subject of high-minded international declarations. They are also, without a doubt, and more fundamentally, recognized by cultural groups themselves. Cultural rights come in many shapes and sizes. There are many ways to be or become a minority. German speakers who live in the far north of Italy are a minority only because of the way national borders are drawn. Basques and Catalans are linguistic minorities without a country, but who live in compact geographical zones. The Romany people, on the other hand, are scattered throughout Europe.[283]

Linguistic minorities are particularly active in the modern world. They demand the right to use their language, and to teach it to their children: Basques in Spain, Berbers in Algeria, Hungarians in Romania, Quechua in Latin America. Other minorities are asking more broadly for the very right to exist, for the right to resist the crushing power of national and global majorities. Indigenous peoples—Brazilian tribes, various groups of Indians ("indigenas") in Latin American countries, Native Americans, Maoris in New Zealand, aborigines in Australia, and many others—it is a sizeable list. Some of these groups have become quite militant. They also have concrete economic demands. They want their land back—land that was stolen from them—or they want the right to hunt and fish or catch whales; or some kind of sovereignty or autonomy; or compensation in cash for the wrongs that were done to them.

There is no shortage of such wrongs. In the age of imperialism, the great powers swept across the continents, extending their power and their sway over most of the world. In some places—Australia, the United States, Chile—they simply swamped the native peoples. They took their land and drove them into remote mountains, outbacks, and arid reservations. In other places, the cadres of civilization established their rule over masses of "primitive" or "backward" people. Ancient civilizations, in Mexico, or India, or Vietnam, were conquered or obliterated. Cathedrals were built on top of Aztec temples. Almost all of Africa was parceled out among the great powers. In Asia, Japan took a leaf from the European book to run its own brand of savage imperialism. Everywhere, imperialism meant plunder and exploitation; at times, butchery and genocide. Even at its best, imperialism showed little or no respect for the cultures and customs of the subject peoples.

Classic imperialism is gone with the wind. So is its mind-set. Today, the academy would drum out any scholar who spoke or wrote about "primitive" people or "savage society." More and more, majority cultures have come to recognize minority cultures and indigenous people, and their rights. "Assimilation" as we said has become a dirty word. Multiculturalism is the new mantra.[284] There is a strong movement in Latin American for indigenous rights.[285] In Chile, for example, the Mapuche Indians are demanding rights to land.[286] Constitutions from the 1990's on, in Colombia, Ecuador, and Peru, all recognize ethnic and cultural diversity. According to the new Bolivian Constitution (2009), the various indigenous communities, including "Afrobolivians," together "constitute the Bolivian people" (Art. 3).[287] Section 27 of the Canadian charter calls for interpretation of the charter "in a manner consistent with the preservation of the multicultural heritage of Canadians." Under the Multiculturalism Act of 1985, it is official Canadian policy "to preserve and enhance the multicultural heritage of Canadians," and to "promote the understanding that multiculturalism reflects the cultural and racial diversity of Canadian society." All "members of Canadian society" have the "freedom...to preserve, enhance and share their cultural heritage"; and the law expresses a promise to "encourage and assist the social, cultural, economic and political institutions of Canada to be both respectful and inclusive of Canada's multicultural character." The act is not terribly specific about how all this is to be done; but the law does give the government discretion to do a lot of supporting and encouraging and sponsoring of research and so on.[288] Mexican law, too, expresses a duty to protect the integrity of indigenous groups.[289] Indigenous rights are widely recognized, as well, in the various declarations and manifestoes of the United Nations. For example, the Convention on the Rights of the Child gives children "of indigenous origin" the right to enjoy their culture, religion, and language.[290]

The "Fribourg Declaration," published in 2007 and produced by the Institute for Ethics and Human Rights of the University of Fribourg, in

Switzerland, asserts the idea of cultural rights in a particularly emphatic way. First comes a ringing preamble, including the (usual) statement that "human rights are universal, indivisible and interdependent," but adding that "cultural rights...are an expression of and a prerequisite for human dignity." This neatly encapsulates two of the basic concepts that undergird the human rights movement: first, that human rights are inherent, and global; in other words, that local law and custom cannot and should not impair them; and second, that people are entitled to develop themselves and their personalities fully and freely, through their own individual choices. It defines (Art. 2) "cultural identity" as the "sum of all cultural references through which a person, alone or in community with others, defines or constitutes oneself." And a "cultural community" is a group whose members share a "common cultural identity." The Declaration goes on, in sweeping language, to spell out what cultural rights it considers essential. Everyone (Art. 4) is free to "choose to identify or not...with one or several cultural communities, regardless of frontiers." Further, that "no one is to have a "cultural identity imposed...against one's will," or to be forced to "be assimilated into a cultural community." The astute reader will notice, however, that there is, at least in theory, a certain tension between universal human rights and the right to choose an identity and a community whose tenets and customs might conflict with "universality." We will return to this point.

If we talk about "cultural rights," we have to have some notion of who and what constitutes a distinct culture. The word "culture" does not exactly have a hard, precise meaning; and what constitutes a "cultural community" is sometimes not obvious at all. In the United States, for example, some interesting litigation has turned on whether a certain group can qualify as a tribe or native community. The Navajo, who have their own language and customs, and who live for the most part in a compact geographical area, obviously form a "cultural community." But many native groups—historically distinct—have tiny numbers; many of them have lost their language and most of their customs; and the members may live, scattered about, in various cities and towns.

Some of these communities are trying valiantly to bring back from the dead their lost identity. Of course, the chance to gain rights to land, fishing and hunting privileges, and sometimes cold cash as well, are powerful stimuli. These benefits seem finally attainable in an age of guilt-ridden majorities. Not that there is any reason to doubt the sincerity of members of these groups or quasi-groups. They feel they were victimized in the past; and indeed they were. They share, too, in the modern passion to discover "roots." Paradoxically, this takes place in a period in which people feel they also have an inherent right to tear themselves up from their roots. to make themselves over completely, to shed the past and adopt a new identity. The ideology of choice allows both of these moves; both are options available in the age of expressive individualism. A person has the right to eat sushi and become a Buddhist, even if she was born to white bread and Methodism. A person also has the right to embrace the culture of his great-great-grandmother, who might have been Armenian or Jewish or a full-blooded Cherokee.

Majority guilt, as we said, plays a role in the politics of indigenous rights. Quite a few countries—the United States, Canada, New Zealand, Australia— have more or less pleaded guilty to treating their "first nations" abominably. All of these countries have good reason to be ashamed of their history of race relations. This is the age, in any event, of civil rights movements; and the minority communities share in the culture that produced these movements, and have themselves become much more militant. But militance of course is not enough. The Apaches and others indigenous groups did not exactly lie down and play dead in the 19th century. They fought for their rights. The result was catastrophe. They were defeated in battle, stripped of their lands, herded into reservations; the white majority community tried to stamp out native languages and religions. In some cases, they even robbed the tribes of their children. This was not only true in the United States; Australia is another egregious example. But the majority culture has dramatically changed. This is the age of plural equality. Plural equality and free choice are fundamental premises of the rights movement and of modern society in general. All of the countries mentioned now make efforts to meet the demands of minority communities. The Canadians have set aside Nunavut for people of the Arctic region. Native Americans, Maoris, and Australian aborigines have gained new rights. The indigenous peoples of Latin America—like the Mapuche of Chile— have risen up as well, to demand land, rights, and a place in the sun.

The Language Issue

A "cultural community" that has lost its language, as we mentioned, stands on much shakier grounds than a community bound together by a common language. Language is, par excellence, the carrier of culture. The Declaration on Minority Rights mentions language rights, and asks states to take "appropriate measures...wherever possible," to give minorities "adequate opportunities to learn their mother tongue or to have instruction in their mother tongue" (Art. 4.3). This is indeed extremely important. When a language dies—and languages are dying at a very rapid rate—the culture either dies with it, or at the very least suffers a mortal blow. Heroic efforts may have brought the California condor back from the brink, and may save the giant panda or the Arabian oryx; but nothing can stop the inexorable destruction of the world's small and precarious languages. Extinction lies just ahead for thousands of these languages. Languages cannot survive without official status and (nowadays) television channels. And if the language is not taught to children in the schools, it has very little chance in the modern world.

In some ways, this is not a new situation. Every major language, whether English, French, Chinese, Arabic, or Spanish, hacked its way to official status over the dead bodies of competing "dialects," many of them old and rich in tradition, many of them in fact independent languages. If the throne of Queen Elizabeth I had not passed to the King of Scotland when she died, and Scotland had remained independent, there would probably be a Scottish language today, with official status and a vibrant literature. It would be related to English as Dutch is to German, or Swedish and Norwegian to each other.

As we said, most minor languages are doomed. No brave words about cultural rights can keep them alive. People who speak a dying language do not pass it on to their children. The old folks often do not want to, and the children want it even less. Why should they? Young people in the modern world feel a strong need to learn and speak the majority language. They no longer live in isolated villages. The same sort of habitat destruction that dooms so many plants and animals dooms the languages spoken in small, isolated corners of the world. As people become connected, through schools, roads, television, and the internet, as they move out into the larger world, they leave behind the tongue of their forefathers. When the old folks die off, the language is gone. Marie Smith Jones died in Alaska in January 2008, at the age of 89; her language, Eyak, died with her.[291] Ned Mandrell died in 1974; that was the end of Manx. The last speaker of Ubykh died in a Turkish village in 1992.[292] Countless tiny languages, in the Americas, in Africa, Asia, and even in Europe, are suffering a similar fate. A handful of elderly people speak these languages; their children speak English, Spanish, or one of the major African languages. Yet language is at the very core of any struggle to keep a minority culture alive.

Language is a clear case of a community or cultural marker, and this is if anything truest of the smaller languages. English of course has enormous cultural meaning, but it is spoken in many countries; it carries somewhat different cultural freight in Ireland, Barbados, British Columbia, or the Falkland Islands. Other great world languages, like Spanish or Arabic, share this trait. Spanish is spoken, after all, in the Dominican Republic, in Chile, in Panama, and in Spain itself. Icelandic and Estonian, on the other hand, are spoken in one country only, and these languages in a sense monopolize the work of carrying on the culture of Iceland or Estonia. This indeed is the norm for most of the world's official languages. Basically, Japanese is spoken only in Japan; Latvian only in Latvia, Polish only in Poland. There are émigré communities; but no language can survive through émigré communities alone.

Language is a unique aspect of culture. It is also deviant, in that it is also the *least* subject to destruction or erosion by mass global culture. The Japanese no longer wear traditional costumes; they have mostly given up Emperor worship and the old-time religion; they drive cars, use computers, play baseball, and even eat French cheeses. In dozens of large and small ways their culture has converged with those of other developed countries. Many old customs are dead or dying. Yet the Japanese still speak Japanese. Modernity has had an impact, to be sure, on the language. It has absorbed large numbers of English and international words. Still, compared to the way modernity has impacted the family, styles of dressing, or business, politics, and ways of life, the impact of modernity on the Japanese language is extremely small. Language, thus, stands as an exception to a powerful trend. Koreans who work for corporations may wear business suits, the Swedes might eat sushi and pizza, elite Panamanians might drive cars and use computers, but at home and in the streets they will still speak, respectively, Korean, Swedish, and Spanish.

Standard languages are themselves, as we pointed out, the result of a kind of convergence. They have crowded out "dialects" and rival languages spoken in the countryside (usually it is the dialect of the capital that prevails— Parisian French, or London English). There are, to be sure, differences between (say) Italy, where dialects are still quite strong, and English, where they are not. Most of the dialects in larger countries—Plattdeutsch, for example—are likely to die out within a generation or two; they have as little chance of surviving as Eyak or Ubykh, or the hundreds of African, Asian, and Latin American languages that do not command official status. Some minority languages—Welsh, or Breton, or Basque—are putting up a more significant struggle. They have larger and more vibrant communities of speakers. In an era of cultural rights, they have won a number of advantages. But the battle is not easy; and they might well lose out in the end. Welsh or Basque or Quechua will survive if the speakers persuade or force central governments to allow them their own schools, TV channels, and newspapers. Some small languages, like Icelandic or Maltese, are in no danger; they have official status. Much bigger languages, which lack this great gift, can be seriously imperiled.

In the age of minority rights, minority languages that have gained some sort of recognition may have at least a fighting chance. Catalan and Basque have full recognition in Spain; Romansch in Switzerland. The French in the past have been extremely hostile to their minority languages, like Breton and Provencal; but this may be changing. Hawaiian is an official language in Hawaii, but very few people speak it at home; it is fighting for life, but there is a strong movement that aims to preserve it and teach it to children. Irish clings to precarious life in Ireland. In Latin America, Spanish (and Portuguese) have crowded out most of the indigenous languages; a few have remained important. Some indigenous languages have millions of speakers—Aymara, Guarani, Quechua—which gives them a strong claim for recognition. Under the Constitution of Paraguay, Spanish ("castellano") is an official language; but so is Guarani.[293] The new Bolivian Constitution (2009) states that the "official languages of the state" are Spanish ("castellano") and all of the indigenous languages; the text goes on to name more than 30 of these languages, from Aymara to Zamuco (Art. 5).[294] The ones with millions of speakers seem fairly safe (for now). The fate of the others is dubious.

Modernity, then, has doomed most small languages; yet the big ones, the powerful ones, like Spanish or Chinese or Arabic, seem not only to thrive, but seem to form an exception to the powerful forces of convergence in modern society. How is this possible? We will explore this question shortly.

Convergence and Society

To quote one author: "the spread of the modern state makes human rights relevant throughout the world."[295] There *are* universal norms of human rights. But they are universal, not because of some natural law, or because of some trait of human nature. They are universal because modernity is universal, or is rapidly becoming universal. They are universal insofar as they have tended to spread all over the world. They are universal because they are global; and they are global because of the presence of a single, overwhelming global culture.

Generally speaking, convergence is the dominant fact of modern life. At any rate, it is the dominant fact of life in the developed countries, and in the elite strata of other countries as well. There is, I think, no question that world cultures are getting more and more alike, at least in the richer countries.[296] To return to an earlier theme: imagine yourself an American visiting Japan. A good deal of what you see strikes you as different—interesting, but different. Foreign. Alien. Strange. When you go home, and talk about your trip, you naturally stress these differences—how odd it all seems. You—also quite naturally—will ignore or gloss over the many obvious similarities.

Some scholars think that, underneath a veneer of modernity, one can detect the throbbing of a unique Japanese heart, the breath of a unique Japanese soul. These elements of Japanese culture, it is said, have persisted through the centuries, and still persist, through all the ups and downs of Japanese history, and will persist presumably forever. Of course, nobody can prove or disprove this thesis. But it seems most unlikely to me. It has of course a grain of truth—which would be true of French culture or Australian culture too. Nonetheless, to me it seems clear that Japan is *more* like other advanced countries than modern Japan is like medieval Japan. And medieval Japan was very different from medieval England or Russia or Thailand. Similarly, modern England is more like modern Japan than it is like medieval England. The movement of culture, in other words, has been *toward* convergence, even though it never reaches complete convergence, and probably never will. I have used Japan as an example, because the Japanese are particularly insistent on this idea of some sort of inner cultural essence. But the Japanese are not alone in thinking of themselves as unique; we mentioned "American exceptionalism," for example. And America *is* exceptional—up to a point, just as other countries are. But the United States too has cars, computers, rock-and-roll, and elevators; it has an income tax and old-age pensions, and the rest of the trappings of a modern social order. American surfaces and Japanese surfaces—and Swedish surfaces, and Spanish surfaces, and Taiwanese surfaces—have an awful lot in common. I have stressed similarities in *looks*, and in technology. But there are also huge convergences in law, in social norms, and ways of life in general.

Convergence is distasteful to anthropologists, among others. One anthropologist, in a study of morals and morality in South Asia, starts out by referring to a scene in Schiller's play, *Don Carlos* (and Verdi's opera *Don Carlo*); in this scene, Don Carlos confesses his love for the queen, who is married to his father, Philip II. This forbidden love is the seed of a tragedy, which ends with "the hero's doom." But, the author says, a "Tibetan audience would not understand what all the excitement is about, for Tibetans see no harm in the sharing of one wife by father and son."[297] Laura Bohannon makes a similar point; on a field trip in West Africa, studying the Tiv, she tried to explain the plot of *Hamlet* to the elders. When she told them that Hamlet's mother rather hastily married her husband's brother, the elder said "He did well... In our country also, the younger brother marries the elder brother's widow." Hamlet's wish to kill his uncle shocked the Tiv: "For a man to raise his hand against his father's brother and the one who has become his father—that is a terrible thing." The idea that a widow should wait a reasonable time—two years, perhaps—before remarrying, was greeted with derision. Too long, one woman said, "Who will hoe your farms for you while you have no husband?" Bohannon had begun with the proposition that "human nature is pretty much the same the whole world over," and that "at least the general plot and motivation of the greater tragedies would always be clear—everywhere." The point of the essay, apparently, is to show that this notion of universality is profoundly wrong.[298]

These are entertaining and even enlightening anecdotes. But they are anecdotes about pre-modern people. Educated people in the developed world have no trouble enjoying literature, for example, which expresses points of view that are completely alien to them. We can admire (and *understand*) Shakespeare, despite the ghosts in *Hamlet*, the witches in *Macbeth*, and Shakespeare's acceptance of monarchy. The audience that enjoys *Don Carlo* might be in Tokyo as well as in Rome or Madrid. Theater-goers, in any modern city, would have no trouble enjoying a Tibetan play that expressed ancient Tibetan values, provided the play had other merits, and provided the program notes explained Tibetan customs to the audience. Over and over again, one hears claims of an unbridgeable gulf between cultures. But in the modern sector of the modern world there is no unbridgeable gulf. Of course, there are violent and non-violent clashes in modern societies over values and interests. There is resistance, backlash, revolt. But the kind of blank failure to understand, which the *Don Carlo* episode implies, an *inability* to grasp cultural differences, is another story. Laura Bohannon would have no trouble peddling *Hamlet* in any part of the developed world.

What this implies is a central idea in this book: cultural convergence. Cultural convergence is not the same as cultural homogeneity. Most countries—modern countries, non-modern countries—are not, in fact, homogeneous. Different languages, races, religions coexist. Some have argued, however, that only culturally homogenous societies are likely to respect human rights. Walker and Poe have tried to test this hypothesis.[299] They concluded that precious little evidence supported it—or supported, for that matter, the opposite idea. Some countries that are split along language or ethnic or religious lines are strong supporters of human rights; some are not.

To begin with, it is not so easy to measure homogeneity. Iceland is a very homogeneous country; Japan and Korea are basically homogeneous, too (though not completely). But so is Somalia—perhaps the most homogeneous in Africa: one language (Somali), and one religion (Islam). Among modern countries, we note that Belgium is split along language lines; Canada, along both religious and linguistic lines. Switzerland has four official languages, and has a strong divide between Catholics and Protestants. Switzerland seems an unqualified success; Canada basically the same; Belgium, however, seems to teeter on the brink of dissolution. On the whole, it is hard to argue, also, that unitary states respect human rights more (or less) than federal states; or that states with more than one official language do worse (or better) than those where there is only one.

Yes, countries that respect human rights are indeed somewhat homogeneous. But not in terms of language, necessarily; or religion; or ethnic diversity. They are more or less homogeneous in terms of modernity. Every religion under the sun can be found in the United States. So too of every race. Yet the vast majority of Americans take part in what we might call the culture of modernity. This refers to ways of thinking, behaving, and living; and it also includes a commitment to at least the basic menu of human rights. And what is true of the United States, is also true of other Western, developed countries. It is certainly true of Switzerland; and Belgium and Canada too, for that matter.

This points to a kind of central paradox that involves the cultural rights movement. More and more, law and society recognize cultural rights. Cultural rights are enshrined in constitutions. They grow stronger and stronger, legally and socially. Canada has given thousands of square miles of land to the Inuit, and created a whole new territory, Nunavut, essentially on behalf of the Inuit. Since 1976, Australia has been granting extensive land rights to its native peoples. The story can be repeated elsewhere as well. Yet, at the same time the cultures themselves become weaker and weaker. Boli and Elliott, as I noted, have argued that the "worldwide celebration and promotion of diversity" is basically a "façade" which obscures "underlying similarity and homogeneity."[300] Behind this veneer, this outer covering, is a cultural convergence, the result of modernity itself. In fact—one more paradox—the movements of native peoples are themselves a sign of convergence. The indigenous peoples advance their cause through thoroughly modern techniques. And the culture they are so carefully preserving is, in many ways, a museum piece. What is lost is lost forever. The forces of modernity, of global culture, are simply too strong to be resisted for long. The old culture can only survive in translation, as it were.

Moreover, convergence is too powerful a force to allow any glaring exceptions—even language. This has led to the search for a universal, artificial language—Esperanto has been the most notable attempt. I think it is fair to say that this experiment has failed. Yet a global language has indeed appeared—it is English. Its dominance is, in many ways, parallel and similar to the dominance of other global features of modern life. Just as everybody in the developed world uses the same technology, the same work habits, the same clothes, and the same architecture, outside the home in many contexts they will all speak the same language, English. International organizations, more and more, conduct their meetings in English. Scientific journals are printed in English. Air traffic controllers, all over the world, give their commands in English. A modern woman in Japan will wear Western dress. She may on occasion, and for some specific reason, wear the kimono that hangs in her closet. Of course she speaks Japanese at home. But if she is in business or government, if she has connections with overseas partners and customers, she will carry this on in English. And in many countries in Europe, English is an essential part of education. Most educated people will try hard to become fluent and competent in the language.

This is not to deny the supreme importance of language rights—no "cultural right" has greater salience. Wars have been fought over language rights. Linguistic minorities are a source of political conflict—in Canada, in Belgium, in Sri Lanka, in Spain, and in many other countries. A Catalan will fight for the right to speak Catalan and educate her children in Catalan. The same for the Basques in Spain, and the Welsh in Wales. But the Catalan or Basque nationalist will also speak Spanish and, more and more, English as well. Indeed, the English language, as it rolls on with oceanic force, can also serve as at least a partial solution to the problem of language rights. English is everywhere in Singapore—in the airport, in department stores, in street signs. It is nobody's native language; and at the same time everybody's. To make Chinese the official language in a small country with two linguistic minorities, the Malays and the Tamils, would have been a recipe for disaster. In Nigeria and in India, English is the language of the elites, and the language of higher education; it serves that function in the former British colonies of other African countries (admittedly, French has a somewhat similar position in its former colonies as well). In the new South Africa, English is pushing Afrikaans into the background, and competes with the various Bantu languages as well. Broadcasting is now more than 50% in English; Afrikaans, Zulu and Xhosa "get just over 5 per cent each." The armed forces decided in 1996 "that English would be the only official language for all training and daily communication."[301] In the European Union, the official languages of all members have in theory equal status. The regulations and directives of the Union may be translated into all of the languages, including Maltese, Estonian, and Slovak. But the actual working language of the Union, more and more, is English. French is in a distant second place—a fading star. In a recent poll of Europeans, almost 70% agreed with the statement that "Everyone in the EU should be able to speak English."[302] Not only should, but do: large numbers in Europe at least claim that they know English—for people under 40, no less than 87% in Finland, and 71% in Greece.[303] Like Western dress, and Western technology, and Western architecture, the English language has become virtually universal, without displacing the local languages, which survive as the bearers of particular cultures and traditions.

The dominance of English is, in a way, an accident of history—in Shakespeare's day, English was a minor European language at best. Its rise to world hegemony is not because there is something special in the language itself. Any language could serve the same purpose.[304] And for those of us lucky enough to be born into English speaking communities, English dominance gives us a head start in life—a birthright advantage which we do not really deserve. It might have been better and less "imperialistic" if Esperanto or some other artificial construct had succeeded. But English it is; and English has become an absolute necessity, for anybody who wants to play the global game, as a business person, an academic, and even to a degree as a tourist. If you doubt this, try checking into a hotel in Tokyo using your native Norwegian or Hausa.

Universalism and Relativity

Some countries have tried to suppress their minority languages, sometimes with catastrophic results. Sri Lanka is an example of this kind of deadly folly. The state can give people the right to speak Navajo or Quechua— or Welsh, Basque, or Sorbian—and to learn it in school, without really hurting the majority culture. Quechua or Aymara are not really threats to Spanish, which has 300,000,000 speakers. Nor does Karelian or Mordvinian threaten Russian. Other kinds of "cultural rights," however, can easily collide with what are understood to be important and "universal" human rights.

Cultural rights, as we have seen, appear prominently on the list of basic human rights. But there is tension, perhaps unavoidable tension, between cultural rights and other rights. After all, the human rights movement asserts a strong claim to universality. Rights belong to everybody, in every society, and on an equal basis. In a sense, this is a rejection of cultural relativism. Or, to be more exact, a rejection of the idea that "culture" can trump fundamental rights. But empirically speaking, if not morally, universality rests on shaky grounds.

Gender is a prime example. Nothing is more basic in the human rights movement than gender equality. Women should have the same rights and opportunities as men. Sex discrimination is evil. Yet in culture after culture, men and women have sharply different roles; and in many of these cultures, the woman's role is distinctly subordinate. Many spokesmen for these cultures reject even the level of equality achieved in, say, Sweden. Human rights activists, however, tend to have a vision of universal truth and justice. Relativism evokes responses ranging from suspicion to fury. Politically, they may have a point. Politics, however, is not the same as truth.

As we saw, those who deny universality often label certain rights as "Western" and, moreover, as crass and cold and alien to their way of life. "Individualism" is denounced as a foreign import. These critics project an image of warm and cozy forms of communal life, which, they say, are traits of many non-Western and traditional societies. Spreading the values of Western countries is really a thinly disguised form of neo-colonialism. Some "post-colonial theorists," argue that "modern liberalism is founded on an assertion of cultural superiority." "Universalized values," like "individualism," stand in (false) contrast to the "supposedly backward, primitive societies that were 'enlightened' by colonialism."[305]

Colonialism has a lot of answer for; no question. But there is no need to romanticize the cultures which colonial powers brutally destroyed. White people from Europe were not the only slave traders. And, granted that "universalized values" are Western (or at least *come* from the West); and even granted that "individualism" is not necessarily better, fairer, more just, than what it replaces in indigenous cultures—still, the question has to be asked, is there any real alternative? The old song asked, how were you going to keep them down on the farm, after they'd seen Paree? It is sad but true that members of "indigenous cultures" have in fact now as it were seen Paris, or New York, or Mexico City. Colonialism was indeed a wrecker of cultures. But equally powerful, or more so, have been the ravenous forces of globalization and modernity. I am not sure why blue jeans, rock-and-roll, Coca-Cola and television soap operas are so seductive; or perhaps addictive. But this seems to be the case. What imperialism began, modern mass culture finishes off.

There is no point denying that imperialism, discrimination, outright genocide, and now modern mass culture have often had a catastrophic impact on indigenous cultures. Cultures have lost their souls along with their traditions. Poverty, alcoholism, and drug-addiction run rampant among the huts and cabins; the school drop-out rates are appalling; there are no jobs and very little economic opportunity. Pride in the culture and education in the culture—a cultural revival, in short—can be therapeutic. It might make at least a dent in local pathology. Even better is restoration of rights to land and to resources. Money and political will can try to restore health to these communities. But this does not mean a genuine restoration of the culture. Nothing can retard the rampant processes of assimilation. Nobody can put Humpty-Dumpty together again.

Of course, the minorities ought to have what they want most: land and resources that were taken away from them. But unless I am badly mistaken, their members also want, on the whole, the same package of "universal" rights that the majority enjoys. This is so, even though "universalized values" were not part of the cultural stock of indigenous peoples. There is no alternative. The descendants of the Aztecs might want recognition, dignity, language rights, land rights; they might make many demands; but human sacrifice is not among them.

Modernization brings about mixed and not always desirable results. It converts millions of people from the old time culture to the wonders of rock-and-roll, blue jeans, hamburgers, and movies about Batman. But it can also convert people to avid fans of human rights. The process is slow and ragged in some places, fast in others, and almost never smooth. Modernization means heightened sensitivity to human rights—not because people have become wiser and better, but because globalization fosters the peculiar modern dialect of individualism; and that implies, for most people, plural equality, human dignity, and legal and social equality. But this is a complex process. It has many facets and takes many forms. Freedom of religion goes down more easily in many countries than women's rights, gay rights, or the rights of the handicapped.

There are cultures—especially religious cultures—that are particularly ardent in resisting modernization, conventional human rights, and assimilation into the new global order. Moslem fundamentalism is a force to be reckoned with. Reborn or renewed fundamentalism is not just a Muslim phenomenon. It has its Christian, Jewish, and Hindu counterparts, though these tend to be less violent. There has been a surprising upsurge in deep faith. Unfortunately, the deep faiths that develop sometimes conflict with tenets of the (secular) human rights movement—tenets about women and gays, very notably. The culture of individualism and human rights has obviously not conquered *everybody*. In underdeveloped and semi-developed countries, the situation is mixed and complex. Thailand is a country that dangles between old and new. Globalization, according to David Engel, has not converted ordinary Thai people to the culture of individualism and human rights. Indeed, the volcanic changes in Thai society have led many people to lean more heavily on forms of Buddhism. They keep and cherish their deep faith in spirits and ghosts and the awesome power of the supernatural.[306]

The Cultural Defense

Modernity and assimilation do not happen overnight. It is not as if people from traditional societies suddenly have visions and are converted to the new order of things. There are many steps in between. Assimilation happens; but not immediately; and perhaps not in the first generation. This has been the experience of immigration countries, like the United States or Australia. But today, there are many more immigration countries. Italy, for example, once a prime exporter of souls, is now an importer. In Europe, there are new minorities—immigrants, mostly—who are suspended, as it were, between two worlds. Or rather, between two cultures, the old and the new; the culture of the ancestral homeland, and the culture of the country where they live, washing dishes, cleaning houses, picking crops, or digging ditches.

In criminal law and criminal justice, there has been heated discussion of the so-called cultural defense. A man has moved to country X, a wealthy developed country, from his traditional and poverty-stricken homeland. He is accused of a crime; but what he did was not a crime in his old country and culture—indeed, it might be treated as a duty there. He makes this point as a defense to the charges brought against him. Should the courts of country X allow this cultural defense? Alison Renteln has argued that it should. Without it, the state would be violating its duty to apply law equally to all of its citizens. "Individual justice," she writes, "demands that the legal system focus on the actor as well as the act, and on motive as well as intent. This, in turn, necessitates the introduction of cultural information into the courtroom."[307]

Dominant cultures, she points out, tend to misunderstand cultural practices that are harmless but strange. Governments, moreover, "are fearful of multiculturalism because it exposes the fiction of any national identity." But democracies "should let people choose their own life plans."[308] The right to choose life plans is at the heart of the ethos of human rights. Renteln advises a policy of tolerance. She gives the example of a man in Fresno, California, a Hmong, whose wife was ill. He tried "the usual offerings—burning paper money, sacrificing a chicken and pig"; he even tried "Western medical techniques." No results. Frantic with worry, the man "decided to sacrifice a three-month-old German shepherd because the dog's night vision and keen sense of smell enabled him to track down spirits." One of the man's neighbors called the police. He was charged with a felony, cruelty to animals. The judge refused to allow a defense based on religious freedom. The defense, however, might have had an impact on the outcome. The man was fined some small amount and put on probation.[309]

In a Maine case, *State v. Kargar* (1996), a refugee from Afghanistan, Mohammad Kargar, was charged and convicted of gross sexual assault. He had kissed the penis of his infant son. There was testimony that people in Afghanistan do this all the time, that it merely shows love for the child, and has nothing at all sexual about it. The conviction was reversed on appeal.[310] Jewish methods of slaughtering animals have led to controversy in some places. Orthodox Jews will only eat meat that has been slaughtered in accordance with Jewish religious law, which involves rapidly cutting the animal's throat. This can run counter to the local rules for slaughtering animals. But in most European countries, in Canada, the United States, Australia and New Zealand, Jewish ritual slaughtering is permitted by law.[311] Sikhs wear a turban, and this is a religious requirement; in England, after considerable discussion, Sikhs were exempted from laws requiring motorcycle crash helmets.[312] There has been controversy, too, over circumcision, both male and female. Male circumcision is an old practice, practiced by Jews and Moslems as a religious duty; but it can also be defended on health grounds (or attacked). Female circumcision is a common practice in parts of Africa. There is a huge, polemical literature on the subject.[313] The debate over female circumcision starkly poses the issue of a conflict between women's rights, and cultural traditions; at least it can be so framed.

A cultural conflict came before the United States Supreme Court in *Santa Clara Pueblo v. Martinez* (1978).[314] Santa Clara Pueblo was a small tribe of Native Americans, with something over a thousand members. Julia Martinez was a full-blooded member of the tribe, and lived on the reservation in New Mexico. She married a Navajo Indian, and had several children. Under tribal rules, if a male member married outside the tribe, the children remained members of the tribe. But if a female member of the tribe married out, the children lost their membership. Julia's children thus had no right to vote in tribal elections, or even the right to remain on the reservation if their mother died.

The law relating to native peoples in the United States, and the rules about tribal power and authority, are a complex jungle of provisions and doctrines. The trend has been toward more and more autonomy for recognized tribal groups, including the Santa Clara Pueblo. But a Congressional law, the Indian Civil Rights Act, extended the reach of much of the American Bill of Rights to the various tribes, including the Santa Clara. The Act also guaranteed to members "equal protection of the laws." The Supreme Court had interpreted this concept to mean that sex discrimination violates constitutional rights.

The trial court turned down Ms. Martinez' claim. Santa Clara culture, the court felt, was traditionally patriarchal. The membership rules were a vital part of the tribe's social structure. To "abrogate tribal decisions, particularly in the delicate area of membership, for whatever 'good' reason, is to destroy cultural identity under the guise of saving it." The people of the tribe had the right to "decide what values are important"; they, after all, "must live with the decision every day."[315] The Court of Appeals, however, reversed this decision. The appeals court stressed that the membership rule was discriminatory (which of course it was). Moreover, it failed to "rationally identify those persons who were emotionally and culturally Santa Clarans." But the United States Supreme Court reversed *this* decision in turn. Technically, the Supreme Court did not reach the substantive issue, that is, sex discrimination; or the exact thrust of the civil rights statutes on tribal law. It simply decided that cases of this type did not belong in the federal courts. They belonged in the tribal courts. The Court felt quite comfortable ceding power to the tribal authorities. They would decide on questions of membership—even if their decisions might seem discriminatory, in the eyes of the larger culture.[316]

There are arguments on both sides of the issue in cases of this sort. In many of them, the impact on society is not great (except to the immediate circle of litigants, and their families). Certainly, the American republic would not totter on its foundations if immigrants were allowed to sacrifice a dog, or slaughter animals kosher-style, or even give a baby's sex organs a perfectly innocent kiss. Whether Julia Martinez' children can remain members of the Santa Clara Pueblo does go a bit deeper, but the decision is certainly defensible; and it concerned only a small number of people.

At one end of the continuum of "cultural practices" we can place such "customs" as the killing of (supposed) witches, or "muti murder" in South Africa. This refers to a "ritual during which a victim, who complies with particular requirements (e.g., child or virgin) is selected in order to obtain specific body parts," eyes or genitals, for example, to be "used for medicinal purposes." South African law treats these killings simply as murder.[317]

More serious and probably more widespread are practices that reflect the subordinate place of women in society. Forced marriages, for example. The parents of Nadia, Moroccans living in Norway, alarmed at the way she was blending into Norwegian culture, took her against her will to Morocco, to make sure she married a proper Moroccan Muslim.[318] Even more reprehensible from a Western standpoint is so-called "honor killing." The victims are women cruelly put to death by their own families, because they have supposedly brought shame and dishonor on their families. Honor killings occur in many countries, especially (but not exclusively) countries with Muslim majorities, such as Jordan.[319] Honor killings are also, for example, a problem in Brazil. Fathers or brothers or husbands kill women who are unfaithful to their husbands, or who simply marry against the wishes of male relatives or who violate the strict norms of their community; or even, in some extreme instances, if they were raped, bringing dishonor quite unwittingly on the family.[320] With the growth of a Muslim diaspora, "honor killing" has now spread to such countries as Germany. Is tradition, and family honor, a valid defense against a charge of murder, if a father from a conservative Muslim country, but living in the United States or Germany, kills a daughter who had sex outside of marriage? Most people in these countries shrink back from the very notion of allowing such a defense. But should the law take the cultural defense seriously as a mitigating factor? It is a difficult question.

Men are the defendants in these cases, for the most part; but not always. In a Georgia case, a Vietnamese woman, who shot her stepdaughter and her husband, tried to defend herself partly on the basis of a battered wife syndrome (but she had suffered only psychological abuse); she also tried to introduce evidence about her Vietnamese religious beliefs, to show that the way her husband treated her in the family resulted in "loss of status, humiliation, and possible adverse spiritual consequences." The Supreme Court of Georgia agreed that such evidence was properly excluded from the trial.[321]

In Germany, there have been instances of Turkish or Kurdish men, or other Muslims, killing wives or daughters to salvage the family's "honor." In 2003, an Albanian Muslim—he had lived in Germany for 14 years—killed his teen-aged daughter, who was rebellious, went to parties, dressed in Western clothes, and had "fallen in love with a young man. Her father strangled her and dumped her body in a lake." He invoked the cultural defense, but he was sentenced to life in prison. German courts, apparently, have never actually acquitted anyone who used a cultural defense; and these courts have made it clear that "reduced sentences for cultural reasons in cases of honour crimes will no longer be tolerated."[322]

Part of the problem, obviously, is the way the label of "culture" gets pasted on all sorts of practices harmful to women, or which buttress a system where men have dictatorial control over women. Not all practices, even common ones, deserve to be venerated as part of some deep cultural tradition. "Culture, moreover, is an "open and flexible system," and one that is constantly changing. A richer and more nuanced conception of culture, as Sally Merry has remarked, does not get rid of conflicts between "rights concepts and cultural beliefs," but it directs attention to the "importance of framing universalistic reforms in local cultural terms" and recognizes that "culture is not static and that there are creative ways to challenge it."[323] The point is not only that culture changes, but also that it is possible to *make* it change. And to make it change in ways that harmonize with the norms of human rights. Some of the push for change comes from outside the culture, to be sure; but a lot of it comes from inside the culture as well. And this is at least partly because the lines between inside and outside are hopelessly blurred in this globalizing age. Women in many "traditional" societies are no longer comparable to members of some isolated tribe, deep in the Amazon jungle. They are more and more part of the wider world, which oozes into all except the most remote and intractable landscapes. Nadia's family no longer lived, cocooned, in a Moroccan village. They lived in Norway, where Nadia—and they themselves—were exposed to new norms and new forces. Truly traditional people do not migrate. The very fact of migration—from Morocco to Norway, from Somalia to Minneapolis—not only exposes men and women to a new way of life; it hints that they are consciously or unconsciously open to that exposure.

Women's rights are, perhaps, the most salient example of the (supposed) clash between "culture" and fundamental rights. Occasionally, the problem is the way in which parents manage, or fail to manage, their children. In one instance, a court ordered surgery to correct a boy's club foot; the parents, who were Hmong, objected vehemently. Apparently, the objection was based on Hmong cultural beliefs. The surgery, the parents felt, might "interfere with the natural order; misfortunes might well befall other members of the family or community." Clubfoot, they believed, was "punishment for wrongs committed by an ancestor."[324]

One might also mention again the great uproar in France over girls wearing headscarves to school. To devout Muslims, the headscarf might be a religious duty; to the French, the practice seemed somehow to threaten the Republic or, in any event, to threaten national solidarity and identity. There was also a campaign in France against the burqa, that is, the "all-enveloping cloak" which some Moslem women wear.[325] A Moslem woman, married to a French citizen, and with three children, applied for citizenship, and was rejected, because of her headdress; the reason was "insufficient assimilation" into France.[326] There is a theory of French identity here which events may be making obsolete. Americans, who generally are respectful of religion—almost any religion—have a hard time seeing what the fuss is all about. But the headscarf was an issue in Turkey, too, where the clash between secularism and Islam is particularly acute.[327] And in Germany, teachers who want to wear headscarves have also stirred up controversy. Local governments have been hostile to such teachers, and the case law is quite mixed.[328] Indeed, some European countries have turned the concept of "cultural defense" on its head: to them, it means defending *their* culture from contamination; the wave of immigrants from traditional societies (especially Muslim societies) is the source of this infection. Citizenship in France, or Germany, or the Netherlands (for example) is not easy to get; the immigrant has to show knowledge of the language (not too unreasonable a demand), but also acceptance of national customs and values. This may mean embracing the ethos of human rights—in Germany, "commitment to the free democratic constitutional system." "Our history," said the Minister of the Interior in the early years of the 21st century, "has developed over a thousand years"; Germany cannot allow the "basis of our community" to "be destroyed by foreigners."[329] Of course, the "thousand years" of German history and culture included a great deal not to be proud of, including Adolf Hitler and the Nazis, but this was not what the Minister had in mind. There *is* a problem of assimilation and culture clash; but the war against the headscarf, and the growing plague of xenophobia, shows that the problem has two sides: the immigrants have a problem adjusting; but so do citizens of the host country.

European countries, historically, were not importers but exporters of people. Millions of people flowed to America, Canada, Argentina, and other immigrant countries. They assimilated, sometimes rather slowly; and they often faced discrimination and the power of nativist movements. But on the whole, they prospered in their new homes, and most of them never looked back. Now the shoe is on the other foot. Europe officially welcomes diversity, and immigrants have in theory equal rights. But Europe is also afraid of multiculturalism. Multiculturalism means, if nothing else, respecting minority cultures. But minority cultures can arouse suspicion and even hatred. And these cultures can at times conflict with what the majority defines as basic, fundamental rights.

The "worldwide surge toward identity politics," has both advantages and disadvantages, with respect to basic human rights. On the one hand, it can give people "uplifting integrity and dignity," which small cultures and indigenous people had lacked in the past. On the other hand, pressure for cultural rights can sharpen the distinction between insiders and outsiders. It can lead to ethnic conflict. So, "For every group that has found strength in a greater sense of common identity, there is a Yugoslavian disaster waiting to happen."[330] The age of multiculturalism is also an age of pervasive conflicts along ethnic, religious, and linguistic grounds. These conflicts exist all over the globe: in Bolivia, in South Africa, in the Middle East. Some countries manage these conflicts well; others do very badly. Spain, Switzerland, and Singapore have found ways to accommodate diversity of language. Sri Lanka has not. Turkey has resisted Kurdish demands for language rights. Belgians are not yet killing each other over language; but the tension is there. Ethnic conflict plagues many African countries. Religious conflict is endemic in many countries, too—India and Nigeria, for example. The successful societies are those which have been able to bend, and compromise, and accommodate.

And what of small groups that do not or cannot make peace with the modern world? In a well-known American case, *Wisconsin v. Yoder* (1972),[331] state law required children to go to high school until a certain age. The Conservative Amish Mennonite Church objected to this law. Yoder and his fellow Amish believed elementary school was quite enough for their children. High school, they felt, would only teach things that had no use in Amish society. The Amish rejected the values of the general society—values (though they did not put it this way) of individualism. The Amish stressed community values, and they wanted to live apart from the big and seductive society around them. The Supreme Court, somewhat surprisingly, agreed with the Amish, citing the constitutional right to the "free exercise of religion." The majority of the justices took a rather romantic view of this small, conservative group—a group that was, in a sense, living in the past. The opinion was drenched in a kind of nostalgia for an old and simple way of life.[332]

Yet the Amish were probably right, in their terms, to be leery of public high school. Education in science and other secular subjects might indeed threaten the Amish way of life. Probably most young Amish could resist the lure of the outside world, even in high school. But some might not. The Amish understood, intuitively, the central problem of minority cultures, in the contemporary world. They understood that only isolation could keep their way of life alive, in its traditional, old-fashioned ways. No amount of "multiculturalism," no platter of rights, no celebration of "roots," can preserve most minority cultures, faced with the overpowering force of modern ways of life. These modern ways—the mass culture which has swept over most of the globe—are enormously attractive, surely in part because they tap into, and stimulate, a kind of individualism which the old-order Amish wished to reject.

The ruling princes of Saudi Arabia seem far removed in their way of life from the Amish of Wisconsin, but they too struggle to prevent the outside world from leaking in, to some extent. No religion other than Islam is tolerated. Women may not drive cars, or work in most occupations. And yet the rulers have felt compelled, for example, to establish a modern University, planned as a carefully quarantined enclave, which will rise up out of the sand dunes, and provide training and skills the kingdom must have to survive.[333]

10
Sovereignty and Rights

In the literature on human rights, and more generally, in discussions of the politics and policies of human rights, the concept of sovereignty casts a long shadow. Sovereignty is a complicated concept, not always easy to define.[334] "Sovereignty" usually refers to an aspect of domestic power of governments, but it has an important international meaning. Here I use the term chiefly in its international sense: the principle that within its borders, a country (more accurately its government) has absolute, total, and final authority, over territory, people, and resources. No other country or institution can invade that authority. No other country or institution can meddle in the affairs of a sovereign nation. Each sovereign state has a monopoly of control over internal affairs. Sovereignty is a "fundamental principle" in the literature of international law. The members of the United Nations are all sovereign states. China and the United States are sovereign states; but so are Andorra or Lichtenstein or Nauru.

Yet of course this has never been entirely true, and is perhaps less so than ever in our times.[335] There is a lot of talk about the decay of sovereignty, or even about the end of sovereignty as we know it. It is "not just the nature of sovereignty but its very existence" that is called into question.[336] As one writer put it, "the back of sovereignty has been broken. Its days as an absolute ordering principle are over."[337] Sovereignty has been "chipped away, both from the outside, as technological changes increased the permeability of borders, and from within, as human rights are recognized as trumping the right of states to...violate these rights."[338]

Sovereignty may be decaying, but it is certainly far from dead. States still jealously guard their authority. They may sign all sorts of Conventions and Declarations with regard to human rights; but (as we noted) they often do so in full knowledge that these pieties cannot and will not be enforced. States resent, and try to repel, any attempt by outsiders to impinge on their control over internal affairs. The Chinese bristle at the merest hint of meddling with Tibet, and regard the Dalai Lama as a serious threat to territorial integrity. Rich countries police their borders vigorously; they try to control immigration; they make strong efforts to keep out illegal immigrants; they limit the numbers and types of people who claim the right to asylum. Poor countries, unlucky enough to live next door to a failed state, or a war-torn state, try to control the flood of refugees. Authoritarian states limit the right of their people to emigrate, or travel abroad, as Cuba does, and as was standard in the Soviet bloc before 1990.

No doubt the decay is most obvious in regard to economic sovereignty. This is, in part, a product of globalization. It would be an exaggeration to say that every country trades with every other country, but certainly the scope and scale of international trade is vastly greater than ever before. Currency flows are, if anything, even more universal. Transfers of billions or trillions occur every day. States have, in some ways, as little power to control these flows as they have to control the wind or the rain. Like so much wealth these days, these currency flows take the form of electronic blips. The large, multinational corporations, whose sales dwarf the GNP of most third-world countries, are almost sovereignties in their own right. They have branches and offices and installations in dozens of countries. They shift personnel and factories about like pawns on a chess board. This form of "stateless" capitalism slips easily beyond the control of nation-states.[339] Complex global systems, "from the financial to the ecological, connect the fate of communities in one locale to the fate of communities in distant regions of the world." The new realities explode and displace the old conception of state power as an "absolute, indivisible, territorially exclusive and zero-sum form of public power."[340]

Of course, it makes a difference whether a country is big or small, rich or poor. A large, rich country has more control over its economy than a small, poor one. A large, rich country can also bully or control small, poor countries, regardless of theories about the nature of sovereignty. This of course is nothing new; and at least the big rich countries no longer gobble up the small poor countries, as they did in the 19th century. When imperial powers did not bother to annex, they (or their big business interests) tended to dominate and control. The United Fruit Company had enormous power over the banana republics. Perhaps more to the point, the United States of America had even more power to control or badger the banana republics. In the 19th century, the big powers carved their own spheres of influences in the huge, weak, flabby body that was China. In our times, the collapse of the Soviet Union robbed Russia of most of its empire, but it can still threaten and even dominate small, weak neighbors like Georgia or Moldova, economically and politically. Some countries are totally dependent on international trade; others are much less so. Big countries have military and political power; small countries do not. The United States refused to tolerate the invasion of Kuwait; but nobody intervened against its own foray into Grenada. When Nicaragua went before the International Court of Justice in the 1980's to complain about American military intervention, the United States denied that the court had jurisdiction; and when the Court ruled in favor of Nicaragua, the United States simply refused to comply with the decision. And nobody could call it to account.

What is new, however, is the sheer scale of connections that bind countries together. Even powerful countries like Japan and Germany are linked to the rest of the world and dependent on other countries, because their wealth rests on a massive export trade. The United States imports far more than it exports, and is much less dependent on export than (say) Germany or Japan. On the other hand, it depends heavily on foreigners—the

Chinese very notably—to buy its Treasury Bills. Most governments are convinced that free trade is (in the long run at least) good for everybody; and so is interdependence. There is, of course, also a dark side. Subprime mortgages collapse in the United States, and Iceland goes bankrupt. The Emirate of Dubai cannot meet its bills, and stock markets tremble in East Asia. Our fates—the fates of all of us—are linked.

The huge traffic in goods, from country to country, is what we usually think of when we talk about globalization. But globalization is much more than trade. It is also—and perhaps most basically—a matter of culture. That is, we live in an age where ideas, customs, images, habits of thought, are themselves highly globalized. Trade was often, in the past, asymmetrical. Europe bought silks and spices from the East; but consumption patterns were vastly different in different parts of the world. In terms of actual products, trade is still asymmetrical. Saudi Arabia exports oil, Japan imports it. Only a few countries manufacture jet airplanes; but most countries must buy from these few manufacturers.

But trade is no longer *culturally* asymmetrical. There is convergence in what people want and buy and consume. Blue jeans are popular all over the world. The Japanese make and sell cars; but they also buy cars, and are blessed or cursed with the same automotive culture as other developed societies. And a computer culture as well. The Japanese are also avid travelers and tourists. They listen to rock-and-roll music. Some of them also listen to Beethoven. Both low culture and high culture have spread all over the world. The traffic is mostly West to East, North to South. But not always. The Japanese have borrowed law, architecture, music, and business practice from the West. But the rest of the world has developed a taste for Japanese art and architecture—not to mention a more recent passion for sushi. And Japanese methods of manufacture have been widely copied in the West.

Technology is at the core of globalization. Television, the internet, email, jet airplanes—all of these have shrunk the world, and made the one-world idea a reality. Whether these technologies are more an effect than a cause is a question not easy to answer. Perhaps both. The globalization of culture is, as we have argued, a matter of convergence, which is in turn the product of modern individualism, and this in turn a product of the capitalist system and its variants—in any event aided, abetted, and molded, if not created, by modern technology. And, in turn, individualism and the modern mind-set have nurtured innovation in technology.

Culture and trade have been globalized; but risk, alas, has been globalized as well. Economic risk, for one thing. Bank failures in one country travel with the speed of light to other countries. Global markets mean global insecurity for labor.[341] There are also more physical, tangible risks that come with globalization. Insect pests travel in cargo ships from country to country. Fish that swim in the wrong place and gobble up native fish, rabbits that invade countries without the right predators, plants that invade waterways and strangle their plant life—these threaten the natural order, and sometimes the economy as well. Countries spend billions fighting tiny moths and beetles that crossed the national border without a visa, so to speak.

Risks from humans have also globalized. Ranchers in South America set fires that "create massive clouds of smog and low-lying ozone," and this contributes to "widespread respiratory problems."[342] Air pollution has no problem moving across national frontiers. No guards or barbed wire can keep out dirty air. The nuclear disaster at Chernobyl, in 1985, was a dramatic illustration of the globalization of risk. Sovereignty and independence "could not prevent radioactive gases from blanketing much of Scandinavia, other parts of Europe, and various other parts of the world."[343] Epidemics of course have never showed respect for national borders—think of the Black Death, the 1918 flu pandemic, and other plagues of the past. Modern medicine has a solution for many of the classic plagues. But the problem of pandemics has not gone away. AIDS began, perhaps, in Africa; and is now truly global. The outbreak of swine flu, in 2009, was first noticed in Mexico, but quickly spread to other places. Very soon, health officials admitted they had no way to "contain" this disease. Too many people travel to too many places; it is impossible to identify, and quarantine, people who might be incubating the disease, or prevent them from getting on a jet and going about their business all over the world. It hardly needs to be said that global warming, and the destruction of rain forests, are world-wide problems, with world-wide consequences.

In short, the facts of modern life make some aspects of sovereignty seem obsolete, irrelevant. This is why scholars argue that sovereignty is not what it used to be (if it ever was). The economic meltdown of 2008-2009 began, perhaps, in the United States. The housing bubble burst, and led to a crisis involving subprime mortgages, "securitization," mysterious bundles of assets, and arcane financial dealings. The crisis led to events that rocked Icelandic society, pushed Ireland and Greece into crisis, raised the unemployment rate in Spain and Germany, shook the euro zone to its foundations, and drove down the export trade of Japan, Korea, Hong Kong, and Singapore.

Sovereignty is weakened when everything is thus connected with everything and everybody else. The weakness shows in a number of ways. Global processes, "both natural and human-made," demonstrate, in a dramatic way, that "artificial, socially constructed borders between states" are "permeable"; and this undermines "the concrete expression of sovereignty."[344] The state, as John Merryman has put it, is losing power in two directions. Once "all political and legal power was focused in the state," but now the world is moving "toward a more uniform distribution of power along a spectrum extending from the unique individual, the bearer of individual legal rights, through local governments, intermediate organizations and the states, to supranational organizations."[345]

The whole concept of human rights is thus also in conflict with sovereignty, and in a double sense. First, it eats away at sovereignty from inside, by insisting that the sovereign state has no power to override these rights. Second, slowly and gradually, an international legal order emerges, which at least *promises* to trump sovereign rights. International norms and practices have a long pedigree, but for most of their history, they were the softest kind of soft law; totally toothless. Now they seem to be sprouting teeth. Rather like baby teeth, but teeth nonetheless. The very existence of the United Nations, with its resolutions and its peace-keeping forces, is a sign of this new development. The United Nations has tried to play a role in keeping the peace on an international scale. It has sometimes been effective, sometimes not. The UN can be bumbling and bureaucratic; corrupt at times; paralyzed by big-power buffoonery; but still it is there, and it functions more or less, at certain levels. One can also point to such institutions as the new International Criminal Court. This Court is a work in progress; but it has indicted, and tried, important political figures—for example, Jean-Pierre Bema, formerly a vice-president in the transitional government of the Democratic Republic of the Congo; and a one-time presidential candidate. Bema was arrested in 2008, on charges of war crimes and crimes against humanity. The ICC has also called for the arrest and prosecution of other important political figures.

At the very least, the Court has symbolic meaning. It stands for universal rights. It makes a statement. It asserts that, in those matters where the Court has jurisdiction, sovereignty is no longer as relevant as before. To be sure, states have to consent to the jurisdiction of the ICC (the UN Security Council can refer matters to it, as well). But the ICC stands for the proposition that there *are* international norms; that basic human rights transcend borders; that in egregious cases at least, norms and rights of justice and humanity are higher and more legitimate than any claims of sovereignty; and, most notably, that humanity can do more than wring its hands and deplore. The Court is new. Whether it will have much of an impact remains to be seen.

The human rights movement contributes to the decay of sovereignty—such as it is. But the decay of sovereignty also, in turn, has an impact on the human rights movement. On the positive side: the massive scope of global trade, and the massive spread of a global mass culture, together with the weakening of economic sovereignty, have a certain tendency to promote democracy and the rule of law. No country exists in isolation. Korea was once called the hermit kingdom. But there are no hermit kingdoms today. Even Bhutan shows signs of entering the big world. If there is such a thing as a hermit kingdom today, the best example is still Korea—North Korea, that is. North Korea works very hard to block out the influence of the outside world, and does this fairly well. The Chinese are engaged in a dramatic experiment—liberalizing their economy, while keeping the lid on political and human rights. This puts them at war with dissidents—but also at war with the new world of the internet and the blogosphere, with Google and other search engines and websites. It is not clear who will win this war.

On the negative side: human rights, as Johan Galtung has pointed out, "are guaranteed by states, and the rights of states are being eroded from without and within by globalization and privatization."[346] This erosion is perhaps most serious with regard to social rights. Globalization limits the power of countries, even very rich countries, to guarantee a high standard of living, including health care, pensions, and the other features of the welfare state. Factories pick themselves up and run off to poor countries with low wages (not to mention low standards of health and safety, and total disregard of the environment). The welfare state depended, in many countries, on a rich supply of factory jobs, paying decent wages, and with benefits; most of these jobs have now vanished. Terrorism has also globalized. Terrorism is nothing new; there were terrorists in the 19th century, and in most of the 20th century. Modern terrorism seems different; it has the feel of a world-wide *movement* and is aimed not to assassinate kings, presidents, and princes so much as to blow up ordinary citizens who live in the developed world, and who are defined as infidels and enemies. The cold, clammy fear of this invisible enemy gives states powerful incentives to cut back on fundamental rights, in the name of the battle against terror. The citizens, by and large, seem to approve.

Globalization has a negative effect, too, on cultural rights. This may seem paradoxical. After all, cultural rights owe much of their strength to the human rights movement. Basic human rights documents recognize cultural rights and minority rights. More to the point, many countries, as we have seen, embarrassed by their history of ruthlessness, have embraced the cultural rights of minorities. The results range from language rights, for Basques, Saami people in Norway, and many more; hunting and fishing rights; grants or regrants of land; rights to kill seals and harpoon whales; even the return of skulls and skeletons from museums of anthropology. In general, as we saw, indigenous people have, for the first time, a voice that can be heard in the corridors of power.

If globalization spreads a culture of human rights—including cultural rights—how can it also be the enemy? Formally, of course, it is not the enemy. It is destructive, not to cultural *rights* so much as to the cultures themselves. Communication is global. TV, the internet, and fast ways of traveling, all tend to make the world a smaller place. And, as we have seen, this has a murderous impact on minority languages, and more generally, on local cultures all over the world. Pizza, blue jeans, and rock-and-roll are symptoms of a universal mass culture, which crowds out everything else. We have argued that cultural convergence is a mighty force, and one which seems almost irresistible. Perhaps in the future it will be less irresistible. But for now, nothing seems to stand in its way. Fundamental religion may be the most formidable enemy. Traditional sovereignty ideas seem incapable of stopping convergence. It is almost impossible to seal the cultural borders—even North Korea may not totally succeed. It is also true that fundamentalist religion pays no attention to national borders. Jihad cannot be reconciled with traditional sovereignty. Swine flu is not the only pandemic. Suicide bombing also seems to be pandemic; and, like swine flu, has little respect for the notion of all-powerful, sovereign states.

Toward Universal Jurisdiction

There are also formal, legal threats to sovereignty. The ethos of human rights is inconsistent with total sovereignty. Sovereignty cannot be an excuse for gross disregard of human rights. This idea follows logically from the very notion of human rights. If people think these rights are inalienable, if they consider them part of everybody's birthright, if they are felt to be beyond the reach of government, then sovereignty does not and should not matter. For norms that are inherent and universal, there ought to be some kind of authority, somewhere, which can punish crimes against humanity, and gross violations of human rights, regardless of borders.

This is slowly coming to life. Real change came only recently. The period of the second World War was a kind of starting point. Nothing similar to the Nuremberg trials took place after the first World War. There were some feeble attempts; but basically no one was punished for war crimes or any crimes. To be sure, the victorious powers set up a commission to investigate war crimes. The commission labeled the Turkish killings of Armenians in the years around 1915 as "crimes against the laws of humanity." But the United States and Japan objected to this concept. The ultimate treaty with the Turkish government said and did nothing about punishing those responsible for these awful acts of murder. Nothing, in other words, was done about these "crimes against... humanity."[347] As for the German Kaiser, the public in the allied countries reviled him, and there were cries to hang him, or worse. He lost his throne, but that was all. He slipped into exile in Holland. He died at a ripe old age, still in exile. He lived long enough to see Hitler conquer the Netherlands, but not long enough, unfortunately, to see Germany crushed and occupied, and its leaders punished for their crimes.

Yet, by the early 21st century, the idea of a universal, enforceable body of norms, punishing crimes against humanity, had gained dramatically. The Nuremberg trials stood for the proposition that evil people could and should be held accountable for their evil acts—and accountable in some transnational way. The victorious governments put the Nazis on trial. The Nuremberg idea contained at least the seeds of an important "corollary": that "an individual might...petition an international forum directly to protect violations of his or her rights."[348] These trials were an important milestone; and a step away from classic notions of sovereignty. But of course the Axis powers had themselves had no respect for sovereignty. The Germans gobbled up small, peaceful countries like Denmark and Holland. The Japanese tried (unsuccessfully) to swallow China, and later overran much of south Asia.

As the second World War came to a close, the Allies had to decide what to do with the Nazi leaders, who were responsible for millions of deaths and unspeakable atrocities. In the end, the United States, Britain, France, and the Soviet Union set up a tribunal to hear the evidence against a group of Nazi leaders. These men were accused of violating international law, and the (customary) laws of war. They were charged with waging wars of aggression (perhaps the most controversial of the charges against the defendants).[349] And they were also charged with crimes against humanity: "murder, extermination, enslavement, deportation, and other inhumane acts committed against [a]...civilian population...whether or not in violation of domestic law of the country where perpetrated."

This was the "most innovative and controversial" of the charges against these men. It is the one that looms largest in our consciousness today (though perhaps not at the time).[350] It is of the greatest historical importance. But still, in many ways, it did not go as far as it might have gone. The question was, could the Allies prosecute these men for committing crimes against German Jews and others, before the outbreak of the war? Weren't these acts, bad as they were, simply internal affairs? In the end, these offenses were left out of the indictments at Nuremberg.[351] There was hardly any precedent, at that time, for punishing men who were responsible for crimes against their own citizens, carried out under their own laws, and during peace time. There were plenty of atrocious crimes committed by the Nazis *during* the war; no need, then, to enter this new and delicate territory, which raised the touchy question of national sovereignty much more acutely.

It was, to be sure, also possible to question the whole idea of punishing men for violating "international law." "International law" after all was a fairly nebulous body of doctrine; or, if not nebulous, more a matter of custom than hard law. Was it even "law" at all, since nobody had power to enforce its rules and practices? Still, books and books had been written about international law; and there were enough treaties and conventions to give international law a certain amount of tangible body.

The Nuremberg trials did not escape criticism, as we mentioned. No doubt many survivors of concentration camps, and relatives of the countless Nazi victims, would have been perfectly happy to line up Hermann Goering and other top Nazis against a wall and shoot them. There were, on the other side, attacks on the trials—arguments that they were unfair (despite the defense attorneys and the regular apparatus of a trial). The *Chicago Tribune* called the tribunal a "kangaroo court," a court that had "no warrant in law," a court that makes up "its rules and its law as it goes along."[352] The tribunal, according to critics, was simply dispensing "victor's justice." Soviet judges sat on the bench along with American, French, and English judges. But the Soviet regime itself was drenched in blood; and, like Hitler, had waged aggressive war (on Finland), swallowed up small peaceful countries (the Baltic states), and in 1939 had seized part of the dismembered corpse of the Polish Republic. Still, there is no denying the fact that men like Goering and the other top Nazis deserved, a thousand times over, whatever punishment the court, or anybody else, inflicted on them. The same goes for the lower level thugs and mass murderers who carried out the Nazi crimes at the level of actual operations. Some of these men were tried and executed, or tried and imprisoned, after proceedings in various countries; but with much less publicity than the big Nuremberg trial. In the so-called SS-Einsatzgruppen Trial, the defendants were responsible for the murder of millions (mostly Jews); yet some German clergymen actually denounced the trials as little better than acts of revenge. These men, the argument went, were tried under ex post facto laws, and the Americans did not have the "moral authority" to put them on trial."[353]

The International Military Tribunal for the Far East—the so-called Tokyo trials—received the same sorts of criticism. General Hideki Tojo, prime minister of Japan, remarked that his trial "was a political trial. It was only victors' justice."[354] Some Japanese critics (and some Americans) agreed, or felt that the trials were tinged with racism—perhaps the war itself was nothing but an "unjust war on the Oriental race," as one Japanese critic put it.[355] Of course, the Japanese did commit incredible atrocities during the war (and in the course of their war with China). One rather compelling criticism could in fact be leveled against the Tokyo trials. The Emperor Hirohito, in whose name the war was fought, was never tried, never accused of war crimes; indeed he kept his throne after the war, and his family also received implicit immunity. This was a political decision, and perhaps a wise one.[356] But it opened the Tokyo trials to a charge of hypocrisy, which was at least mildly plausible.[357]

The Nuremberg and Tokyo trials were the most visible of the war crimes trials, but there were many others.[358] Between 1946 and 1949, the United States put on trial nearly 200 Germans who had held important positions in the Nazi regime. The American army tried as many as 1700 defendants.[359] Many countries victimized by Germany or Japan ran their own war-crimes trials. Norway, for example, put Vidkun Quisling, the Norwegian Nazi leader, in the dock in 1945, accused of high treason. Poland put the commandant of Auschwitz on trial, and sentenced him to death. The Dutch tried war criminals both in Europe and in the Far East. Australia ran military courts, with many Japanese as defendants. There were in all 296 of these Australian trials. Some of the defendants were acquitted; most were convicted, and 148 were sentenced to death. A Japanese non-commissioned officer, for example, was convicted and sentenced to death for massacring prisoners of war. In a bizarre trial, conducted in New Guinea, Australia accused a Japanese officer of cannibalism; he pleaded starvation as his defense; nonetheless, he was sentenced to be hanged.[360]

In the so-called Doctors' Trial, held in Nuremberg, the defendants were accused of sadistic and unnecessary experiments on human beings.[361] The United States conducted it, in an American military court. Most of the defendants were medical men, for example, Karl Brandt, Hitler's physician, and Waldemar Hoven, chief doctor at the concentration camp in Buchenwald. The most infamous of the Nazi doctors, Josef Mengele, the "angel of death," was probably the worst and most sadistic of these doctors; but Mengele had managed to escape (he was never captured, and lived out his life in South America). There were twenty-three defendants at the trial, which ended in August, 1947. Fifteen defendants were found guilty; seven were sentenced to death. The judges also formulated the so-called Nuremberg Code, an ethical code for medical researchers. Here too the tribunal, faced with acts of monstrous evil, condemned the acts of the defendants, even though Nazi law, which was in force when the doctors conducted their experiments, would have absolved them completely. Indeed, they were in many ways only carrying out Nazi policy.

Dr. Leo Alexander had drafted a document on the limits of medical research; the trial adopted his points, and added others. The Nuremberg Code has been influential ever since, as a basic document of medical ethics. The heart of the Code is the notion that people cannot be treated like lab rats. The "voluntary consent of the human subject is absolutely essential," in the words of the Code. A doctor or scientist cannot conduct experiments on human beings, unless this stringent requirement is met. And any experiment must take pains to avoid unnecessary suffering. The experimenter, if he feels there is any chance of injury or death to the subject, has to end the experiment.

The Code, then, is in some ways the grandparent of all those human subjects committees at Universities and other research institutions, which monitor medical, biological, and social science research. The doctrine of "informed consent" in American tort law, which we mentioned earlier, dates from more or less the same period.[362] Doctors have a duty to tell their patients about the risks and the benefits of any medical procedure; and cannot go forward if the patient says no. Doctors are professionals; they have a license to practice medicine, and an aura of authority. But the patient has ultimate responsibility for life-choices. Informed consent, thus, is a doctrine which, as we pointed out, reflects the ethos underlying the human rights movement: a doctrine of individual autonomy and dignity, a doctrine that asserts the primacy of choice.

All in all, thousands of defendants were tried in Germany, in the allied occupation zones, in the Soviet Union, and in many other countries. Most of these trials were held soon after the end of the war. As time went on, the Cold War and a resurgent Germany helped dampen enthusiasm for these trials.[363] There were sporadic trials over the years. Some of these were trials of Nazis who had escaped and hidden out, often in Latin America, only to be sniffed out and discovered later on. The most famous of these men was Adolf Eichmann. Eichmann, a key figure in the slaughter of Europe's Jews, was captured in South America by Israeli intelligence, brought to Israel, put on trial in 1961, and executed in 1962. Klaus Barbie, head of the Gestapo in Lyon, France, during the Nazi occupation, was caught, extradited to France, and sentenced to life imprisonment in 1987. By the early 21st century, almost all escaped Nazis were dead. In a few trials, wretched old men were still called to account for the horrible crimes of their youth. In late 2009, for example, John Demjanjuk went on trial in Munich. Demjanjuk, it was alleged, had been a prison guard in a notorious concentration camp, where he helped the Nazis murder thousands of prisoners. Demjanjuk, 89 years old, came to the court in a wheelchair. All of the survivors of the camp who might have testified were already dead. But their families were eager to show that they had not forgotten or forgiven.

The Nuremberg trials, as we said, broke new ground; but only up to a point. These were real trials, with real procedures, and a real defense for those in the dock. A few of the defendants were actually acquitted; this happened in other war crimes trials as well. The trials avoided, as we said, the most delicate issues of sovereignty. One crucial aspect of the trials deserves further mention. The defendants were on trial as *individuals*.[364] They were held responsible for what they themselves had done. Many of the defendants—particularly the small fry—argued that they were just following orders. The Nuremberg Charter, however, under which they were tried, specifically provided otherwise: "The fact that the Defendant acted pursuant to orders of his Government or of a superior shall not free him from responsibility"; it could, however "be considered in mitigation of punishment" (Art. 8). Nor was sovereignty a shield for these defendants. They could not say, in their own defense, that what they did, at the time they did it, was legal under the law of a sovereign state; or that they were officials of the government (Art. 7). The central message, then, was not a message of revenge; it was a message about universal norms of conduct, norms that outranked domestic laws and rules. There is no right to commit "crimes against humanity," even if a superior commands you to do it, and even when these crimes conform to the law of a sovereign state.

Is it realistic to expect people to disobey orders to kill—orders from higher up in the hierarchy of some ruthless, dictatorial state? The famous Milgram experiments at Yale University specifically had this question in mind. These experiments attempted to explore the psychology of obedience.[365] Stanley Milgram's subjects were brought into what looked like a laboratory and instructed to carry out the orders of a man who seemed to be a scientist. He wore a white coat, at any rate. They were told they were taking part in an experiment about the learning process. The "learner" answered questions; when he made a mistake, the subjects were supposed to pull a lever, and give the man an electric shock. The more errors, the more shocks—and at higher and higher levels. Most people slavishly followed the orders of the man in the white coat, even when the poor, innocent man who was (mis)answering the questions was screaming with pain. (In reality, of course, this man was an actor, simply pretending to be hurt, and there were no electric shocks at all; but the subjects of the experiment *thought* they were inflicting real pain.) Milgram was testing a common opinion: that is, that the men who committed the Nazi crimes, the thousands who took part in actions that killed millions of people, were thugs, gangsters, psychopaths. Milgram thought otherwise. His experiments seemed to prove his point; ordinary people, it seems, would obey orders from legitimate authority, even when these orders seemed immoral or even criminal. And this kind of misguided obedience could be found everywhere, in every country.

Obeying illegal orders—orders to kill innocent people—is not, unfortunately, a purely historical issue. It figured in the dispute over the My Lai massacre during the Vietnam War. It was not allowed as a defense in the Eichmann trial; but it surfaced during the outcry over American mistreatment of Iraqis detained as prisoners in Abu Ghraib. And of course, there was and is a lively debate over the infamous torture memo, hatched by government lawyers during the administration of George W. Bush. There is debate, too, about the way the CIA and comparable agencies in other countries treat prisoners, how they extract or try to extract information. "I was just obeying orders" has never been accepted as a defense; and this is generally recognized in international criminal law.[366] The reality, however, is otherwise. Countless government leaders, CIA agents, generals who organize death squads, and heads of paramilitary groups are guilty of all sorts of atrocities. Such people rarely go on trial. Or perhaps it is more accurate to say, rarely *went* to trial. As we will see, heads of states no longer have quite so much immunity.

More than fifty years after Adolf Hitler died in a bunker under the ruins of Berlin, and after the Nuremberg trials, and the death of Joseph Stalin, genocide and crimes against humanity are still major problems in the world. There have been horrific massacres in Cambodia, under the notorious Khmer Rouge; there was genocide also in Rwanda, and in the former Yugoslavia, to name some egregious examples. The awful situation in Darfur, in the Sudan, may also amount to genocide. Whatever the label, these have been crimes committed on a gigantic scale—merciless suffering inflicted on tens of thousands of helpless people, sometimes millions. The death squads of Guatemala and the "disappearances" in Argentina under military rule were on a smaller scale; but that is about all that can be said for these episodes in which standards of decency and human rights were trampled on, and the lives of the innocent snuffed out.

These events certainly suggest that Milgram was right. Evil regimes, murderous regimes, can find hands to do their dirty work, either eagerly, or simply as slavish followers of authority. This is, to say the least, a depressing conclusion. But in a way, it has its optimistic side. Perhaps people in Norway or New Zealand could also be cruel, ruthless, murderous, under certain circumstances. Why, then, is it almost impossible to imagine such crimes in Norway or New Zealand? Partly because these countries have strong institutions and solid political structures; these structures act as a firewall against such massive crimes. At least we can hope so. The post-war history of Germany and Japan gives some grounds for this kind of hope. These are now solidly democratic countries, with solid democratic institutions. Imagining crimes on the scale of Hitler for either country is now almost as unthinkable as it is for Norway or New Zealand.

Institutional structure is, however, only part of the story. Another part is the human rights movement itself. The norms that underlie the human rights movement, if taken seriously, are utterly inconsistent with "crimes against humanity." Insofar as these norms gain traction in any given society these crimes are less likely to occur. Or, if they do occur, less likely to enjoy immunity and impunity. Moreover, today, in the age of the human rights movement, the taboo against outside intervention in domestic oppression and slaughter, on the grounds that these are "internal affairs," has been slowly weakening. A sovereign nation may more or less lose sovereignty, if it goes beyond a certain limit; and certainly if it engages in mass murder, even of its own citizens. The worse the behavior, the more corpses piled up on the streets or in the territories, the stronger the case for humanitarian intervention. The "notion of human rights is axiomatic to today's liberal citizens." Justice for the Bosnian Muslims, or the Tutsi, or the people of Kosovo rest on "universal rights.... Universal human rights do not respect 'geographical morality' or sovereignty."[367]

On the legal front, there is much discussion of so-called "universal jurisdiction." Exactly what this entails is a matter of debate. A country like Belgium normally has the right to punish only crimes committed inside Belgium; or, under some circumstances, if committed by a Belgian; or, again under some circumstances, if the crime in some way threatened Belgium. Belgium, therefore, has at least some authority to deal with events that took place outside its national borders, so long as there is some connection to Belgium itself. States have tried to prosecute mass murderers who either give themselves up or wander into the state's jurisdiction. They might even, at times, try these mass murderers *in absentia* if the proper link is there.

Can there be an even more expansive form of *universal jurisdiction*? Could Belgium try to punish people for crimes against humanity and the like, even if there is absolutely no link between the crime and Belgium or the Belgians?[368] This would be a powerful kind of jurisdiction; and it would greatly extend the Nuremberg idea. This kind of universal jurisdiction has not had much traction so far. And, if the idea spread, there would be plenty of problems: for example, the messy possibility that many courts in many countries would try, or try to try, the same people for the same crimes at the same time.

Moreover, it is not easy to provide an exact definition of "crimes against humanity." The Rome Conference listed a number of acts—murder, extermination, enslavement, torture, rape, persecution against "any identifiable group or collectivity on political, racial, national, ethnic, cultural, religious, [or] gender...grounds," when "committed as part of a widespread or systematic attack directed against any civilian population."[369] The charters and statutes creating various special courts and tribunals often attempt to define "crimes against humanity."[370] The Geneva Conventions, for example, which deal with victims of war, include strictures against mistreatment of civilians, and inhuman treatment of civilians in general.

There have been, and will be, borderline cases; but for the worst offenders, the case is often clear enough. General Pinochet was a case in point. The general had seized power in Chile, in a coup that overthrew the government of Salvador Allende. Pinochet then instituted a rather brutal and bloody dictatorship. Pinochet was foolish enough in 1988 to allow free elections, which he imagined he was bound to win. But in fact he lost; and a democratic government took over in Chile. Pinochet, however, remained a Senator, and there was at least an implicit understanding that he would not be called to account. But in 1998, a Spanish judge, Baltasar Garzón, accused Pinochet of human rights violations and demanded that he answer for his crimes. Garzón's excuse was that there were Spanish citizens among the victims of Pinochet's regime. Pinochet at that time was in England, on a visit, and Spain asked England to extradite him. The case went up to the House of Lords. The English government found the situation embarrassing, and refused to extradite him to Spain, on the grounds that he was not medically fit to stand trial. Pinochet immediately left for Chile. He never stood trial, however, because of his advanced age. The Pinochet affair, however, made headlines all over the world. It struck many people as a dramatic illustration of the noble idea that human rights could leap over oceans and national borders.[371]

Very few countries seem willing to take the next step, however, and allow jurisdiction without any link to the country that asserts jurisdiction. But Belgium, in 1993, passed a law "concerning the punishment of serious violations of international humanitarian law." This law gave the courts of Belgium universal jurisdiction over crimes of genocide, war crimes, and crimes against humanity.[372] In 2000, a Belgian judge sitting in Brussels issued an international arrest warrant against Abudlaye Yerodia Ndombasi, a cabinet member in the Congo. The charge was that Yerodia had incited hatred against the Tutsi, resulting in a massacre of several hundred members of this group.

At the time the arrest warrant was issued, Yerodia was foreign minister of the Congo. The Congo claimed the warrant was illegal, and brought its case before the International Court of Justice. That court decided in favor of the Congo, and against Belgium. The majority opinions said surprisingly little about the concept of universal jurisdiction. Some of the dissenting opinions did. The majority rested its opinion for the most part on a doctrine of immunity. A foreign minister in office is normally immune from criminal prosecution; the warrant, therefore, should not have been issued.

The decision is clearly a blow to universal jurisdiction. But Belgium was already an outlier. If Spain can prosecute a Latin American dictator, for crimes committed in his own country, whenever he wanders into their country, or if he committed a crime against a citizen of Spain, and travels to a country from which he can be extradited to Spain, that is already a big step; and it was taken in the case of General Pinochet. After all, if you murder enough people, you are likely to include at least a few foreigners among your victims; and that would legitimate a cluster of trials in a cluster of countries. Getting hold of the defendant may be a trickier proposition. But these trials, at the very least, can put a crimp in the travel plans of dictators. And indictments might embarrass or even frighten dictators,[373] and might have some political impact, both in the dictator's country and abroad. Countries have "no choice but to take account of the growing internationalization of criminal justice."[374]

Governments, in general, do not care much for the idea of universal jurisdiction. They especially do not like the idea that ordinary judges might take it on themselves to indict evildoers all over the world, least of all when there is no real link to their country. Such action on the part of judges is, in a way, a kind of foreign policy, and judges do not usually make and carry out foreign policy. Some countries, however, have accepted the weaker form of "universal jurisdiction": that is, they allow it but require some minimal link to their country. In Spain, however, the crusading judge, Baltasar Garzón, who began the Pinochet saga (and which made him famous), was busy in 2009 investigating torture at Guantánamo Bay. Another Spanish judge was looking into charges that Israel had violated the laws of war in Gaza. Still another was trying to get the Chinese government to defend its actions in Tibet. All of this was extremely embarrassing to the Spanish government. The Chinese and Israeli governments voiced extreme disapproval. In May, 2009, the Spanish Congress acted to rein in these judges. "Universal jurisdiction" was to cover only certain crimes (for example, genocide, terrorism, piracy or the hijacking of airplanes—"apoderamiento illicito de aeronaves"—illegal drug traffic, and crimes concerning female genital mutilation). But these were cognizable only if the defendants were actually in Spain, or if there were Spanish nationals among the victims, or some link relevant to Spain ("algún vínculo de conexión relevante con España"); and only in the absence of proceedings going on in some international tribunal, or some other competent jurisdiction.[375] Clearly, Tibet or the Gaza strip was unlikely to qualify under the new Spanish rules.[376] And, the Spanish Supreme Court has accused Garzón of overstepping his powers, when he planned to investigate atrocities committed during the Franco regime.[377]

Oddly enough, there is a kind of universal jurisdiction which the United States seems to recognize. This is indeed peculiar, since the United States has an almost allergic reaction to international treaties, and notoriously refuses to sign on to many of them—the International Criminal Court, for one; a convention barring land mines for another. A powerful current of conservative opinion treats anything international as if it threatened American liberty, or, God forbid, could put Americans at risk of trial conducted by foreigners in foreign countries. Yet the Alien Tort Claims Act, originally passed in 1789, gives the federal district courts original jurisdiction over tort suits by aliens, if the tort was in violation of a treaty, or was "committed in violation of the law of nations."[378] In 1991, the Torture Victim Protection Act seemed to give a cause of action to victims of torture in "any foreign nation," provided the plaintiff had "exhausted adequate and available remedies" in the country where the torture took place, and so long as the torture took place "under actual or apparent authority, or color of law," in the offending country.[379] What impact these laws have had is another question. It is (alas) unlikely that they have done much to deter torture. Some cases have been won; some evil men have been deported. The hoary old doctrine of sovereign immunity has not been a major stumbling-block so far.

The broader form of universal jurisdiction, in short, is not on the horizon, at least for now. But the milder form may be gaining more acceptance. The Canadian parliament, for example, enacted a statute in 2000, the "Crimes Against Humanity and War Crimes Act."[380] The statute applied to "crimes against humanity," "genocide," and "war crime." A violator can be prosecuted (section 9) if he was a Canadian citizen, or "employed by Canada in a civilian or military capacity," or if the victim was a Canadian, or if the violator happened to be "present in Canada."[381] In the United States, the Center for Justice and Accountability has brought civil cases against some of the worst Latin American abusers, who had taken up residence in the United States; and has won some notable suits for damages against them.[382]

INTERNATIONAL TRIBUNALS

If the problem with "universal jurisdiction" is that it might result in a messy cacophony of lawsuits, most of them futile, then the future of "universal jurisdiction" might lie, not in national courts, but in international tribunals. And here there is definitely some movement and some forward evolution.

The Arrest Warrant case (against the foreign minister of the Congo) was brought in Belgium, under Belgian law; but it was finally decided before the International Court of Justice. This is not the only tribunal with "international" in its title. The International Criminal Tribunal for the Former Yugoslavia, established by the UN in 1993, was authorized to prosecute men guilty of genocide and "crimes against humanity."[383] The tribunal sits in the Hague. In 1999, this tribunal convicted a Croatian general of crimes against humanity. Later, Serbia extradited Slobodan Milosevic, who had been the leader of that country, to face charges of genocide and crimes against humanity.[384] He died in captivity. The tribunal has issued over 150 indictments, and has convicted quite a few defendants. A few remain at large. Resolution 955 of the Security Council, of November, 1994, creating the International Criminal Tribunal for Rwanda, expressed "grave concern" over reports of "genocide and other systematic, widespread and fragrant violations of international humanitarian law," committed in Rwanda. The tribunal has been actively at work, and has (for example) convicted the former prime minister of Rwanda of genocide.

A kind of hybrid national and international tribunal is the Special Court for Sierra Leone. This court came into existence pursuant to an "Agreement between the United Nations and the Government of Sierra Leone" in August 2000. Charles Taylor, the former President of Liberia, accused of carrying out atrocities in Sierra Leone, is (at the date of this writing) on trial in The Hague, before this tribunal. A second hybrid national and international tribunal is at work in Cambodia as of 2009, another country where an evil regime slaughtered an astonishing number of Cambodians. This is the Extraordinary Chambers in the Courts of Cambodia for the Prosecution of Crimes Committed during the Period of Democratic Kampuchea, usually called ECCC (or the Khmer Rouge Tribunal).[385] This hybrid, which combines national and international staff, is not carrying on its work in The Hague; rather, it is located in the country where the murders were carried out; and promises to be much cheaper to run than the Rwanda and Yugoslavian tribunals. The ECCC, however, has been dogged with claims of incompetence and downright corruption. The first trial—of Kaing Guek Eav (usually called Duch), who ran a notorious Khmer Rouge prison—began in March 2009, and has attracted a lot of attention in Cambodia. Hybrid courts, like hybrid cars, may have a real future.

The General Assembly of the United Nations called a conference in Rome, in June 1998; and in July of that year, the Rome conference adopted a treaty to establish an International Criminal Court. Most countries who were there voted in favor of this idea; 21 countries abstained, and seven voted no, including the United States and China. But enough countries had ratified it by 2002 for the Court to select judges and open up for business. Its mandate was to try individuals—not states—who were guilty of crimes against humanity. It would, hopefully, end the paradox pointed out by Robin Cook, the British Foreign Secretary, that a person who killed one other person was more likely to be tried and punished than "those who plot genocide against millions."[386]

As of 2010, more than 100 countries recognize the jurisdiction of the Court. Most European countries have agreed to sign on, along with most Latin American countries. The Rome treaty lists four types of crime: genocide, crimes against humanity, war crimes, and aggression. The court sits in The Hague. In 2009, as we mentioned earlier, it called for the arrest of the President of the Sudan, Omar al-Bashir, accused of crimes against humanity (the atrocities in Darfur).[387] Bashir reacted to this call with defiance. He certainly has no intention of surrendering to the International Court; at the present time, the court has no way to force him to come. It does, to be sure, make his travel plans a bit more iffy. The Court has been active in other ways: it prosecuted, for example, two Congolese militia leaders, who allegedly sent child soldiers into a village and wiped it out, killing more than 200 men, women and children; some were burned alive in their houses.[388]

It is too early to tell much about the success or failure of these international tribunals. They face many difficulties, including financial ones. A careful study by Gary Jonathan Bass posed the question whether "war crimes tribunals work." Basically, his answer was no. But, he added, "they have clear *potential* to work"; and a "well-run legalistic process," he felt, is better than "apathy or vengeance."[389] These tribunals grow out of, and expand, the basic ideas that animated the Nuremberg trials. We talk about "rogue states," and "failed states"; but the rogues and the failures are people, not abstract entities. People who run states give the orders to kill; and people who obey them, sometimes eagerly, do the actual killing. And these are the people who, under the social norms that animate the human rights movement, can and should be held responsible for their blood-soaked acts of mass murder. Also, the very fact that these tribunals are *international* makes them unusually significant.

Like such NGO's as Amnesty International and Human Rights Watch, they grow out of the general human rights movement. They reflect its basic premises, and its underlying assumptions: that there are fundamental rights; that these rights belong to every human being; and that they are superior to the will of parliaments, kings, presidents, and whoever flies the flag of state sovereignty.

These are also—and this is especially important—courts of *law*. People can argue and quibble over whether it is good law or bad law, just as they argued over the procedures in Nuremberg and in Tokyo. But in the end, these are real courts and they run real trials with real procedures and a real chance for the men in the dock to defend themselves. The legalism of these trials may be "an elite phenomenon"[390] — surely some victims and relatives of victims would be willing to tear these evil people apart limb by limb, or shoot them on sight. But calling these trials an "elite phenomenon" does not make them unimportant. The trials, complete with learned judges, prosecutors, defense counsel, and rules of evidence, tell the world that these men will be held accountable, but in an orderly way. *They* may have ruled through terror and raw power, but it is the rule of law that will condemn them. National law is no defense; nor is obedience to orders; nor is authority to do what they are accused of doing. The Resolution setting up the Rwanda tribunal made this explicit:[391] the "official position of any accused person, whether as Head of State or Government or as a responsible Government official," does not "relieve such person of criminal responsibility" (Art. 6.2).[392] International tribunals override national ones; and international norms override national ones.

11
Some Concluding Remarks

In this chapter, I would like to sum up some of the arguments I have tried to advance in earlier chapters; and add a few comments by way of prediction or, as you will see, non-prediction.

This book has tried to put the human rights movement into some sort of social and historical context. There is, as we noted, a huge and daunting literature about human rights. This literature, to be sure, does not neglect history. But its history is usually intellectual history. It is a history of thinkers and philosophers and their writings; secondarily, it is a history of texts: who drafted them, when, whose hand was behind this or that sentence or provision. As I pointed out, much of the literature has been written by philosophy professors and political theorists. The literature has a highly normative flavor. I have nothing against that. The scholars who write about human rights are usually quite passionate about the subject. They want more justice, more humanity, more human dignity. This is all to the good. I applaud them. But I began this enterprise by assuming there was room in the tent of scholarship for other ways to look at this important subject.

The other way is, in a word, sociological. This too is not terra incognita, but here too there are many ways to look at the subject. What intrigued me was the macro-question: why? Why is the human rights movement so powerful? Why have its ideas been so seductive? In the past—and not that long ago—almost *nobody* accepted (for example) the equality of men and women as a fundamental premise. Or, for that matter, the equality of black and white. Why have so many people changed their mind about gender and race relations? It will not do to invoke some sort of evolution theory, some story of human progress. There may well be human progress; but if so, this only defers the question. *Why* are we progressing? I will not repeat the answers I have tried to give. Heaviest emphasis was placed on the rise of expressive individualism, in developed countries; and more and more, in the rest of the world as well. I have tried to show how the premises of the human rights movement grow out of a particular type of soil; and I have put forward my own notion of why this has happened.

INDIVIDUALISM AND ITS DISCONTENTS

I promised in the introductory chapter to say a bit more about individualism. This troublesome concept has been, after all, central to my argument.

I want to distinguish between three uses of the term. First, individualism can be treated as a normative ideology. By this I mean, individualism as a prescription for the way people and the world ought to be or behave. This sense seems to me largely a straw man, something to argue against. It would be repulsive to suggest that people and economies are and ought to be isolated, atomic, every dog for himself. People who consider themselves "communitarians" reject this ideology (which almost nobody actually espouses). Possibly some libertarians might fit into this category, but no doubt in a more benign form. Certain economists come dangerously close to assuming this type of individualism, at least in some of their model-building enterprises. But economists would insist that they are describing human behavior, not telling people how they ought to behave.

The second meaning is as an empirical ideology, that is, an ideology that people, real people, actually believe in, for themselves at any rate. Not the belief that this is a dog eat dog world, not the belief in a Hobbesian state of nature—which would be, as he said, nasty and brutish if not short. Rather, it is the belief that what people need is the right and the chance to be whatever kind of dog they choose to be. Faith that we—all of us—need space to grow, to develop, to expand our horizons; to maximize our possibilities, to develop our own personalities, to strive for our personal best. So long as we don't interfere with or harm other people, of course.

Obviously, in the world we live in, this kind of personal development is at best possible only to a limited degree. Many of the games of life are zero-sum games. There are winners and losers. That much is perfectly plain. And equally plain is the fact that people are not really on their own. After all, we *are* social animals, we do live in families, we do help each other, we do need each other; we do make sacrifices, and other people in turn make sacrifices for us. But this philosophy of trying to achieve our "personal best" is certainly popular; and it rests on the *third* meaning, that is, individualism as a social fact.

This too is a matter of more or less. Societies are complicated. Every one of us is also complicated. Millions of people are passive, hide-bound, traditional, timid, afraid to make changes; some of these people can hardly be called individualists at all. Society also contains a dazzling rainbow of occupations, hobbies, and ways of life; contains artists, entrepreneurs, hair stylists, as well as axe-murderers, cloistered nuns, and professional soldiers. All of these stand in different relations to other people—and to themselves. Yet on the whole, it seems to me that expressive individualism is a powerful force in developed societies; and more so than was true in the past. There is abundant evidence, in many areas of life, suggesting the power of expressive individualism. Religion for example. The astonishing percentage of Americans who change religions is one piece of this evidence. The astonishing numbers of Europeans who change jobs, countries, habits of food and drink is also a piece of evidence. We must remember, though, that all modal changes in personality and in culture tend to be relative, not absolute. They never apply to everybody everywhere at every time.

But what about "community" in an age of individualism? Nobody could deny that "community" is valuable; and that people should have the right to choose whatever "community" suits them. Is there anything more painful than utter loneliness? People long for attachments—to family and friends, and failing that, to some sort of community (or to both family and friends *and* community). And, in fact, modern society provides plenty of opportunity to choose community—the community of your choice. You can (if you qualify) enlist in the Marine Corps or the French Foreign Legion. You can become a civic activist. You can attach yourself to an actual commune, or enter a monastery or a convent, for that matter. You can certainly try to be close to your family and friends. You can work hard to expand the circles in which you revolve.

Historically, few "communities" have been communes or Utopian settlements, or collective settlements like the classic Israeli kibbutzim. Most, if not all, communities have been based on hierarchies and social distinctions. Indeed, some modern "communes" are in effect little dictatorships, ruled by some guru, who tells the members what to do and when to do it. Most people find this way of life repulsive. They might find a career in the Army equally repulsive, and for the same reason. People will always be social animals, but this does not mean that they necessarily want to live in a structured, hierarchical "community." Friends, yes; groups and circles of like-minded people, yes; social clubs and family gatherings, yes; but organized "communities," no.

THE END OF HISTORY; AND THE BEGINNING

The future is a mystery, a blank, a voyage into the unknown: this much is completely obvious and banal. We can extrapolate things a little; but we cannot really predict. What will happen next year is impossible to guess; and what will happen next century or next millennium is worse than unknown, it is totally inconceivable. But somehow it is easy to forget this simple fact. It is tempting to imagine that we have come to some sort of climax—the end of history. It is easy to assume that some sort of mopping up is all that is left to do.

The "end of history" idea is all the more seductive when we see, or think we see, some sort of long-term trend. The world has been evolving in the direction of freedom, liberal democracy, welfare states, and expanded human rights. The divine right of kings was not that long ago. First nobles, then men of property, earned rights, and then they gained the vote. Men without property came next, as voters; followed by women and various out-groups. It would be only natural to imagine that this trend will inevitably continue. Democracy seems to be on the march. The Nazi dream of a thousand-year

Reich turned into a dozen years and ended in total destruction; Germany today is a democratic state, with a constitutional court and a charter of basic rights. The Soviet Union, a massive and powerful empire, disintegrated toward the end of the 20th century. Today, more and more countries have become democracies, with more or less respect for the rule of law. The rest are certain to fall into line. At least we think so. We are confident that eventually even Saudi Arabia or China or Laos or Zimbabwe will mend their ways and end up democratic and committed to human rights, the same as Sweden or Australia. And, along the way, the last tribe in the Amazon jungle will put on blue jeans and T-shirts, eat hamburgers, and join the rest of the world.

These are natural thoughts (or dreams). But enlightened people have been wrong many times before. A solid citizen of Victorian England was probably just as convinced about the end of history. He knew where the world was heading, and why. The good Victorian could look back on an imperial century, and extrapolate from what he saw; the natural trend was clear. Advanced peoples (all of them European) would take over the rest of the world, and gradually (perhaps) bring civilization to the benighted souls in Africa and Asia. Or at least to those that *could* be civilized. The rest would work for and serve their betters. Free trade was another universal given. And so was the advance of civilized morals — the end, perhaps, of crime, prostitution, and other forms of vice. The sex drive would be tamed, and shut up inside the marital cage where it belonged. Science and technology, and perhaps eugenics, would help to bring about a better world, and certainly a more civilized world.

In a very interesting movie, *Iceman*,[393] scientists discover a man from the ice age, frozen in an Arctic glacier. They somehow manage to revive him and bring him back to life. The scientists keep him in an artificial environment, designed to look more or less like the environment in which he lived long before. But later in the movie, he manages to escape. Out the door of the laboratory, he finds himself suddenly in the midst of a modern city. The movie brilliantly portrays his total bafflement at this world: a world of shopping centers, cars and buses whizzing by, and all the paraphernalia of life in the developed world. What on earth could the poor iceman make of all of this?

If we somehow managed to extract DNA from some solid British corpse of the 19th century, and brought him or her back to life, the poor Victorian would be almost equally bewildered and disoriented. This is a world in which Burundi and Vanuatu are members of the United Nations and in which Belize has an embassy in London. It is also a world, of course, of automobiles and jets and computers and antibiotics; a world of the internet and instant communication across great distances. And it is also a world of triple X movies, and gay rights—and, probably most dramatic of all, a world of women's rights, a world in which relations between men and women have changed dramatically, not in all countries, to be sure, but very much so in his own. Almost none of this was predictable; in some cases, as I said, men and women would have made exactly the opposite sort of prediction. And I have no doubt that if we became icemen and icewomen, and came to life in the distant future—and even the not so distant future—we would find ourselves equally at sea, unable to grasp (perhaps only at first) what this brave new world was all about, and how to cope with it.

So I will resist trying, however feebly, to make guesses about where the human rights movement is going. We know where it has gone. We know where it *seems* to be heading. But to say anything more would be foolish. We do know, or can guess, that technology will play a massive role in whatever the future has in store. Technology is responsible for much of what our world is like. It will surely be responsible for the shape of the world to come. And technology can upset our comfortable assumptions and predictions. As I have said elsewhere, technology could already furnish a dictator with tools of oppression that Hitler or Stalin, let alone Genghis Khan, could hardly have dreamed of. How to control and master these tools is an issue that will have to be faced someday. And soon.

A second point: we live in what Ulrich Beck has called a risk society.[394] Great risks, global risks, are all about us. Risks of nuclear war, of course. The world has lived with this threat since 1945. It still exists. But the world is more likely, perhaps, to end not with a bang but with a whimper, to steal a line from T. S. Eliot. Not with an explosion, in other words, but by virtue of slow erosion; decay of the conditions that make life comfortable for those of us who live in comfortable countries: degradation of the environment, or poisons in air and water or the melting of icecaps or massive induced change in climate and weather. Or, perhaps, with a bang of another sort: a total collapse of the financial system, in a world tied together, with lethal consequences; or an explosion of poverty, desperation, and outright hunger; then, in the face of greater and greater inequality, violent revolutions and wars might erupt and spread. Bombs can destroy in minutes roads, schools, buildings, and cities that took years to build. Wars can tear apart the fabric of societies that were patiently created by whole generations. This kind of apocalypse is also possible.

And yet a third point: this book has underscored a set of social norms, and a modal personality. These were central to understanding how and why the human rights movement came about, developed, and spread. The movement rests, I have argued, on a few basic premises, premises widely shared by people in developed countries, and by the elites in less-developed countries. These norms and premises show every sign of expanding their reach to other populations as well. And these norms and premises rest in turn on changes in society that have altered the way people think and behave. The human rights movement is unthinkable, I believe, without the rise of expressive individualism. But this personality type hardly existed, as far as we can tell, in medieval Europe or classic China or among the Inca or the Aztecs. So here too we have to resist the seductive notion of the end of history. What has come to be can also pass away. Human personality is plastic and malleable. There is no reason to think some kind of modal personality will stay the same, forever and ever.

I have assumed, for example, that people in the modern world, generally speaking, value privacy very highly. They want space, they want to be (in a sense) alone; and they want to be free to craft their own lives. And yet and yet.... The younger generation is in a sense never really alone. They are always connected, to someone or something. Their iPads and smart phones give them constant access to everybody they know and care about. I already find it hard to put myself, psychologically, in the shoes of the people on Facebook and who text and twitter obsessively; or the people who are willing to expose their bodies and souls on blogs or on the internet, or who populate reality TV. By the same token, I find it hard to understand the mindset of people who blow themselves to bits in the name of religion, taking with them dozens of innocent people who happened to be in the wrong place at the wrong time. Or the mindset of the throngs who took fatal doses of Kool-Aid in Guyana, at the twisted behest of their guru. These people—the jihadists, the suicidal fanatics—are, one hopes, a tiny minority. But nobody can predict which way the winds of personality will blow.

This book has assumed that the human rights movement taps into social norms that are, in some sense, quite fundamental. How deep these norms go, how firm they are, is another question. These *are* norms of Western elites (I see nothing wrong in that). And these norms rest on even more basic norms of individual autonomy. As I said, these norms are spreading. International groups carry these norms to remote villages and to traditional societies; local groups that sign on to the ethos. Global mass culture prepares the way. Sally Merry, for example, has vividly documented the process of global infection, so to speak, that has carried norms against gender violence from West to East. Men have been punching and raping and dominating women for centuries. But now, many women in many countries show themselves willing to resist. Change seems to be on the way. It is a "slow process," because it means changing the way you think of yourself, and the way you behave. It requires, for the woman, a "rights-defined self," and this is a "substantial identity change both for the woman and for the man." Women are "invited to take on a more autonomous self."[395] This is not easily done. The human rights ethos— and the human rights personality—has expanded quite dramatically in my lifetime (though never without resistance); but it has a long way to go.

Nonetheless, so far, the human rights movement is genuinely *popular*, certainly so in the developed world. Millions of people want these rights for themselves; and also for other people. But this too can change, even in these countries. In some regards, for many people, the mentality that underlies the movement may be paper thin. Or may become thin, in the future. It may be strong now—this is hard to tell—but this does not guarantee its future strength. There are powerful competitors. There always have been. In some ways, the ethos of individual autonomy is profoundly unsatisfying. Young people may enjoy doing their thing, leaving home and roaming about the world with a backpack; older people may enjoy changing directions (and spouses) and starting over with a new skin, after molting the old one. But millions of other people surely feel a hunger for something else, more satisfying, more basic. In some ways, and at some times, nothing can be more fulfilling than abject subjection to a movement or a goal or a belief that is higher than oneself; or to a guru, a leader, a hero, with charisma and a cause.

But this is not the only problem the human rights ethos might face. There are other dangers. It is already easy to persuade many people, or even most people, that the war on terror calls for strong measures. Or that the overwhelming risks and dangers of modern life call for a new approach. The old attitudes toward rights may come to seem naïve and unrealistic. Fighting crime is another popular excuse for erosion of rights. Or battles against evil ideologies. People were willing to tolerate outrageous behavior in the United States, in the name of the war against communism; and this excuse was used in some Latin American countries to justify even worse offenses against civil liberties—death squads and military dictatorships, for example. Communism lost its grip; but terrorism replaced it as an all-purpose bogeyman. If the risks, or the panic, increase, stronger measures against "terror" might be put on the table. And this might erode some of what the movement for human rights has achieved.

The punchline is this: technology, and the crushing weight of circumstances, may make majorities out of far-fetched and deviant minorities. Or not. Perhaps the last paragraphs paint much too bleak a picture. Perhaps the world community will find ways to solve its most pressing problems. Perhaps the future *will* see more progress toward a just and generous world order. In either case, I end this book, as I must, with a riddle that can be solved only with the passage of time.

ABOUT THE AUTHOR

Lawrence M. Friedman is the Marion Rice Kirkwood Professor of Law at Stanford University. An internationally renowned, prize-winning legal historian, Friedman has for a generation been the leading expositor of the history of American law to a global audience of lawyers and lay people alike—and a leading figure in the law and society movement. He is particularly well known for treating legal history as a branch of general social history. From his award-winning *History of American Law*, first published in 1973, to his *American Law in the 20th Century*, published in 2003, his canonical works have become classic textbooks in legal and undergraduate education.

Friedman is a prolific author on crime and punishment, and his numerous books have been translated into multiple languages. He is the recipient of six honorary law degrees and is a fellow in the American Academy of Arts and Sciences. Before joining the Stanford Law School faculty in 1968, he was a professor of law at the University of Wisconsin Law School and at Saint Louis University School of Law.

In addition to his position at Stanford Law School, he has an appointment (by courtesy) with the Stanford University Department of History and the Department of Political Science.

NOTES

CHAPTER 1

[1] Emilie M. Hafner-Burton, Kiyoteru Tsutsui, and John W. Meyer, "International Human Rights Law and the Politics of Legitimation," *International Sociology* 23:115, 119 (2008). On the impact of treaties, conventions, and the like on the rights of children, see Elizabeth Heger Boyle and Minzee Kim, "International Human Rights Law, Global Economic Reforms, and Child Survival and Development Rights Outcomes," *Law and Society Review* 43:455 (2009).

[2] Oona A. Hathaway, "Do Human Rights Treaties Make a Difference?" *Yale Law Journal* 111:1935, 1989 (2002).

[3] In the United States, conservatives have successfully resisted economic and social rights; and even mainstream human rights documents are viewed with suspicion—as an interference with states' rights, for example. Tony Evans, "Introduction: Power, Hegemony, and the Universalization of Human Rights," in Tony Evans, ed., *Human Rights Fifty Years On: A Reappraisal* (1998), pp. 2, 9-10.

[4] Jack Donnelly, *Universal Human Rights in Theory and Practice* (2d ed., 2003), p. 7.

[5] Helen M. Stacy, *Human Rights for the 21st Century: Sovereignty, Civil Society, Culture* (2009), p. 29.

[6] Emilie M. Hafner-Burton and Kiyoteru Tsutsui, "Human Rights in a Globalizing World: The Paradox of Empty Promises,"*American Journal of Sociology* 110:1373 (2005).

[7] Wade M. Cole, "Sovereignty Relinquished? Explaining Commitment to the International Human Rights Covenants, 1966-1999," *Am. Sociological Rev.* 70:472 (2005); Hafner-Burton and Tsutsui, op. cit. *supra*.

[8] Beth A. Simmons, *Mobilizing for Human Rights: International Law in Domestic Politics* (2009), pp. 12, 373.

[9] Oona Hathaway, op. cit., at 2019, 2020. She does admit that where there is (as there usually is) "little monitoring or enforcement... treaty ratification can serve to offset, rather than enhance, pressure for real change in practices."

[10] Todd Landman, *Protecting Human Rights: A Comparative Study* (2005), p. 6.

[11] Hafner-Burton and Tsutsui, "Human Rights," op. cit. *supra*.

[12] For a trenchant critique of the two fields, and their work, see Neil Stammers, *Human Rights and Social Movements* (2009), pp. 11-14.

[13] Michael Freeman, *Human Rights: An Interdisciplinary Approach* (2002), pp. 6-7. See also Eva Brems, "Methods in Legal Human Rights Research," in Fons Coomans et al., eds., *Methods of Human Rights Research* (2009), p. 77. Brems surveyed human rights researchers, asking them about their "methodology," and mostly found that they basically had none; and that their work was strongly normative.

[14] There are, to be sure, critiques of the human rights movement; those who consider it biased and imperialistic and so on, as we shall see. But these are almost never attacks on the basic or core substance of human rights.

[15] For example, Paul Gordon Lauren, *The Evolution of International Human Rights* (2d ed., 2003); Lynn Hunt, *Inventing Human Rights: A History* (2007).

[16] Among the words that try to fill this gap between the social sciences and the study of human rights, one might mention Michael Freeman, op. cit., and Lydia Morris, ed., *Rights: Sociological Perspectives* (2006). But even the essays in Morris' collection seem, frankly, not particularly sociological. A welcome addition to the literature is Neil Stammers, *Human Rights and Social Movements* (2009). I want to also mention Fons Coomans et al., eds., *Methods of Human Rights Research* (2009).

[17] See Gunnar Beck, "The Mythology of Human Rights," *Ratio Juris* 21:312 (2008). For Beck, Human rights "lack the overriding normative status that is commonly assumed in justifying their privileged legal status.... [J]udges make rights, and their choices remain political." Ibid., 346.

[18] Jack Donnelly, "Human Rights, Globalizing Flows, and State Power," in Alison Brysk, ed., *Globalization and Human Rights* (2002), pp. 226, 228.

[19] Colm O'Cinneide, "The Right to Equality: A Substantive Legal Norm or Vacuous Rhetoric?" in *UCL Human Rights Review* 1:80 (2008).

[20] District of Columbia v. Heller, 554 U.S. 570 (2008). See also McDonald v. City of Chicago, 561 U.S. 3025, 130 S. Ct. 3020 (2010) (extending second amendment to the states as well).

[21] This is also true of a few American states, for example, Massachusetts and Iowa.

[22] 1 Cranch (5 U.S.) 137 (1803).

[23] For example, in Sturges v. Crowninshield, 4 Wheat. (17 U.S.) 122 (1819), the Supreme Court struck down a New York insolvency statute.

[24] The German *Grundgesetz* went into effect in 1949. On the history of this document, see Maximilian Steinbeis, Marion Detjen and Stephan Detjen, *Die Deutschen und das Grundgesetz: Geschichte und Grenzen unserer Verfassung* (2009). For Japan, see John W. Dower, *Embracing Defeat: Japan in the Wake of World War II* (1999), pp. 346-404.

[25] C. Neal Tate, "Why the Expansion of Judicial Power?" in C. Neal Tate and Torbjorn Vallinder, eds., *The Global Expansion of Judicial Power* (1995), pp. 27, 30.

[26] Ran Hirschl, *Towards Juristocracy: The Origins and Consequences of the New Constitutionalism* (2004), p. 43.

[27] C. Neal Tate, "Why the Expansion of Judicial Power?" in Tate and Vallinder, *Global Expansion of Judicial Power*, pp. 27, 28-29, 36.

[28] Art. 3 (3); on the political movement behind this, see Katharina C. Heyer, "The ADA on the Road: Disability Rights in Germany," *Law and Social Inquiry* 27:723 (2002).

[29] There is a large literature on the South African constitution; see, for example, Mark S. Kende, *Constitutional Rights in Two Worlds: South Africa and the United States* (2009).

[30] See the figures in James L. Gibson, *Overcoming Apartheid: Can Truth Reconcile a Divided Nation?* (2004), p. 307.

[31] Of course, the distinction may not be artificial in one sense—that is, if it corresponds to an actual fact of legal culture, that is, to a notion that exists as a social fact.

[32] See, for example, Peter Jones, "Human Rights, Group Rights, and Peoples' Rights," *Human Rights Quarterly* 21:80 (1999).

[33] See the discussion of this point in Kenneth Karst, *Belonging to America: Equal Citizenship and the Constitution* (1989), pp. 160-162.

[34] Rory O'Connell, "Let's Talk: Dealing with Difference in Human Rights Law," in Koen De Feyter and George Pavlakos, eds., *The Tension Between Group Rights and Human Rights: A Multidisciplinary Approach* (2008), pp. 131, 141.

[35] See also the discussion in Stephan Breitenmoser, "The Protection of Groups and Group Rights in Europe," in De Feyter and Pavlakos, eds., *The Tension Between Group Rights and Human Rights* (2008), p. 245.

[36] John Boli and Michael A. Elliott, "Façade Diversity: The Individualization of Cultural Difference," *International Sociology* 23:540, 542 (2008).

CHAPTER 2

[37] See Brian Z. Tamanaha, *On the Rule of Law: History, Politics, Theory* (2004), pp. 114ff.

[38] For a review of the literature, see Stephan Haggard, Andrew MacIntyre, and Lydie Tiede, "The Rule of Law and Economic Development," *Annual Review of Political Science* 11:205 (2008).

[39] Frank R. Upham, "Speculations on Legal Informality: On Winn's 'Relational Practices and the Marginalization of Law,'" *Law and Society Review* 26:233, 237 (1994); the reference is to Jane Kaufman Winn, "Relational Practices and the Marginalization of Law: Informal Financial Practices of Small Businesses in Taiwan," *Law and Society Review* 28:193 (1994). Winn argues that Taiwan's quite remarkable growth owed little or nothing to the formal legal system.

[40] Ibid., at 221.

[41] One classic text is James Buchanan and Gordon Tullock, *The Calculus of Consent: Logical Foundations of Constitutional Democracy* (1962).

[42] Ran Hirschl, *Toward Juristocracy* (2004), *supra* note 26.

[43] Mutua, *Human Rights*, p. 151. The Constitution "robs [the ANC]...of any ability to carry out major reforms."

[44] Ran Hirschl, "The 'Design Sciences' and Constitutional 'Success,'" *Texas Law Review* 87:1339 (2009).

[45] Hirschl, op. cit., at 1373.

[46] See Lawrence M. Friedman, *The Legal System: A Social Science Perspective* (1975), pp. 193-194. I have no doubt that "legal culture," as so defined, is real, and important. The phrase itself is perhaps not ideal, because the word "culture" is so slippery and carries so much baggage. For this reason, the concept has been subject to a good deal of criticism, see, for example, Roger Cotterrell, "The Concept of Legal Culture," in David Nelken, ed., *Comparing Legal Cultures* (1997), p. 13.

[47] Guenter Bierbrauer, "Toward an Understanding of Legal Culture: Variations in Individualism and Collectivism between Kurds, Lebanese, and Germans," *Law and Society Review* 28:243 (1994).

[48] *Pew Global Attitudes Project* (2009), p. 65; www.pewglobal.org, visited April 15, 2010.

[49] Arif Payaslyoglu and Ahmet Icduygu, "Awareness of and Support for Human Rights among Turkish University Students," *Human Rights Quarterly* 21:513 (1999).

[50] The source is *Pew Global Attitudes Project* (2002). That 77% said yes in Egypt, and 70% in Iran does, however, raise some suspicions as to what exactly people thought they were responding to. Curiously enough, India had the lowest percentage of yeses—53%.

[51] These figures are also from *Pew Global Attitudes Project* (2002). But Turkey, with 80% yes, and Indonesia, with 65% yes, show that some Muslim countries are more tolerant. Surprisingly, in the Ukraine only 30% said yes; and in South Korea, only 48%. Again, this leads one to wonder how the question was understood by different respondents.

[52] James L. Gibson and Gregory A. Caldeira, "The Legitimacy of Transnational Legal Institutions: Compliance, Support and the European Court of Justice," *Am. J. Political Science* 39:459, 470 (1995).

CHAPTER 3

[53] There is a huge literature on the human rights ideas of the Enlightenment. See, for example, Paul Gordon Lauren, *The Evolution of International Human Rights* (2d ed., 2003); Lynn Hunt, *Inventing Human Rights: A History* (2007); Stephen James, *Universal Human Rights: Origins and Development* (2007).

[54] On this point, see in particular Neil Stammers, *Human Rights as Social Movements* (2009).

[55] These courts are treated in Jenny S. Martinez, "Antislavery Courts and the Dawn of International Human Rights Law," *Yale Law Journal* 117:550 (2008).

[56] Ibid., at 590.

[57] Ibid., at 632.

[58] Wiktor Osiatynski, *Human Rights and Their Limits* (2009), p. 63. He remarks that "humanitarian action implies a passive victim who needs to be protected and assisted; a crucial word here is *need* rather than *right*." Ibid., p. 61.

[59] 17 Stats. 598 (act of March 3, 1873); on the background, see Donna Dennis, *Licentious Gotham: Erotic Publishing and its Prosecution in Nineteenth-Century New York* (2009).

[60] See, in general, Lawrence M. Friedman, *Guarding Life's Dark Secrets: Legal and Social Controls over Reputation, Propriety, and Privacy* (2007).

[61] The defense of slavery by Southern apologists was in part based on the sacredness of property rights.

[62] Lochner v. New York, 198 U.S. 45 (1905).

[63] Anthony Woodiwiss, *Human Rights* (2005), p. 55.

[64] "Certain communities formerly belonging to the Turkish Empire" had, however, "reached a stage of development where their existence as independent nations can be provisionally recognized," though with help from mandatory powers until "such time as they are able to stand alone."

[65] Elizabeth Borgwardt, *A New Deal for the World: America's Vision for Human Rights* (2005), pp. 14-45.

[66] Borgwardt, *A New Deal*, treats the Atlantic Charter and its history in detail.

[67] See, in general, Johannes Morsink, *The Universal Declaration of Human Rights: Origins, Drafting, and Intent* (1999); also, Mary Ann Glendon, *A World Made New: Eleanor Roosevelt and the Universal Declaration of Human Rights* (2001).

[68] The article adds as a purpose "strengthening of respect for human rights and fundamental freedoms"; and education shall also "promote understanding, tolerance and friendship among all nations."

[69] Paul Gordon Lauren, *Evolution of International Human Rights*, p. 191.

[70] Mrs. Roosevelt "was consistently instructed to avoid any measures of implementation that might conflict with domestic law"; and later, during the McCarthy era and beyond, "fears of world government," particularly among conservatives, pushed in the same direction. Roger Normand and Sarah Zaidi, *Human Rights at the UN: The Political History of Universal Justice* (2007), p. 237.

[71] Mary Ann Glendon, op. cit., p. 235.

[72] Christopher Harland, "The Status of the International Covenant on Civil and Political Rights (ICCPR) in the Domestic Law of State Parties: An Initial Global Survey Through UN Human Rights Committee Documents," *Human Rights Quarterly* 22:187 (2000).

[73] On the role of CEDAW in campaigns to combat violence against women, see Sally Engle Merry, *Human Rights and Gender Violence: Translating International Law into Local Justice* (2005), especially ch. 3.

[74] In March and April, 1993, Asian countries met, and adopted what came to be called the Bangkok Declaration, which reaffirmed a commitment to the Universal Declaration of Human Rights, but which also reaffirmed "principles of respect for national sovereignty...and non-interference in the internal affairs of States," spoke of the "right to development as a universal and inalienable right," and emphasized the "non-use of human rights as an instrument of political pressure." The Bangkok Declaration had something for almost everybody—it denounced racism, colonialism apartheid, "neo-nazism, xenophobia and ethnic cleansing"—everybody that is, except Israel, in that the Declaration affirmed "support for the legitimate struggle of the Palestinian people," and denounced "grave violations of human rights" in the occupied territories.

[75] Michael Ignatieff, *Human Rights as Politics and Idolatry* (Amy Guttmann, ed., 2001), p. 6.

[76] Eric Neumayer, "Is Respect for Human Rights Rewarded? An Analysis of Total Bilateral and Multilateral Aid Flows," *Human Rights Quarterly* 25:510 (2003).

[77] See, in general, Maria T. Baldwin, *Amnesty International and U.S. Foreign Policy* (2009).

[78] Baldwin, ibid., p. 23.

[79] Michael Freeman, *Human Rights* (2002), p. 143.

[80] 347 U.S. 483 (1954). The case is, of course, the subject of an enormous literature; very notable are Richard Kluger, *Simple Justice* (1975); and Michael J. Klarman's comprehensive history, *From Jim Crow to Civil Rights: The Supreme Court and the Struggle for Racial Equality* (2004).

[81] Gerald N. Rosenberg, *The Hollow Hope: Can Courts Bring About Social Change?* (2d ed., 2008).

[82] Sally Engle Merry, *Human Rights and Gender Violence: Translating International Law Into Local Justice* (2005), pp. 218-219.

[83] Merry, op. cit., pp. 144-146.

[84] See Norbert Loesing, *Die Verfassungsgerichtsbarkeit in Lateinamerika* (2001).

[85] See Part 1, section 4 of the NZBORA: no court can declare any law "to be impliedly repealed or revoked, or to be in any way invalid or ineffective," merely because it is "inconsistent with any provision of this Bill of Rights."

[86] See Ran Hirschl, *Toward Juristocracy: The Origins and Consequences of the New Constitutionalism* (2004), pp. 24-25. The law also provided that the Attorney General was to bring to the attention of the House of Representatives any provision in a proposed law that appeared to be "inconsistent" with the rights and freedoms in the Bill of Rights.

[87] The Communist regime in Albania ended in 1991; and in 1996, Albania agreed to pay compensation; the British in turn released assets of Albania that they had held back.

[88] Gentian Zyberi, *The Humanitarian Face of the International Court of Justice* (2008), p. 282.

[89] Bosnia and Herzegovina v. Serbia and Montenegro, case 91, ICJ (Feb. 2007).

[90] On the matter of the separation barrier, see Gentian Zyberi, *The Humanitarian Face*, pp. 212-226.

[91] For example, on the issue of the consular rights of Mexican nationals, tried in American courts and sentenced to death, the ICJ judgment in Mexico v. United States (2004) was ignored; and the prisoner in question was executed.

[92] Nina-Louisa Arold, *The Legal Culture of the European Court of Human Rights* (2007), p. 20.

[93] Alec Stone Sweet and Helen Keller, "The Reception of the ECHR in National Legal Orders," in Helen Keller and Alec Stone Sweet, eds., *A Europe of Rights: The Impact of the ECHR on National Legal Systems* (2008), pp. 3, 5.

[94] Nina-Louisa Arold, *The Legal Culture of the European Court of Human Rights* (2007), pp. 26-27.

[95] Steven Greer and Andrew Williams, "Human Rights in the Council of Europe and the EU: Toward 'Individual,' 'Constitutional' or 'Institutional' Justice?" *European Law Journal* 15:462, 464 (2009).

[96] Alec Stone Sweet and Helen Keller, "The Reception of the ECHR in National Legal Orders," in Helen Keller and Alec Stone Sweet, eds., *A Europe of Rights: The Impact of the ECHR on National Legal Systems* (2008), pp. 5, 6-7.

[97] Keller and Stone Sweet, "Assessing the Impact of the ECHR on National Legal Systems," in ibid., p. 677.

[98] Nina-Louisa Arold, *The Legal Culture of the European Court of Human Rights* (2007), p. 160.

[99] Arold, *The Legal Culture*, p. 161.

[100] Aileen Kavanagh, *Constitutional Review under the UK Human Rights Act* (2009), p. 3.

[101] Christian Tomuschat, *Human Rights: Between Idealism and Realism* (2d ed., 2008), p. 113; Human Rights Act 1998, ch. 42. A comprehensive treatment of the case law is in Cavanagh, *Constitutional Review.*

[102] Jeffrey Jowell and Jonathan Cooper, "Introduction," in Jeffrey Jowell and Jonathan Cooper, eds., *Delivering Rights: How the Human Rights Act is Working* (2003), pp. 1, 3.

[103] But of course this is expensive and time-consuming; and in the British courts, the litigant might find costs awarded against him, so that, in the opinion of some scholars at least, litigation in England is "unlikely to provide a substantial benefit to a claimant," even if he or she ultimately wins in the European court. Richard Clayton, "Remedies for Breach of Human Rights: Does the Human Rights Act Guarantee Effective Remedies?" in Jowell and Cooper, *Delivering Rights*, pp. 147, 159.

[104] On this point, see Nina-Louisa Arold, *Legal Culture*; and Alastair Mowbray, "The Creativity of the European Court of Human Rights," *Human Rights Law Review* 5:1 (2005).

[105] See Katharina Gebauer, *Parallele Grund- und Menschenrechtsschutzsysteme in Europa?* (2007).

[106] European Court Reports 2002, page 1-06279.

[107] Dinah Shelton, "The Promise of Regional Human Rights Systems," in Burns H. Weston and Stephen P. Marks, *The Future of International Human Rights* (1999), pp. 351, 353.

[108] For an elaborate discussion, see Eva Brems, *Human Rights: Universality and Diversity* (2001), pp. 91-182.

[109] Lucy Bannerman, "Former Slave, Hadijatou Mani, is Suing State of Niger Over Cruelty," *The Times of London*, April 9, 2008, at http://www.timesonline.co.uk/tol/news/world/africa/article3708849.ece (last visited May 2, 2011).

[110] Blake v. Guatemala, 1998 Inter-Am. Ct. H. R. (ser. C) No. 36 (Jan. 24, 1998).

[111] Lawrence R. Helfer and Anne-Marie Slaughter, "Toward a Theory of Effective Supranational Adjudication," *Yale Law Journal* 107:273, 329 (1997).

[112] Helen Stacy, *Human Rights for the 21st Century*, p. 169.

[113] H. Abigail Moy, "The International Criminal Court's Arrest Warrants and Uganda's Lord's Resistance Army: Renewing the Debate over Amnesty and Complementarity," *Harvard Human Rights Journal* 19:267 (2006).

[114] Marlise Simons and Neil MacFarquhar, "Warrant Issued for Sudanese Leader over Darfur War Crimes," *New York Times*, March 5, 2009, p. A6.

[115] Stephanie McCrummen and Colum Lynch, "Sudan Ousts Aid Groups After Court Pursues President," *Washington Post*, March 5, 2009, p. A1; Eric Reeves, "Arrest Warrant Too Costly for Darfur," *Boston Globe*, Mar. 21, 2009, p. A11.

[116] For the argument that the "universality of human rights is derived from the universality of the capacity for human suffering," see Eva Brems, *Human Rights: Universality and Diversity* (2001), p. 306.

[117] Diane Elson, "Women's Rights are Human Rights," in Lydia Morris, ed., *Rights: Sociological Perspectives* (2006), 94, 96.

[118] Michael Ignatieff, *Human Rights as Politics and Idolatry* (2001), p. 79.

[119] Lynn Hunt, *Inventing Human Rights: A History* (2007), p. 33-34.

[120] See, in general, Eva Brems, *Human Rights: Universality and Diversity* (2001).

[121] Cosmo Howard, "Introducing Individualization," in Cosmo Howard, ed., *Contested Individualization: Debates about Contemporary Personhood* (2007), pp. 1, 2.

[122] Anna Yeatman, "Varieties of Individualism," in Cosmo Howard, ed., *Contested Individualization*, p. 45.

[123] Robert Bellah et al., *Habits of the Heart: Individualism and Commitment in American Life* (1985), pp. 334, 336, 382.

[124] Michael Les Benedict, "Victorian Moralism and Civil Liberty in the Nineteenth-Century United States," in Donald G. Nieman, ed., *The Constitution, Law, and American Life: Critical Aspects of the Nineteenth-Century Experience* (1992), pp. 91, 104.

[125] Ronald Inglehart, Christian Welzel, *Modernization, Cultural Change and Democracy: The Human Development Sequence* (2005), p. 152.

[126] David Riesman, *The Lonely Crowd: A Study of the Changing American Character* (1950). By way of contrast, the 19th century American was "inner-directed," following norms of hard work and character implanted in him or her when young; and even earlier people were "tradition-directed." Ibid., pp. 11, 14.

[127] See Sheena S. Iyengar and Mark R. Lepper, "Rethinking the Value of Choice: A Cultural Perspective on Intrinsic Motivation," *J. Personality and Social Psychology* 76: 349 (1999).

[128] See Michael J. Rosenfeld, *The Age of Independence: Interracial Unions, Same-Sex Unions, and the Changing American Family* (2007).

[129] Ulrich Beck and Elisabethe Beck-Gernsheim, *Individualization: Institutionalized Individualism and its Social and Political Consequences* (2002), p. 7.

[130] Constanza Tobio, "Marriage, Cohabitation, and the Residential Independence of Young People in Spain," *International Journal of Law, Policy, and the Family* 15: 678 (2001).

[131] Rhoda E. Howard-Hassmann, "The Second Great Transformation: Human Rights Leapfrogging in the Era of Globalization," *Human Rights Quarterly* 27:1, 34-35 (2005). Howard-Hassmann points out that in the past, the Western countries as they modernized were able to engage in some very dubious "wealth-creating activities," including "slavery, colonialism, genocide, massive population transfers, or deportations of citizens they do not want." The "newly industrializing countries" are not supposed to do these things (though, I might add, some of them pay little or no attention to these strictures); but "what is lost as an advantage of states is gained as an advantage of [their] citizens." Ibid.

[132] Paul Gordon Lauren, *The Evolution of International Human Rights: Visions Seen* (2d ed., 2003), pp. 279-280. Clifford Bob remarks that the "new technologies and new international norms may be a boon for victims and activists, binding the world together and making it harder for repressive regimes to act with impunity against their own citizens." But on the other hand, the "ideology of free trade" and the "spread of multinational corporations" can negatively affect "labor rights...vulnerable environments, and...local control." Clifford Bob, "Globalization and the Social

Construction of Human Rights Campaigns," in Alison Brysk, ed., *Globalization and Human Rights* (2002), pp. 133, 144.

CHAPTER 4

[133] On the tension this idea creates in the human rights field, see Christian Tomuschat, *Human Rights: Between Idealism and Realism* (2d ed., 2008), pp. 86-87.

[134] Shmuel N. Eisenstadt, "The Resurgence of Religious Movements in Processes of Globalization–Beyond the End of History or the Clash of Civilizations," in Koenig and de Guchteneire, *Democracy and Human Rights in Multicultural Societies* (2007), pp. 239, 242.

[135] "British Leader Stirs Debate with his Call to Raise Veils," *New York Times*, Oct. 7, 2006, p. 8.

[136] Janice Gross Stein, in Janice Gross Stein et al., *Uneasy Partners: Multiculturalism and Rights in Canada* (2007), pp. 5-6. It is not entirely true that there are no norms of modesty for men; a young man in the Gaza strip reported, in 2009, that "when he asked friends for a back massage on the beach recently," he was told by a "man wearing civilian clothing" that there "should be no touching," and that he should put his shirt on; another time, on the street, a man told him "not to wear shorts or a sleeveless shirt." Taghreed El-Khodary and Ethan Bronner, "Hamas Fights, Often Within its Ranks, Over Gaza's Islamist Identity," *New York Times*, Sept. 6, 2009, p. A4.

[137] In Spain, 76.4% of adults considered themselves Catholic as of 2006; but only 17% of these "self-declared Catholics" went to religious services regularly; civil marriages were common, the fertility rate was low, and though the Church "prohibits homosexual sex," a survey in 2004 found that 79% of the adults in Spain agreed that "Homosexuality is a personal option as respectable as heterosexuality." Celia Valente, "Spain at the Vanguard in European Gender Equality Policies," in Silke Roth, ed., *Gender Politics in the Expanding European Union* (2008), pp. 101, 107-108.

[138] These tables from the World Values Survey are quoted in Rolf Nygren, "Can We Predict the Future of Family Law?" in Harry N. Scheiber and Laurent Mayali, eds., *Japanese Family Law in Comparative Perspective* (2009), pp. 21, 25.

[139] The Pew Forum on Religion & Public Life, *U.S. Religious Landscape Survey. Religious Affiliation: Diverse and Dynamic* (February, 2008), p. 22. This figure includes changes *within* the ranks of Protestantism, for example, from Methodist to Baptist; excluding these changes, it is still the case that many (28%) change from "one major religious tradition to another." And the 44% may understate the matter, because it does not include "individuals who have changed affiliation within a particular denominational family, say, from the American Baptist Churches in the USA to the Southern Baptist Convention." Nor does it include people who switched "at some point in their lives but then returned to their childhood affiliation," nor do the figures "capture multiple changes in affiliation on the part of individuals." Ibid.

[140] Pew Forum, p. 12. Another 2.4% call themselves "agnostic," though 12.1% define their religion as "nothing in particular."

[141] Thorleif Pettersson, "Religion in Contemporary Society: Eroded by Human Well-being, Supported by Cultural Diversity," in Yilmaz Esmer and Thorleif Pettersson, eds., *Measuring and Mapping Cultures: 25 Years of Comparative Value Surveys* (2007), pp. 127, 131-133.

[142] See, in general, Edwin B. Firmage and Richard C. Mangrum, *Zion in the Courts: A Legal History of the Church of Jesus Christ of Latter-Day Saints* (1988); Sarah Barringer Gordon, *The Mormon Question: Polygamy and Constitutional Conflict in Nineteenth Century America* (2002).

[143] Shawn F. Peters, *Judging Jehovah's Witnesses: Religious Persecution and the Dawn of the Rights Revolution* (2000). In Minersville School District v. Gobitis, 310 U.S. 586 (1940), the Supreme Court held that a school district could expel a student who was a member of this religion, for failure to salute the flag. But three years later, in West Virginia State Board of Education v. Barnette, 319 U.S. 624 (1943), the Supreme Court reversed itself, and declared the local law requiring the salute unconstitutional.

[144] Makau Mutua, *Human Rights*, pp. 110-111.

CHAPTER 5

[145] Herbert McClosky and Alida Brill, *Dimensions of Tolerance: What Americans Believe About Civil Liberties* (1983), p. 49.

[146] David G. Barnum and John L. Sullivan, "Attitudinal Tolerance and Political Freedom in Britain," *British Journal of Political Science* 19:136, 139 (1989). But about half would allow the group to make a public speech. The results were strikingly similar to results in a comparable survey in the United States.

[147] See Paul M. Sniderman et al., *The Clash of Rights: Liberty, Equality, and Legitimacy in Pluralist Democracy* (1996), p. 236.

[148] The study is Alfred Winslow Jones, *Life Liberty and Property: A Story of Conflict and a Measurement of Conflicting Rights* (1941).

[149] James L. Gibson, "Truth, Reconciliation, and the Creation of a Human Rights Culture in South Africa," *Law and Society Review* 38:1 (2004).

[150] Stephen F. Szabo, "Social Perspectives and Support for Human Rights in West Germany," *Universal Human Rights* 1:81 (1979); see Table 1, at 84. The study did find *class* differences in the degree of support for human rights—wealthy and educated people showed more support than the working class; but the differences were not huge.

[151] Barnum and Sullivan, op. cit., p. 145. For example, 70% of the MP's thought members of the least-liked group should be able to run for office (27% of the public did); and other results were equally striking. The authors concluded that "political elites are primarily responsible for safeguarding and perpetuating the principles of democracy in Britain." Ibid., at 146.

[152] Michal Shamir, "Political Intolerance among Masses and Elites in Israel: A Reevaluation of the Elitist Theory of Democracy," *Journal of Politics* 53:1018, 1036 (1991).

[153] Darren W. Davis and Brian D. Silver, "Civil Liberties vs. Security: Public Opinion in the Context of the Terrorist Attacks on America," *American J. of Pol. Sci.* 48:28, 33 (2004).

[154] Alex Inkeles, *One World Emerging? Convergence and Divergence in Industrial Societies* (1998), p. 239.

[155] On the question, should the government have the right to "prohibit certain political or religious views," only 13% in the United States said yes, as against 27% in France, 39% in Great Britain, 41% in Germany. Only 14% said yes in South Korea, and 16% in

Taiwan. But in Kenya the yeses were 67%, and in Thailand 63%. Of course, one wonders how the question was understood in these various countries. *Pew Global Attitudes Project* (2002). Huge majorities in most countries supported the right to demonstrate peacefully (and against the government's right to "ban peaceful demonstrations that it thinks would be politically destabilizing").

[156] John Boli and Michael A,. Elliott, "Facade Diversity: The Individualization of Cultural Difference," *International Sociology* 23:540, 542 (2008).

CHAPTER 6

[157] Makau Mutua, *Human Rights: A Political and Cultural Critique* (2002), p. 15. Mutua also argues that the West was largely indifferent to "the enslavement of Africans, with its barbaric consequences and genocidal dimensions," and the colonization of Asians, Africans, and Latin Americans, with all of the "bone-chilling atrocities"; the West was not moved to create a human rights movement, until it confronted the "genocidal extermination of Jews in Europe—a white people." Ibid., at p. 16.

[158] Takeyoshi Kawashima, "The Status of the Individual in the Notion of Law, Right, and Social Order in Japan," in Charles A. Moore, ed., *The Status of the Individual in East and West* (1968), pp. 429, 431.

[159] Christian Tomuschat, *Human Rights: Between Idealism and Realism* (2d ed., 2008), p. 81.

[160] Michael Ignatieff, *Human Rights as Politics and Idolatry*, p. 60.

[161] Kawashima, op. cit., at 437, 438.

[162] Neil A. Englehart, "Rights and Culture in the Asian Values Argument: The Rise and Fall of Confucian Ethics in Singapore," *Human Rights Quarterly* 22:548, 549 (2000).

[163] Helen Stacy, *Human Rights for the 21st Century*, p. 167.

[164] Englehart, ibid., at 559.

[165] Ibid., at 564.

[166] Stephen James, *Universal Human Rights: Origins and Development* (2007), p. 251.

[167] Ibid. In fact, Stephen James argues, the "incorporation" of universal human rights into "international law was achieved in the face of widespread and persistent Western—including American—resistance," ibid.

[168] Volker H. Schmidt, "One World, One Modernity," in Volker H. Schmidt, ed., *Modernity at the Beginning of the 21st Century* (2007), pp. 205, 213.

[169] S. N. Eisenstadt, "Multiple Modernities," in S. N. Eisenstadt, ed., *Multiple Modernities* (2002), pp. 1, 3.

[170] See Alex Inkeles, *One World Emerging? Convergence and Divergence in Industrial Societies* (1998), especially pp. 19-23. Inkeles argues that the "industrial societies of the world are converging on a common social structure," ibid., p. 26.

[171] Eisenstadt, op. cit., at 5.

[172] For an excellent account of the Confucian version, see Tu Weiming, "Implications of the Rise of 'Confucian' East Asia," in Eisenstadt, ed., *Multiple Modernities* (2002), p. 195.

[173] Sally Engle Merry, *Human Rights and Gender Violence: Translating International Law Into Local Justice* (2005), p. 3.

CHAPTER 7

[174] Blackstone, *Commentaries*, Bk. 1, Ch. 15: "By marriage, the husband and wife are one person in law, that is, the very being or legal existence of the woman is suspended during the marriage."

[175] On these laws see, for example, Norma Basch, *In the Eyes of the Law: Women, Marriage, and Property in Nineteenth-Century New York* (1982); Lawrence M. Friedman, *A History of American Law* (3d ed., 2005), pp. 146-148.

[176] See, in general, Sally G. McMillen, *Seneca Falls and the Origins of the Women's Rights Movement* (2008).

[177] Dorothy McBride Stetson, *Women's Rights in France* (1987), pp. 34-36.

[178] "Women Finally Join Men as Voters in Swiss State," *Chicago Tribune*, April 29, 1991, p. M4.

[179] Bill Marsh, "The Basics: Women Gain Votes (Some Even Matter)," *New York Times*, May 22, 2005.

[180] Susan Deller Ross, *Women's Human Rights: The International and Comparative Law Casebook* (2008), pp. 7-8.

[181] On the campaigns for and against the ERA, see Deborah L. Rhode, *Justice and Gender* (1989), pp. 63-80.

[182] 208 U.S. 412 (1908).

[183] The case was Reed v. Reed, 404 U.S. 71 (1971). As is often the case, a great principle was established in a case that in itself affected very few people. The case came up out of Idaho. If an Idaho resident died without a will, the court would appoint an administrator, to handle the estate. Under the statute, males were preferred over females for this job. The Reeds were separated. Their son died, leaving a tiny estate. Cecil Reed was appointed administrator; and his estranged wife, Sally, objected.

[184] There is a large literature on the subject. See, for an overview, Deborah L. Rhode, *Justice and Gender* (1989). In Craig v. Boren, for example, 429 U.S. 190 (1976), an Oklahoma law allowed women to buy beer at 18; men could not do so until they reached 21. The Supreme Court struck down the statute, ending what was a form of discrimination against young men.

[185] 442 F.2d 385 (5th Cir. 1971).

[186] 458 U.S. 718 (1982).

[187] This was a narrow, 5-4 decision; the dissenters felt that "single-sex education is an honored tradition," and pointed out that there were other state schools where Hogan could get a nursing education.

[188] Bradwell v. Illinois, 83 U.S. 130 (1873).

[189] Statistisches Bundesamt, *Justiz auf einen Blick* (2008), p. 43.

[190] Stetson, op. cit., pp. 145-151.

[191] Allgemeines Gleichbehandlungsgetsetz (AGG), August 14, 2006. The law also is aimed at discrimination on the basis of ethnic origin, religion, handicap ("Behinderung"), age, or "sexual identity."

[192] Ronald Inglehart and Christian Wetzel, *Modernization, Cultural Change and Democracy* (2005), p. 284.

[193] On the German movement in general, see Stefanie Ehmsen, *Der Marsch der Frauenbewegung durch die Institutionen* (2008), which compares Germany and the United States.

[194] See above, at page 75.

[195] Beth Simmons, *Mobilizing for Human Rights: International Law in Domestic Politics* (2009), p. 255.

[196] 410 U.S.113 (1973); the basis for the decision was the so-called right of privacy. On this, and the issue of privacy in general, see below, chapter 8.

[197] BVerfGE 39, No.1 (1975).

[198] Myra Marx Ferree et al., *Shaping Abortion Discourse: Democracy and the Public Sphere in Germany and the United States* (2002), pp. 42-43.

[199] Kathrin Zippel, "Violence at Work? Framing Sexual Harassment in the European Union," in Silke Roth, ed., *Gender Politics in the Expanding European Union* (2008), pp. 60, 68.

[200] Myra Marx Ferree, "Framing Equality," in Silke Roth, *Gender Politics*, pp. 237, 234-235.

[201] See John Dupre, "Global versus Local Perspectives on Sexual Difference," in Deborah L. Rhode, *Theoretical Perspectives on Sexual Difference* (1990), p. 47; and Deborah L. Rhode, "Definitions of Difference," ibid., p. 197.

[202] Rebecca Pates, "Are Women Human? Prostitution and the Search for the Right Rights," in Koen De Feyter and George Pavlakos, eds., *The Tension Between Group Rights and Human Rights: A Multidisciplinary Approach* (2008), pp. 175, 178-179.

[203] 1992 Australia Act 135, section 3.

[204] Lawrence M. Friedman, *The Republic of Choice: Law, Authority, and Culture* (1990), p. 160.

CHAPTER 8

[205] In this chapter, I am indebted to Scott Schackelford and to Andrew Shupanitz for valuable assistance.

[206] Daniel J. Solove, "Conceptualizing Privacy," *California Law Review* 90:1087 (2002). Solove does not really give up, however; rather he attempts to approach privacy in a "pragmatic" and "contextual" way.

[207] 277 U.S. 438 (1928). Olmstead was the head of a "conspiracy of amazing magnitude"; it employed "not less than 50 persons," along with "two sea-going vessels for the transportation of liquor," smaller vessels for "coastwise transportation," a central office, and a "large underground cache for storage," among other things. No doubt the Court was reluctant to exclude the evidence that was used to break up such a large and brazen operation.

[208] Section 605 of the Federal Communications Act, 48 Stat. 1064, 1103-1104 (act of June 19, 1934).

[209] 389 U.S. 347 (1967). See also Berger v. New York, 388 U.S. 41 (1967), decided shortly before *Katz*. Here a lawyer's office had been bugged, in the search for evidence of bribery. This was done under a New York statute which authorized this kind of eavesdropping when there was "reasonable ground to believe that evidence of a crime may be thus obtained."

[210] 488 U.S. 445 (1989).

[211] 533 U.S. 27 (2001).

[212] Wolfgang Kilian, "Germany," in James B. Rule and Graham Greenleaf, eds., *Global Privacy Protection: The First Generation* (2008), pp. 80, 81.

[213] Skinner v. Oklahoma, 316 U.S. 535 (1942); the case and its background are discussed in Victoria F. Nourse, *In Reckless Hands: Skinner v. Oklahoma and the Near Triumph of American Eugenics* (2008).

[214] 381 U.S. 479 (1965).

[215] 405 U.S. 438 (1972).

[216] 410 U.S. 113 (1973). There is a huge literature on this case, and the politics of abortion. See, especially, David J. Garrow, *Liberty and Sexuality: The Right to Privacy and the Making of Roe v. Wade* (1994).

[217] 478 U.S. 186 (1986).

[218] 539 U.S. 558 (2003).

[219] On privacy protection in the Republic of Korea, see Whom-Il Park, "Republic of Korea," in James B. Rule and Graham Greenleaf, eds., *Global Privacy Protection: The First Generation* (2008), p. 207.

[220] The clause adds: "except in the cases and pursuant to procedure provided by law to protect health, morals, public order, or the rights and freedoms of others, to prevent a criminal offence, or to apprehend a criminal offender."

[221] The Arizona Constitution and the Washington State Constitution both have a section of their bill of rights that provides that "No person shall be disturbed in his private affairs, or his home invaded, without authority of law." Ariz. Const. Art. 2, sec. 8; Wash. Const. Art. 1, sec. 7.

[222] Gryczan v. State, 283 Mont. 433, 942 P.2d 112 (1997). Privacy, said the court, was a "fundamental right" under the Montana Constitution. The Montana Supreme Court has in fact used the privacy provisions of the Montana Constitution with some vigor, and in late 2009, was considering whether the Montana Constitution gave a man dying of lymphocytic leukemia the right to die, with his doctor's help. Kirk Johnson, "Montana Court to Decide Claim of Right to Doctor's Aid in Dying," *New York Times*, Sept. 1, 2009, p. A1.

[223] Samuel D. Warren and Louis D. Brandeis, "The Right to Privacy," *Harvard Law Review* 4:193 (1890).

[224] See Robert E. Mensel, "'Kodakers Lying in Wait': Amateur Photography and the Right of Privacy in New York, 1885-1915," *American Quarterly* 43:24 (1991).

[225] On this point, see Lawrence M. Friedman, *Guarding Life's Dark Secrets* (2007), pp. 214-215.

[226] 115 Cal. App. 4th 425, 9 Cal. Rptr. 3d 257 (2004).

[227] Judge Sills dissented on this point, refusing to "go along with this emasculation of our state Constitutional right to privacy." Sills felt that "there is an expectation of privacy even as to one's *identity* when using a cyber café."

[228] Tily B., Inc. v. City of Newport Beach, 69 Cal. App. 4th 1, 81 Cal. Rptr. 2d 6 (1998).

[229] Williams v. City of Minneola, 575 So. 2d 683 (Fla. App., 1991).

[230] Liability at the trial court level could rest on "outrageous inflictions of emotional distress by reckless conduct." There were, to be sure, some difficult fact issues which a jury (or judge) would have to decide—for example, "was it reasonably foreseeable that the appellants would learn of the events involving the pictures of their dead family member"?

[231] See Diane Zimmerman, "Requiem for a Heavyweight: A Farewell to Warren and Brandeis's Privacy Tort," *Cornell Law Review* 68:291 (1983).

[232] 376 U.S. 254 (1964).

[233] Curtis Publishing Co. v. Butts, 388 U.S. 130 (1967).

[234] 5 U.S.C. sec. 552, as amended.

[235] Lawrence M. Friedman, *The Republic of Choice: Law, Authority, and Culture* (1990).

[236] The leading case was Salgo v. Leland Stanford Jr. University Board of Trustees, 317 P.2d 170 (Cal. App. 1957); see Lawrence M. Friedman, *American Law in the 20th Century* (2002), pp. 365-367.

[237] Lawrence M. Friedman, *Private Lives: Families, Individuals, and the Law* (2004), pp. 114-123.

[238] Lawrence M. Friedman, "The One-Way Mirror: Law, Privacy, and the Media," *Washington University Law Quarterly* 82:319 (2004).

[239] Friedman, *Guarding Life's Dark Secrets*, p. 228.

[240] 113 F.2d 806 (2d Cir. 1940).

[241] In *Briscoe v. Reader's Digest*, 4 Cal. 3d 529, 483 P.2d 34 (1971), the plaintiff had been convicted of hijacking a truck. Eleven years later, the magazine published a story that revealed this fact. The plaintiff won his case. The plaintiff, said the court, had led an exemplary life; a lot of time had gone by; he no longer had any obligation to "satisfy the curiosity of the public."

[242] The case is *Entscheidungen des Bundesverfassungsgericht* 35, no. 16, p. 202 (1973).

[243] The court stressed a number of factors which seemed important to it. The plaintiff had no criminal record; seemed genuinely penitent; and the documentary would advertise to the world that he was homosexual, which would (the court felt) injure his standing in the community.

[244] On this case, see Lawrence M. Friedman & Nina-Louisa Arold, "Cannibal Rights," forthcoming in *Northwestern Interdisciplinary Law Review*. And see generally A. W. Brian Simpson, *Cannibalism and the Common Law* (1985).

[245] Meiwes' defense—such as it was—rested on the notion that his victim had asked to be killed which, under German law, would reduce the crime from murder to a kind of manslaughter.

[246] Mark D. West, *Secrets, Sex, and Spectacle: The Rules of Scandal in Japan and the United States* (2006), p. 65.

[247] Available at http://www.guardian.co.uk/media/2008/jul/24/privacy.newsoftheworld2 (last visited Jan. 30, 2011).

[248] Von Hannover v. Germany, App. No. 59320/00, 40 Eur. H. R. Rep. 1 (2005).

[249] James Q. Whitman, "The Two Western Cultures of Privacy: Dignity Versus Liberty," *Yale Law Journal* 113:1151, 1219 (2004).

[250] Laura K. Donohue, *The Cost of Counterterrorism: Power, Politics, and Liberty* (2008), pp. 216, 218.

[251] Peck v. United Kingdom, 36 ECHR 28/04/2003.

[252] R. v. Brentwood Borough Council, ex parte Peck [1998], EMLR, CO/1673/96, 1997.

[253] The damages were 11,800 euros "in respect of non-pecuniary damages," and 18,075 euros "in respect of costs and expenses."

[254] The British courts, as we noted, are not exactly *bound* by the European Convention; but under British law, courts must interpret British statutes, if at all possible, in conformity with the Convention. See above, at page 41.

[255] See Mark Andrejevic, *iSpy: Surveillance and Power in the Interactive Era* (2007), pp. 11-14.

[256] Sarah Lyall, "Britons Weary of Surveillance in Minor Cases," *New York Times*, October 25, 2009, at http://www.nytimes.com/2009/10/25/world/europe/25surveillance.html (last visited May 21, 2011).

[257] Ibid., "British Public Tires as Role of Big Brother Gets Bigger," p. 6.

[258] Laura K. Donohue, *The Cost of Counterterrorism: Power, Politics, and Liberty* (2008), p. 3.

[259] Rolf Goessner, *Menschenrechte in Zeiten des Terrors: Kollateralschaden an der "Heimatfront"* (2007), p. 47.

[260] See James Q. Whitman, *Harsh Justice: Criminal Punishment and the Widening Divide between America and Europe* (2003).

[261] See James Cavallaro and Mohammad-Mahmoud Ould Mohamedou, "Public Enemy Number Two? Rising Crime and Human Rights Advocacy in Transitional Societies," *Harvard Human Rights Journal* 18:139 (2005). The authors point out that in authoritarian states the police "tend to suppress not only dissent but also criminality," and "they are widely perceived as being effective at crime control." Ibid., at 145. And when "public outrage against crime leads to the demand for harsh justice, those who defend rights...become themselves open to attack." Ibid., at 151.

CHAPTER 9

[262] See, for example, the discussion in Tara Usher, "Adjudication of Socio-Economic Rights: One Size Does Not Fit All," *UCL Human Rights Review* 1:155 (2008).

[263] *Pew Global Attitudes Project* (2002): 97% in Argentine and Indonesia, well over 90% in most European countries; lowest in India (70%) and the United States (77%).

[264] Bivitri Susanti, "The Implementation of the Rights to Health Care and Education in Indonesia," in Gauri and Brinks, eds., *Social Justice* (2008), pp. 224, 233.

[265] Article 8 adds: "Effective measures should be taken to ensure that women have an active role in the development process"; and "reforms" should be carried out with "a view to eradicating all social injustices." Under Article 2, "The human person is the central subject of development and should be the active participant and beneficiary of the right to development."

[266] Stephen F. Szabo, "Contemporary French Orientations Toward Economic and Political Dimensions of Human Rights," *Universal Human Rights* 1:61 (1979).

[267] Sandra R. Levitsky, "'What Rights?' The Construction of Political Claims to American Health Care Entitlements," *Law and Society Review* 42:551 (2008).

[268] Sandra Fredman, *Human Rights Transformed: Positive Rights and Positive Duties* (2008), p. 30.

[269] Fiona Robinson, "The Limits of a Rights-Based Approach to International Ethics," in Tony Evans, ed., *Human Rights Fifty Years On: A Reappraisal* (1998), pp. 58, 72.

[270] Though obviously this is still a contested issue in the United States (as of 2010).

[271] Indeed, in the United States (rather exceptionally), the Constitution, in the hands of a conservative Supreme Court in the late 19th and early 20th century, impeded the development of social legislation. The most famous, or notorious, instance was Lochner v. New York, 198 U.S. 45 (1905), which struck down a New York state law regulating conditions of work in bakeries. Another notable case was Hammer v. Dagenhart, 274 U.S. 251 (1918), which struck down a Congressional act designed to prevent the flow of goods across state lines that had been manufactured with child labor.

[272] See, in general, the essays in Malcolm Langford, ed., *Social Rights Jurisprudence: Emerging Trends in International and Comparative Law* (2008); and Varun Gauri and Daniel M. Brinks, eds., *Courting Social Justice: Judicial Enforcement of Social and Economic Rights in the Developing World* (2008).

[273] See, in general, Jamie Cassels, "Judicial Activism and Public Interest Litigation in India: Attempting the Impossible," *Am. J. Comparative Law* 37:495 (1989).

[274] Minister of Health v. Treatment Action Campaign, 2002 (10) BCLR 1033 (CC), in the Constitutional Court of South Africa.

[275] Sandra Fredman, *Human Rights Transformed* (2008), pp. 128-131.

[276] Olga Tellis and Others v. Bombay Municipal Corporation and Others, AIR 1986, SC 18, in 1985 Indlaw SC 161.

[277] Sigrun I. Skogly, "Is There a Right Not to Be Poor?," in *Human Rights Law Review* 2:59 (2002).

[278] Skogly, "Is There a Right Not to Be Poor?," at 77.

[279] See Cassels, "Judicial Activism," supra, note 273.

[280] Koen De Feyter, "In Defence of a Multidisciplinary Approach to Human Rights," in Koen De Feyter and George Pavlakos, eds., *The Tension Between Group Rights and Human Rights: A Multidisciplinary Approach* (2008), pp. 24-25.

[281] Fredman, *Human Rights Transformed*, p. 80.

²⁸² States are supposed to "take measures" to make these rights a reality; but of course, as usual, there is no mode of enforcement. There is a large literature on minority and cultural rights. See, for example, Michael Freeman, *Human Rights: An Interdisciplinary Approach* (2002), pp. 114-123.

²⁸³ There is widespread prejudice against "Gypsies"; the main image of "Gypsies" is as nomads, beggars, fortune-tellers, and thieves. On the issue of their culture, see Joke Kusters, "Criminalising Romani Culture through Law," in Foblets and Renteln, eds., *Multicultural Jurisprudence* (2009), p. 199.

²⁸⁴ Though not without a lot of criticism of the "multi-kulti" trend; see *The Economist*, Nov. 11, 2010, at http://www.economist.com/node/17469563 (last visited May 3, 2011).

²⁸⁵ See the collection of essays in Rachel Sieder, ed., *Multiculturalism in Latin America: Indigenous Rights, Diversity, and Democracy* (2002).

²⁸⁶ "Chile's Mapuche: The People and the Land," *The Economist*, Nov. 7, 2009, p. 39.

²⁸⁷ The Constitution of Ecuador states that the country is a "pluricultural and multiethnic state" (Art. 1); and the Peruvian state "recognizes and protects the ethnic and cultural plurality of the Nation" (Art. 2). Quoted in Donna Lee Van Cott, "Constitutional Reform in the Andes: Redefining Indigenous-State Relations," in Sieder, ed., *Multiculturalism in Latin America*, pp. 45, 47.

²⁸⁸ "An Act for the Preservation and Enhancement of Multiculturalism in Canada," R.S. C. 1985, c. 24, as amended.

²⁸⁹ Francisco López Bárcenas, "Derechos Indigenas en México," in Manuel Calvo García, ed., *Identidades Culturales y Derechos Humanos* (2002), p. 161.

²⁹⁰ S. James Anaya, "The Human Rights of Indigenous Peoples," in Felipe Gomez Isa and Koen de Feyter, eds., *International Protection of Human Rights: Achievements and Challenges* (2006), pp. 593, 600. Anaya gives other examples, for example, a Convention on Biodiversity, which "affirms the value of traditional indigenous knowledge in connection with conservation, sustainable development, and intellectual property rights," op. cit., pp. 600-601.

²⁹¹ "Marie Smith, last speaker of the Eyak language," *The Economist*, Feb. 7, 2008.

²⁹² Daniel Nettle and Suzanne Romaine, *Vanishing Voices: The Extinction of the World's Languages* (2000), pp. 1-2.

²⁹³ Constitution of Paraguay, 1992, Art. 140. This article provides that Paraguay is a "bilingual and pluricultural country" and that the "indigenous languages...are part of the cultural patrimony of the nation." Under Article 77, there is a right to education in the mother language, though in the case of ethnic minorities whose mother language is not Guarani, a choice can be made between Guarani and Spanish.

²⁹⁴ This section of the Constitution also provides that the central government, and the departmental governments, should use at least two official languages—one of them Spanish; and the other to be decided on, taking into account local circumstances and the needs and preferences of the local population. The Constitutions of Colombia, Bolivia, Ecuador, and Peru call for the promotion of bilingual education and (except for Bolivia) make the indigenous languages official in indigenous territories. Donna Lee Van Cott, "Constitutional Reform in the Andes," in Sieder, ed., *Multiculturalism in Latin America*, pp. 45, 47.

[295] Marie-Bénédicte Dembour, "Following the Movement of a Pendulum: Between Universalism and Relativism," in Jane K. Cowan et al., *Culture and Rights: Anthropological Perspectives* (2001), pp. 56-59.

[296] Convergence of values is difficult to measure; see, for example, Yilmaz Esmer, "Globalization, 'McDonaldization' and Values: Quo Vadis," in Yilmaz Esmer and Thorleif Pettersson, eds., *Measuring and Mapping Cultures: 25 Years of Comparative Value Surveys* (2007), p. 79.

[297] Christoph von Fuerer-Haimendorf, *Morals and Merit: A Study of Values and Social Controls in South Asian Societies* (1967), p. 1.

[298] Laura Bohannon, "Shakespeare in the Bush," in James P. Spradley and David W. McCurdy, eds., *Conformity and Conflict: Readings in Cultural Anthropology* (1971), p. 22.

[299] Scott Walker and Steven C. Poe, "Does Cultural Diversity Affect Countries' Respect for Human Rights?" *Human Rights Quarterly* 24:237 (2002).

[300] John Boli and Michael A. Elliott, "Façade Diversity: The Individualization of Cultural Difference," *International Sociology* 23:540, 542 (2008).

[301] Suzanne Romaine, "The Impact of Language Policy on Endangered Languages," in Matthias Koenig and Paul de Guchteneire, *Democracy and Human Rights in Multicultural Societies* (2007), pp. 217, 228.

[302] Chris Longman, "English as Lingua Franca: A Challenge to the Doctrine of Multilingualism," in Dario Castiglione and Chris Longman, eds., *The Language Question in Europe and Diverse Societies: Political, Legal and Social Perspectives* (2007), pp. 185, 206.

[303] Philippe Van Parijs, "Europe's Linguistic Challenge," in Castiglione and Longman, *The Language Question in Europe* (2007), pp. 217, 229.

[304] Chinese, however, is held back by its cumbersome system of writing.

[305] Colin Samson and Damien Short, "The Sociology of Indigenous Peoples' Rights," in Lydia Morris, ed., *Rights: Sociological Perspectives* (2006), pp. 168, 183.

[306] David M. Engel, "Globalization and the Decline of Legal Consciousness: Torts, Ghosts, and Karma in Thailand," *Law and Social Inquiry* 30:469 (2005).

[307] Alison Dundes Renteln, *The Cultural Defense* (2004), p. 187; State v. Kargar, 679 A.2d 81 (Me., 1996).

[308] Renteln, *The Cultural Defense*, p. 218.

[309] Ibid., p. 99.

[310] Alison Renteln, *The Cultural Defense*, pp. 59-60.

[311] See the discussion in Sebastian Poulter, *Ethnicity, Law and Human Rights* (1998), pp. 123-146.

[312] Sebastian Poulter, *Ethnicity, Law and Human Rights*, pp. 291-301.

[313] See, for example, Leslye Obiora, "Bridges and Barricades: Rethinking Polemics and Intransigence in the Campaign Against Female Circumcision," *Case Western Reserve Law Review* 47:275 (1997).

[314] 436 U.S. 49 (1978), discussed in Ayelet Shachar, *Multicultural Jurisdictions: Cultural Differences and Women's Rights* (2001), pp. 18-20.

[315] Martinez v. Romney, 402 F. Supp. 5, 18, 19 (D.N.M. 1975).

[316] See Santa Clara Pueblo v. Martinez, 436 U.S. 49 (1978). Of course, many experts on Indian law defend this decision, for example, Alvin J. Ziontz; see his book, *A Lawyer in Indian Country: A Memoir* (2009), in which he describes how the Northern Arapahoe tribe debated the issue, and voted overwhelmingly to adopt "new and more liberal enrollment standards." This, says Ziontz, is the way these issues should be decided: by the tribes themselves, "not by a non-Indian judge in a federal court hundreds of miles away." Ibid., p. 235.

[317] Pieter A. Carstens, "The Cultural Defence in Criminal Law: South African Perspectives," in Marie-Claire Foblets and Alison Dundes Renteln, eds., *Multicultural Jurisprudence* (2009), pp. 175, 186.

[318] Alison Renteln, *The Cultural Defense*, p. 123-124. Forced and arranged marriages are common, of course, in many societies.

[319] Catherine Warrick, "The Vanishing Victim: Criminal Law and Gender in Jordan," *Law and Society Review* 39:315 (2008); see also Douglas Jehl, "Arab Honor's Price: A Woman's Blood," *New York Times*, June 20, 1999, p. 1.

[320] But a "new generation of activists has quietly begun to battle these honor killings," Jehl, op. cit., and the royal family in Jordan has spoken out against the practice, see Warrick, op. cit.

[321] Nguyen v. State, 271 Ga. 475, 476, 520 S.E.2d 907 (1999) (expert testimony regarding defendant's cultural traditions regarding status and respect inadmissible to support claim of self-defense where "there was no evidence that individuals sharing [her] cultural background would believe themselves to be in danger of receiving any physical harm as a result of loss of status and disrespectful treatment").

[322] Sylvia Maier, "Honor Killings and the Cultural Defense in Germany," in Foblets and Renteln, eds., *Multicultural Jurisprudence: Comparative Perspectives on the Cultural Defense* (2009), pp. 229, 242-244.

[323] Sally Engle Merry, *Human Rights and Gender Violence: Translating International Law into Local Justice* (2006), p. 28.

[324] Alison Renteln, *The Cultural Defense*, p. 62.

[325] Steven Erlanger, "Burqa Furor Scrambles the Political Debate in France," *New York Times*, Sept. 1, 2009, p. A6.

[326] Conseil d'Etat, 27 Juin 2008, no. 2008, cited in Liav Orgad, "'Cultural Defence' of Nations: Cultural Citizenship in France, Germany and the Netherlands," *European Law Journal* 15:719, 723 (2009).

[327] In Sahin v. Turkey, 44 E.H.R.R. 5 (2007), the European Court of Human Rights was called on to rule on the legality of a rule refusing admission to lectures and courses at the Faculty of Medicine of Istanbul University to students with beards, and with Islamic headscarves. The Grand Chamber of the ECHR refused to interfere with the Turkish regulation, and allowed the University to exclude women like the plaintiff, who wanted to wear the headscarf.

[328] See, in general, Kirsten Wiese, *Lehrerinnen mit Kopftuch* (2008). Wiese thinks that a Muslim woman can claim that her motive for wearing the headscarf is religious, and that she therefore can claim "the protection of freedom of religion"; forbidding the

scarf to women in public service, therefore, impairs the religious freedom of such teachers. Ibid., p. 322. This is a normative and doctrinal conclusion; the law in action is more complicated, and it is plain from the material Wiese discusses that school authorities and others resist the headscarf, sometimes successfully.

[329] Quoted in Liav Orgad, "'Cultural Defence' of Nations," at 726.

[330] James N. Rosenau, "The Drama of Human Rights in a Turbulent, Globalized World," in Alison Brysk, ed., *Globalization and Human Rights* (2002), pp. 148, 157.

[331] 406 U.S. 205 (1972).

[332] Justice Douglas dissented. He pointed out that the majority opinion paid no attention to the rights of the *children* who arguably would be deprived of a decent education.

The same issue came up in Canada, with regard to Evangelical schools in Quebec—which also refused to teach sex education and evolution. The Minister of Education of Quebec told them that they had to conform with the official curriculum; and that children had to attend school until age 16. Janice Gross Stein, "Searching for Equality," in Janice Gross Stein et al., *Uneasy Partners: Multiculturalism and Rights in Canada* (2007), pp. 1, 10.

[333] Michael Slackman, "A Saudi Gamble to See if Seeds of Change Will Grow," *New York Times*, Nov. 20, 2009, p. A8.

CHAPTER 10

[334] Stephen D. Krasner, in *Sovereignty: Organized Hypocrisy* (1999), pp. 3-4, distinguishes between four meanings: "international legal sovereignty, Westphalian sovereignty, domestic sovereignty, and interdependence sovereignty." The first refers to the international recognition of sovereignty; the second to the "political organization based on the exclusion of external actors from authority structures within a given territory"; domestic sovereignty "refers to the formal organization of political authority within the state"; and the state's "effective control" within its territory; and "interdependence sovereignty" refers to the "ability of public authorities to regulate the flow of information, ideas, goods, people, pollutants, or capital across the borders of their state."

[335] As Michael Freeman puts it, "The myth of international law is that the world is divided into sovereign, independent states. It is not, and never has been." The imperialists "denied sovereignty to colonized peoples," and imperialism was also a system of "powerful private economic organizations...and cultural entrepreneurs (e.g., missionaries)." Freeman, *Human Rights: An Interdisciplinary Approach* (2002), p. 154.

[336] Helen Stacy, *Human Rights for the 21st Century* (2009), p. 77.

[337] Kurt Mills, *Human Rights in the Emerging Global Order: A New Sovereignty?* (1998), p. 194.

[338] Kurt Mills, op. cit., pp. 41-42.

[339] States find it "difficult to regulate the operations of global corporations effectively," due to the "extensive network of decision-making and operational structures formed by their headquarters, branches, subsidiaries and other forms of investment in independent units throughout the world; and to their flexibility in moving seats of production as well as profits." Kamal Hossain, "Globalization and Human Rights: Clash

of Universal Aspirations and Special Interests," in Burns H. Weston and Stephen P. Marks, eds., *The Future of International Human Rights* (1999), pp. 187, 192-193.

[340] Anthony G. McGrew, "Human Rights in a Global Age: Coming to Terms with Globalization," in Tony Evans, ed., *Human Rights Fifty Years On: A Reappraisal* (1998), pp. 188, 192, 193.

[341] "The feared disasters which may play havoc with one's livelihood...are not of the sort which can be staved off by joining forces, making a united stand.... The most dreadful disasters strike now at random, picking their victims with a bizarre logic or no logic at all.... [T]here is no way to anticipate who will be doomed and who saved." Zygmunt Bauman, *The Individualized Society* (2001), p. 24.

[342] Kurt Mills, *Human Rights in the Emerging Global Order*, p. 20.

[343] Mills, *Human Rights in the Emerging Global Order*, pp. 19-20.

[344] Mills, *Human Rights in the Emerging Global Order*, p. 21.

[345] John Henry Merryman, "On the Convergence (and Divergence) of the Civil Law and the Common Law," *Stanford J. International Law* 17:357, 373 (1981).

[346] Johan Galtung, "The Third World and Human Rights in the Post-1989 World Order," in Tony Evans, ed., *Human Rights Fifty Years On: A Reappraisal* (1998), p. 211.

[347] M. Cherif Bassiouni, "Strengthening the Norms of International Humanitarian Law to Combat Impunity," in Burns H. Weston and Stephen P. Marks, eds., *The Future of International Human Rights* (1999), pp. 245, 250-251.

[348] Elizabeth Borgwardt, *A New Deal for the World: America's Vision for Human Rights* (2005), p. 75.

[349] Apparently, neither the British nor the French were eager to make crimes against peace one of the charges, or to make the waging of aggressive war a crime. The Soviets were also reluctant. But the Americans insisted, and their view carried the day. Bert V. A. Roeling, "The Nuremberg and the Tokyo Trials in Retrospect," in Guénaël Mettraux, ed., *Perspectives on the Nuremberg Trial* (2008), pp. 455, 458-459.

[350] David Luban argues that "for those who conceived of the trial . . . its great accomplishment was to be the criminalization of aggressive war," rather than putting flesh onto the concept of crimes against humanity. Luban, "The Legacies of Nuremberg," in Guénaël Mettraux, ed., *Perspectives on the Nuremberg Trial*, pp. 638, 639.

[351] Borgwardt, pp. 197-198.

[352] *Chicago Daily Tribune*, Oct. 2, 1946. I am indebted to Brandon Marsh for this reference.

[353] Hilary Earl, *The Nuremberg SS-Einsatzgruppen Trial, 1945-1958: Atrocity, Law, and History* (2009), p. 273. These critics included quite prominent clergymen, including at least one bishop.

[354] Quoted in Richard H. Minear, *Victor's Justice: The Tokyo War Crimes Trial* (1971), p. 3. Minear feels that the trial was "highly defective." This is not to say that Japan's policies were "reasonable, or even defensible"; but he finds "serious" questions about "the integrity of the tribunal" and some basis for saying that the trial "was a biased proceeding." Ibid., pp. 177, 160. General Tojo was executed in 1948.

[355] Tim Maga, *Judgment at Tokyo: The Japanese War Crimes Trials* (2001), p. 12.

[356] On Hirohito's role in the war, see Herbert Bix, *Hirohito and the Making of Modern Japan* (2000); and John W. Dower's superb study of the period, *Embracing Defeat: Japan in the Wake of World War II* (1999).

[357] Of course, the Allies in Germany did not exactly have clean hands. The Cold War started almost immediately, and the Allies found it expedient to make use of German rocket scientists, and even certain Nazi agents.

[358] On the trials in Guam, see Naga, *Judgment at Tokyo*, pp. 93-119. One hundred and forty-eight Japanese citizens and residents of the Pacific Islands were tried. Thirty received death sentences. There were ten acquittals. Ibid., pp 118-119.

[359] Thomas Alan Schwartz, *America's Germany: John J. McCloy and the Federal Republic of Germany* (1991), p. 157.

[360] Philip R. Piccigallo, *The Japanese on Trial: Allied War Crimes Operations in the East, 1945-1951* (1979), pp. 128-129, 139.

[361] See, in general, George J. Annas and Michael A. Grodin, eds., *The Nazi Doctors and the Nuremberg Code: Human Rights in Human Experimentation* (1992).

[362] A leading case was Salgo v. Leland Stanford Jr. University Bd. of Trustees, 317 P.2d 170 (Cal. App. 1957); see Lawrence M. Friedman, *American Law in the Twentieth Century* (2002), pp. 366-367.

[363] Thomas Alan Schwartz, *America's Germany*, pp. 158-160.

[364] Six organizations, however, were also indicted by the Allies as criminal organizations, which meant that mere membership was presumptive evidence of guilt. Three of the organizations, including the Gestapo and the SS (Schutzstaffel), were found guilty.

[365] Stanley Milgram, *Obedience to Authority: An Experimental View* (1974). Very relevant to the issue Milgram raised is Christopher R. Browning, *Ordinary Men: Reserve Police Battalion 101 and the Final Solution in Poland* (1992), which discusses how and why men of a German reserve battalion carried out orders, in 1942, to slaughter well over a thousand Jews, mostly women, children, and old men, in a Polish village. A different view was espoused by Daniel Goldhagen, in *Hitler's Willing Executioners: Ordinary Germans and the Holocaust* (1996).

[366] For example, under Canadian war crimes law, a "military commander" is guilty if he "fails to exercise control properly over a person under...effective command," and that person commits a crime against humanity or the like; or if the commander is "criminally negligent" in "failing to know" about the commission of the offence or that the offence is about to happen, and fails to prevent it. *Crimes Against Humanity and War Crimes Act*, S. C. 2000, ch. 24, s. 5.

[367] Gary Jonathan Bass, *Stay the Hand of Vengeance: The Politics of War Crimes Tribunals* (2000), p. 22. Bass sees the idea of "crimes against humanity" as "not just an invention of Nuremberg"; he mentions, for example, the Armenian massacres in 1915, which evoked widespread condemnation.

[368] Roger O'Keefe, "Universal Jurisdiction: Clarifying the Basic Concept," *J. International Criminal Justice* 2:735 (2004).

[369] Quoted in Margaret McAuliffe deGuzman, "The Road from Rome: The Developing Law of Crimes Against Humanity," *Human Rights Quarterly* 22:335, 352 (2000).

[370] So, for example, the "Statute of the Special Court for Sierra Leone" (2000), Article 2, defines it as crimes which are "part of a widespread or systematic attack against any civilian population" and include murder, extermination, enslavement, deportation, imprisonment, torture, rape, sexual slavery, enforced prostitution, "forced pregnancy and any other form of sexual violence"; plus "Persecution on political, racial, ethnic or religious grounds," and "Other inhumane acts."

[371] The impact of the case, of course, is difficult to pin down. Even its impact on the human rights situation in Chile is far from obvious. See Rebecca Evans, "Pinochet in London—Pinochet in Chile: International and Domestic Politics in Human Rights Policy," *Human Rights Quarterly* 28: 207 (2006).

[372] On this law, and on the Arrest Warrant case, see David Turns, "Arrest Warrant of 11 April 2000 (Democratic Republic of the Congo v. Belgium)," *Melbourne J. of Int'l Law* 3:383 (2002).

[373] The French newspaper *Le Monde* remarked that the Pinochet episode meant that fear was beginning "to change sides." Fear was "no longer reserved for the victims." Quoted in Paul Gordon Lauren, *Evolution of International Human Rights*, p. 269.

[374] The quote is from "Welcome to London—Except if You're an Israeli Official," *The Economist*, December 19, 2009, p. 81. A London judge had issued an arrest warrant for Tzipi Livni, who was foreign minister during the Israeli assault on the Gaza strip. The warrant was withdrawn when the judge found out that Ms. Livni was not going to be in Britain after all. The incident (which was not the first of its kind) "drew apoplectic protests from Israel and much abject apologizing from the British government."

[375] Amendment to sections 4 and 5 of Art. 23 of the Organic Law on the Judiciary.

[376] Thomas Catan, "Spain is Moving to Rein in its Crusading Judges," *Wall Street Journal*, May 20, 2009, p. A6; "PP y PSOE se alían para recortar la aplicación de la justicia universal," *El País*, May 19, 2009; "El Congreso límita la jurisdicción universal de la justicia Española," *El País*, June 25, 2009.

[377] See "Justice Wars," *The Economist*, April 15, 2010. Ironically, according to this article, a "writ was presented to a court in Buenos Aires asking it to investigate crimes against humanity and genocide committed in Franco's Spain"; this writ "mirrors" those of Garzón, at the same time that Garzón himself is in trouble in his home country.

[378] 28 U.S.C. section 1350; discussed in Christian Tomuschat, *Human Rights*, pp. 376-379.

[379] The act is 106 Stat. 73 (act of Mar. 12, 1992). The act also gives a kind of wrongful death action to representatives of victims of "extrajudicial killing," and the act includes an elaborate definition of torture.

[380] "An Act respecting genocide, crimes against humanity and war crimes...." S. C. 2000, ch. 24; with amendments in 2001, S. C. 2001, ch. 32, ss. 59-61; ch. 34, s. 36.

[381] Punishment follows also if the violator was "a citizen of a state that was engaged in an armed conflict against Canada," or the victim was a "citizen of a state that was allied with Canada in an armed conflict."

[382] See Matt Eisenbrandt, "The Center for Justice & Accountability: Holding Human Rights Abusers Responsible in the United States and Abroad," in Alice Bullard, ed., *Human Rights in Crisis* (2008), p. 87.

[383] The tribunal also had the power to prosecute for "grave breaches of the Geneva conventions" and "violations of the laws or customs of war."

[384] Paul G. Lauren, *The Evolution of International Human Rights*, p. 272.

[385] Carolyn Dubay, "Evaluating the Khmer Rouge Tribunal," *International Judicial Monitor*, http://www.judicialmonitor.org/archive_summer2009/sectorassessment.html (last visited April 30, 2011).

[386] Quoted in Paul G. Lauren, *The Evolution of International Human Rights*, p. 268.

[387] Marlise Simons and Neil MacFarquhar, "Warrant Issued for Sudanese Leader over Darfur War Crimes," *New York Times*, March 5, 2009, p. A6.

[388] *New York Times*, Nov. 25, 2009, p. A17.

[389] Gary J. Bass, *Stay the Hand of Vengeance*, p. 310.

[390] Gary J. Bass, op. cit., p. 280.

[391] But, according to the Resolution, acting pursuant to orders might be "considered in mitigation" if the Tribunal "determines that justice so requires" (Art. 6.4).

[392] General Pinochet's argument, before the House of Lords in England, was "very simple: what he did, he did as government policy, not in a private capacity. And the policies of one government were traditionally sacrosanct against judgement by any other... No state should interfere in the affairs of another." Frances Webber, "The Pinochet Case: The Struggle for the Realization of Human Rights," *Journal of Law and Society* 26:523, 533 (1999). This argument did not prevail.

CHAPTER 11

[393] *Iceman* (1984), directed by Fred Schepisi.

[394] Ulrich Beck, *Risikogesellschaft: auf dem Weg in eine andere Moderne* (1986).

[395] Sally Engle Merry, *Human Rights and Gender Violence* (2005), p. 181.

INDEX

A

abolitionist movement. *See* slavery
abortion, 27, 59, 83, 93
Abu Ghraib, 150
affirmative action, 14, 16, 87
Afghanistan, 34, 82, 133
Africa
   colonial rule, 22
   courts of human rights, 43
   See also Congo; South Africa
African Charter on Human and
   Peoples' Rights, 43
African Court of Human and
   Peoples' Rights, 43
African Court of Justice and Human
   Rights, 43
African Union, 43
African-Americans. *See* equality,
   racial; Equal Protection
AIDS, epidemic and treatment, 117,
   142
al-Bashir, Omar, 46, 155
Alexander, Leo, 148
Alien Tort Claims Act, U.S., 153
American Convention on Human
   Rights, 44
"American exceptionalism," 74
American Revolution, 7, 25
Americans With Disabilities Act,
   U.S. (ADA), 86
Amin, Idi, 45
Amish, 56, 138
Amnesty, 13, 33, 35, 155
anomie, 52
Aquinas, St. Thomas, 71
Arab Charter of Human Rights, 43
Arabic, language, 123, 124, 125
Argentina, 22, 44, 73, 137, 150
Armenia, and Armenian, 123, 145

Arold, Nina-Louisa, 40, 172n, 181n
assimilation, 17, 56, 121, 71, 131-132,
   136-137
   See also convergence

B

Australia, 50, 78, 85, 86, 120-121, 123,
   128, 132-133, 147, 160

bankruptcy law, as second chance,
   115
Barbie, Klaus, 148
Barnum, David, 64, 65
Basque, 16, 125, 129, 130
Bass, Gary, 155
Beck, Ulrich, 161
Beethoven, 72, 73, 141
Belgium, 128-129, 137, 151-152, 154
Bellah, Robert, 48, 174n
Benedict, Michael Les, 48
Bill of Rights
   Canadian, 37
   U.S., 10, 12, 55, 89-90, 92, 112, 134
   European Convention acting as,
   40
Blake v. Guatemala, 44
Bohannon, Laura, 127, 185n
Boli, John, 18, 128, 169n, 177n, 185n
Bolivia, 121, 137
Bosnia, 38, 45
Bowers v. Hardwick, 93, 95
Bradley, Joseph, 80
Bradwell, Myra, 80
Brandeis, Louis, 92, 95, 98, 103, 180n
Brazil, 44, 85, 120, 135
Brennan, William, 93
Brill, Alida, 64, 65
Brown v. Board of Education, 36
Brussels, 42, 152
Buddhism, 28, 51, 56, 57-58, 122, 132
Bush, George W., 107, 150

C

Caldeira, Gregory, 24
Cambodia, 24, 45, 150, 154
Canada, 17, 23, 28, 34, 37, 57, 63, 74,
   78, 81, 85, 116, 121, 123, 128-129, 133,
   137, 153-154
capitalism, 15, 17, 19, 28, 49, 69, 71,
   113, 116, 140-141
Caroline, Princess of Monaco, 103-
   104
*Carpenter v. Secretary of State for the
   Home Department*, 42

Catalan, language, 125, 129
Catholicism, 26, 28, 49, 51, 55, 56-60, 86, 128
celebrities, and celebrity society, 99-101, 103-104
Center for Justice and Accountability, 154
Charles, Prince of Wales, 104
Charter of Fundamental Rights of the European Union, 42
checks and balances, U.S., 21
children, rights of, 9, 12, 32-33, 121
Chile, 12, 17, 22, 34, 44, 74, 121, 123-124, 151
China
    generally, 3, 20, 21, 22, 45-46, 58, 64, 70, 72, 74, 77, 82, 99, 123, 125, 129, 139-141, 143, 145, 147, 153, 160-161
    rule of law, 20
    vote against ICC, 155
choice
    social and individual, 51
    See also right to choose
Christianity, 8, 56-58, 61, 86, 132
Churchill, Winston, 29
circumcision, female, 133
Civil Rights Act, U.S., 80
civil rights movement, 36
    See also equality, racial
civil society, necessity of, 22
Colombia, 82, 121
colonialism, 22, 61, 121, 131
communism, 11, 23, 44, 69, 163
communitarianism, 16
Community Court of Justice of the Economic Community of West African States (Ecowas), 43
Comstock Act, U.S., 27
Confucianism, 70, 72, 74
Congo, 143, 152, 154-155
Congress, U.S., 37, 79, 107, 134
consent, informed, in medical decisions, 99, 148
Constitution, U.S., as source of social rights, 111
constitutional courts, 5, 10-11, 13, 21, 24, 37, 40, 43, 63, 83
Constitutional Court, German, 41, 91, 102, 104, 160

Constitutional Court, South African, 41, 119
"constitutional design," 22
constitutions, 1, 4-5, 7, 10, 12-13, 21-22, 27-28, 33, 36-37, 55, 63, 66, 77, 82, 89, 94-95, 111-114, 116, 121, 128
contract, as choice, 51
Convention on the Elimination of all Forms of Discrimination against Women (CEDAW), 32-34, 82
convergence, 17-18, 40, 42, 53, 66, 69, 72-75, 125-128, 141-144, 160
Cook, Robin, 155
Corfu Channel case, 38
corporations, rights of, 11
Corruption, effect on rule of law, 19
Costa Rica, 44
Council of Europe, 39, 41
"crimes against humanity," 17, 45, 143, 145-146, 149, 150-155
criminal law
    cultural defense to charges in, 132-133, 135-137
    international, 45
Croatia, 112, 154
Cuba, 35, 44, 139
cultural convergence. See convergence
cultural defense, in criminal law, 132-133, 135-137
cultural homogeneity, distinguished from convergence, 127
cultural identity, 122, 134
cultural rights
    generally, 7, 12, 17-18, 75, 120, 122, 124-125, 128, 130, 137, 144
    as affected by globalization, 144
culture, definition of a distinct, 122
culture, legal, 17, 23, 40, 49, 101, 104
Czech Republic, 22, 37, 41, 58, 86

D

Dalai Lama, 100, 139
Darfur, 45, 150, 155
De Gaulle, Charles, 78
De Tocqueville, Alexis, 7, 77
death penalty, 9, 42
Declaration of Independence, 7, 25, 78

Declaration of the Rights of Man, 25-26

Declaration on the Right to Development, UN, 112

declarations, international and regional, on human rights, 1, 5-6, 10, 34, 36-37, 46, 63, 69, 82, 87, 120-121

defamation, 9, 98-99

Demjanjuk, John, 148

Denmark, 43, 78, 145

desegregation. *See* equality, racial; segregation

dialects, 28, 53, 74, 125, 132

Diaz v. Pan American World Airways, 80

dignity. *See* privacy

disability, rights of people with, 1, 9, 12, 16-17, 33, 48, 77, 85-87, 132

discrimination. *See* equality

District of Columbia v. Heller, 168n

Don Carlos, 127

Donnelly, Jack, 4, 8, 167n

double jeopardy, laws against, 12

E

economic rights, 111, 113, 117

economics, classical, 53, 115-116, 158

Ecuador, 78, 121

education, right to, 7, 12, 29-30, 111, 114-117, 119

Egypt, 24

Eichmann, Adolf, 148, 150

Eisenstadt v. Baird, 93

Eisenstadt, Schmuel, 56, 72, 74

Eliot, T. S., 161

Elliott, Michael, 18, 128, 169n, 177n, 185n

Elson, Diane, 46

employment, right to, 111

Engel, David, 132

Englehart, Neil, 70

English language, as global or dominant, 129-130

entertainment, as industry, 50

Equal Employment Opportunity Commission, U.S., 80

Equal Rights Amendment, U.S., 79

equality

age discrimination, 48, 85, 87

as product of individualism, 52

equality, gender, 1, 2, 7, 9, 12, 14-15, 25, 32-33, 36, 39, 42, 48-49, 57, 60, 63, 66, 73, 77-87, 93, 111, 130, 132-133, 136, 138, 157, 159-160, 162

plural, 8, 37, 74, 85-87, 114, 123, 132

racial and ethnic, 7-8, 12, 15-16, 19, 21, 32-33, 36, 39, 42, 48, 63, 65, 77, 83, 85-87, 120, 144, 157

tolerance distinguished, 86

estado del derecho, 19

Estonia, 11, 22, 94, 124, 129

European Commission on Human Rights, 39

European Convention on Human Rights, 37, 39, 41

European Court of Human Rights (ECHR), 24, 37, 39-43, 103-106

European Court of Justice (ECJ), 24, 41-42

European Union (EU), 9, 37, 41-43, 86, 129

expressive individualism. *See* rights, individual; individualism

F

Failure to Launch, 53

Ferree, Myra Marx, 83, 85

Finland, 3, 9, 21, 41, 43, 71, 78, 129, 146

Florida v. Riley, 91

food, right to, 111

Fourteenth Amendment, to U.S. Constitution, 36, 80

Fourth Amendment, to U.S. Constitution, 90, 107

France, 74

assimilation required for citizenship, 136-137

controversy over scarves, 57

end of World War II, 145

generally, 3, 7, 24, 26, 28, 45, 48, 53, 71, 78, 81, 83, 86, 113-114, 116, 136-137, 148

judges in Nuremberg trials, 146

Franco, Francisco, 29, 153

Freedom of Information Act, U.S. (FOIA), 99

freedom of movement, 12, 30
freedom of speech, 2-3, 17, 7, 9, 12-14,
   17, 24, 26-27, 30, 39-40, 42, 64, 66,
   72, 111, 113-114, 119
freedom to choose, 148
Freeman, Michael, 6, 167n
French Revolution, 25
Fribourg Declaration, 121
fundamentalism, 55-56, 58, 132, 144,
   162
fundamental rights. *See* human rights

G

Galtung, Johan, 143
Garzón, Baltasar, 17, 152-153
gay marriage, 63, 93
gay rights, 1, 9-10, 52, 63, 93, 132, 160
gay rights movement. *See* gay rights;
   gay marriage; sexual minorities
gender discrimination. *See* equality,
   gender; gender violence
gender essentialism, 83, 85
gender violence, 36, 162
Geneva Conventions, 151
Germany
   generally, 10-12, 17, 19, 22-23, 27, 29,
     37, 39, 41, 45, 57, 63, 65, 72, 74, 78,
     81-84, 91, 102-104, 113, 119-120, 124,
     135, 137, 142, 145-148, 150, 160
   assimilation required for
     citizenship, 137
   Constitutional Court, 41, 91, 102,
     104, 160
   dependence on exports, 140
   privacy law in, 102, 104, 108
Gibson, James, 24, 65
Glendon, Mary Ann, 31
globalization
   generally, 53, 131-132, 140-144
   effect on cultural rights, 144
   of risk, 142, 144, 161
Google, and Google Earth, 90, 143
Great Britain
   adoption of regional declarations,
     39
   attitudes toward civil liberties,
     64-65
   colonialism, 22
   constitution, 37

end of World War II, 145
established church in, 55
generally, 29, 45, 86
gun ownership, 9
Human Rights Act, 41
judges in Nuremberg trials, 146
privacy law in, 103
public housing, 117
reaction to Muslim dress, 57
religious freedom, 27
social rights and health care, 28
suit in ICJ, 38
surveillance, 105, 107-108
voting rights of women, 78
Greece, 53, 71, 129, 142
Griswold v. Connecticut, 92
Grotius, Hugo, 25
Grundgesetz, 12, 82-83, 168n
Guantánamo Bay, 107, 153
Guatemala, 34, 44, 150
guns, right to own, 9

H

Hafner-Burton, Emilie, 167n
Hague, The, 46, 154-155
Haiti, 26
Hamlet, as example of cultural
   convergence, 127
Hathaway, Oona, 5, 167n
Havana, 26
headscarves
   controversy over in France, 57, 136-
     137
   controversy over in Germany, 137
health care, 7, 12, 23, 28-30, 69, 82,
   111-113, 115, 116-119, 144
Helfer, Lawrence, 44
Hinduism, 56, 72, 132
Hirschl, Ran, 11, 21, 22
Hitler, Adolf, 6, 17, 29, 57, 137, 145-
   147, 150, 161
Holocaust, 72, 146-147
Honduras, 44
Hong Kong, 20, 142
honor killing, 135
housing, right to, 7, 12, 29, 111, 117
Howard, Cosmo, 48
Howard-Hassmann, Rhoda, 54

human nature, relation to human rights, 115-116, 161

human rights
attitudes toward political rights vs. social rights, 113-114
conflict with state sovereignty, 142
consciousness, 3, 13, 27, 34-37, 40, 45-47, 52, 70, 75, 86, 116, 119, 146
culture of, pervasive, 63, 65-66, 69. *See also* human rights culture, human rights movement
culture of, uniformity and variation of views, 65-66, 70, 72, 83
definition, 2, 10, 17
future risks to ethos of, 162-163
genesis and history of, 46-47
normative consideration of, 6, 10
practice, 6
regional documents of, 38
relation to human nature, 115-116, 161
scholarship on, 1, 6, 19, 115, 139, 157
social movement as opposed to economic or political, 21
sociology of, 1-2, 157
status as law, 4
treaties, 1, 3-6, 17, 26, 32-34, 37, 63, 82, 146, 153, 167n
universalistic claims, 44
universality of, 47, 66, 69, 126, 130, 149, 151

human rights culture, origins of, 46-47, 66, 71

human rights movement
as a sociological phenomenon, 1-2, 157
as contributing to decline of sovereignty, 143
as affecting cultural rights, 144
as global and related to globalization, 17, 53
conflict with state sovereignty, 155
criticisms of, 69-70
international character of, 17, 53
future of, 160-161
origins, 15, 25-27, 46, 87, 157
pervasiveness, 157
popularity of and demand for, 162
premises, 157

social and historical context, 157
social origins of, 15
universality, 122

Human Rights Watch, 13, 33, 36, 155
Hungary, 11-12, 21-22, 119-120
Hunt, Lynn, 47

I

Iceland, 78, 124, 128, 141
Iceman, 160, 161
Ignatieff, Michael, 34, 46
illegitimate children, 8, 48, 64
immigration. *See* assimilation
imperialism, 22, 61, 121, 131
India, 23, 41, 51, 56, 64, 71, 99, 114, 117-119, 121, 129, 138
Indian Civil Rights Act, U.S., 134
indigenous groups, rights of, 1, 7, 9, 15, 66, 85, 87, 121, 123, 128, 131, 134
individualism, and individual rights, 15-17, 23, 27, 31-34, 48-53, 59, 69, 74, 81, 83, 85, 87, 92, 94, 97, 105, 114-115, 122, 131-132, 138, 141, 157-159, 161-162
Indonesia, 24, 112
Industrial Revolution, 15, 28, 49, 71
Inter-American Court of Human Rights, 44
International Court of Justice (ICJ), 38, 39, 140, 152, 154
International Covenant on Civil and Political Rights, 31
International Covenant on Economic, Social, and Cultural Rights, 31
International Criminal Court (ICC), 17, 24, 45, 143, 153, 155
international law
human rights law as subset of, 4
violation of, as crime, 146
International Military Tribunal for the Far East. *See* Tokyo War Crimes trials
International Monetary Fund (IMF), 21
international organizations, 13, 46
international tribunals, 17, 26, 46, 154-155

internet, 49, 51, 54, 98, 101-102, 124, 141, 143-144, 160, 162
Iran, 74, 99
Irish Republic, 39, 58, 63, 124-125, 142
Islam, 28, 32, 35, 55, 56-57, 60-61, 70-74, 82, 86, 128, 132, 136-138
Islamic radicalism, 55
Israel, 35, 38, 53, 55-56, 65, 116, 148, 153, 159
Italy, 18, 22, 24, 29, 53, 58, 60, 72-73, 78, 119-120, 125, 132

J

Japan
  generally, 3, 11, 17, 22, 28, 34, 45, 53, 70-74, 82, 119, 121, 124-126, 140-141, 145, 147, 150
  cultural distinctiveness, 53, 70, 72-73, 126, 141
  culture generally, 101, 126, 129, 141
  dependence on exports, 140, 142
  homogeneity, 128
  importation of oil, 141
  language, 124, 126
  privacy law in, 103
  travel and tourism, 141
Japanese Americans, 34
Jefferson, Thomas, 3, 7, 9, 27, 90, 100
Joyce, James, 27
Judaism, 17, 28, 45, 55-58, 86, 123, 132-133, 148
judicial review, constitutional power of, 10-11, 21-22, 37-38, 41, 43, 60, 63
jurisdiction, universal. See universal jurisdiction
jury, trial by, 9

K

Katz v. United States, 90
Kawashima, Takeyoshi, 69-70
Khan, Genghis, 161
Khmer Rouge, 150, 154
Kuwait, 78, 140
Kyllo v. United States, 91

L

landlords, rights of, 13
language
  English as universal, 128-129

language rights, 1-2, 7, 12, 39, 61, 72, 120-125, 127-131, 137, 144, 165
Latin America, 11, 22, 26, 37, 44, 55, 78, 85, 120-121, 123, 125, 148, 152, 154-155, 163
Lauren, Paul, 30, 54, 168n, 170n 174n, 190n, 191n
Lawrence v. Texas, 93
Lawrence, D. H., 27
League of Arab States, 43
League of Nations, 29
legal systems, complexity of, 20-21
Levitsky, Sandra, 113
libertarianism, 16, 158
Lochner v. New York, 28
Locke, John, 3, 25, 27
Lord's Resistance Army, 45
Luxembourg, 41

M

Magna Charta, 25
Maine, Henry, 51
mainstreaming, 87
Marbury v. Madison, 10
marriage, gay, 63, 93.
  See also gay rights
Martin Luther King, Jr., 9
Martinez, Jenny, 9, 26, 170n
Marxism, rejection of certain freedoms, 69
McCloskey, Herbert, 64-65
Mein Kampf, 6
Meiwes, Armin, 102
Mengele, Josef, 147
Merkel, Angela, 63
Merry, Sally, 36, 75, 82, 136, 162, 171n, 172n, 177n, 178n, 186n, 191n
Merryman, John, 142
Mexico, 24, 44, 72, 74, 121, 134, 142
Milgram experiments, on compliance, 149-150
Mill, John Stuart, 78
Milosevic, Slobodan, 154
Milton, John, 27
Minorities
  linguistic. See language rights
  racial. See equality, racial
  sexual, 8, 10-11, 48, 65, 85, 87

Mississippi University for Women v. Hogan, 80
modernity, and modernization, 2, 15, 34, 37, 38, 48, 49, 51, 53, 56, 61, 63, 71, 72, 74, 75, 124, 125, 126, 128, 131, 132, 162
Mormonism, 27, 49, 58, 60-61
Morocco, 135-136
Mott, Lucretia, 78
Muller v. Oregon, 79
multiculturalism, 17, 66, 121, 133, 137-138
Muslims, 10, 15, 24, 55-58, 86, 132, 135-137, 151
"muti murder," 135
Mutua, Makau, 21, 61, 69, 169n, 177n

N

Navajo, 122, 130, 134
Nazis, and Nazism, 11, 17, 45, 64-65, 72, 92, 137, 145-149, 159
Ndombasi, Abdulaye Yerodia, 152
negative rights, 111
Netherlands, 37, 50, 63, 93, 106, 120, 137, 145
New York Times v. Sullivan, 98
New Zealand, 15, 37, 48, 71, 74, 78, 120, 123, 133, 150
Nicaragua, 44, 140
Nine-eleven (9/11 attacks), 66, 91, 107
North Korea, 38, 82, 143-144
Norway, 39, 41, 45, 58, 60, 78, 124, 135-136, 144, 147, 150
Nuremberg trials, 17, 26, 45, 145-151, 155-156
Nuremberg Code, for medical research, 147-148

O

O'Connell, Rory, 16
Obama, Barack, 29, 63, 113
Olmstead v. United States, 90
Organization of American States (OAS), 43
Osiatynski, Wiktor, 26

P

Pakistan, 38, 54, 64
Palestinians, 35

paparazzi, 89, 95, 98, 103-104
Paraguay, 94, 125
Pates, Rebecca, 84
Peace of Augsburg, 57
Peace of Westphalia, 57
Peck v. United Kingdom, 105
personal development. *See* rights, individual; individualism
Peru, 121
Philippines, 42
Pinochet, Augusto, 17, 34-35, 151-153
Plato, 71
plural equality, 8, 37, 74, 85-87, 114, 123, 132
pluralism, 57, 59
Poland, and Polish language, 58, 60, 124, 146-147
pollution, as globalization of risk, 142
pornography, 27, 64-65
Portugal, 11, 24, 37, 71, 74, 78
positive rights, 111, 114
press, freedom of the, 12, 117
prisoners, rights of, 31, 150
privacy
    generally, 7, 9, 12-13, 29, 31-32, 40, 54, 72, 89-107, 162
    and the right to know, 97
    as space, 105, 162
    constitutional law of, in U.S., 91-92, 94-98, 100
    constitutional provisions on, various, 94-96
    definition, 89
    Europe, 91, 101-108
    history of, in U.S., 90-96
    medical, 96
    relation to defamation and libel law, 98
    tort law of, 89, 95-96, 98
property rights, 11, 19-21, 28, 42
prostitution, 84-85
Protestantism, 28, 55, 57-59, 128
public figures, 95, 97-104

Q

Quechua, 120, 125, 130
Quisling, Vidkun, 45, 147

R

racial discrimination. *See* equality, racial; segregation

Rechtsstaat, 19-20

religion
cults, 60
diversity of, in U.S., 128, 158
freedom of, 2-3, 7-8, 10, 12, 24, 26-31, 39-40, 42, 55-61, 65, 72, 79, 86, 111, 117, 121, 124, 128, 132-133, 136, 138, 144
fundamentalism, 55-56, 58, 132, 144, 162

Renteln, Alison, 133, 184n, 185n, 186n

retirement, as problem for financing social rights, 120

retirement, mandatory, 120

Rhode, Deborah, 178n, 179n

Riesman, David, 50-51, 174n

"right to choose," 12, 83, 99-100, 114, 122, 133, 159

right to counsel, 12

right to education, 7, 12, 29-30, 111, 114-117, 119

"right to equality," 8

Right to Information Act, India, 99

right to know, 97-101

rights
balancing of, 14
consciousness, 22, 24
cost of, 111
group, 15-16, 87
history of, 111
individual, 15-17, 23, 27, 31-34, 48-53, 59, 69, 74, 81, 83, 85, 87, 92, 94, 97, 105, 114-115, 122, 131-132, 138, 141, 157-159, 161-162
negative & positive. *See* social rights

rock-and-roll music, as example of convergence, 73, 126, 131-132, 141, 144

Roe v. Wade, 83, 93

Roosevelt, Franklin Delano, 29

Rosenau, James, 137

rule of law, 19-21, 31, 39, 42, 47, 65, 107-108, 143, 156, 160

Russia, 21-22, 39, 41, 43, 74, 126, 140

Rwanda, 24, 45, 150, 154-156

S

Santa Clara Pueblo v. Martinez, 134, 186n

Saudi Arabia, 4, 18, 30, 33, 55, 70, 78, 82, 138, 141, 160

Schlafly, Phyllis, 79

Second Amendment. *See* guns, right to own

Security Council, UN, 4, 143, 154

segregation, 11, 36

separation of church and state. *See* religion, freedom of

sex discrimination. *See* equality, gender; gender violence

sexual harassment, 83

sexual minorities, 10-11, 48, 65, 85, 87

Shakespeare, William, 5, 127, 130

Shaw, Bernard, 27

Sidis v. F-R. Publishing Corp., 101

Sierra Leone, 26, 154

Singapore
generally, 20-21, 70, 117, 129, 137, 142
rule of law in, 20

Skinner v. Oklahoma, 92, 180n

Skogly, Sigrun, 118

Slaughter, Anne-Marie, 44

slavery, 7, 26-27, 50, 131

social rights, 7, 12, 29-31, 69, 111-120, 144, 167n

Social Security, U.S., 113, 114

sociology, of human rights, 1-2, 157

Somalia, 128, 136

South Africa, 11-12, 21-22, 41, 65, 71, 78, 111, 114, 117, 119, 129, 135, 137
See also Constitutional Court, South African

South Korea, 11, 17, 22, 70, 72, 94, 125, 128, 142

sovereignty
generally, 17, 139, 146
as a defense to war crimes, 149, 156
conflict with concept of human rights, 142
definition, 139
economic, 140
legal and formal threats to, 145
loss of, in modern times, 139, 142, 151

Soviet Union, 22, 29-31, 35, 40, 45, 69, 139-140, 145-146, 148, 160
Spain, 18, 21, 22, 24, 29, 32, 37, 53, 56, 63, 72, 74, 93, 120, 124-125, 129, 137, 142, 152-153
Spain, Constitution of, 37
Spanish, language, 17, 19, 72, 74, 123-126, 129-130, 152-153
speech, freedom of, 2-3, 17, 7, 9, 12-14, 17, 24, 26-27, 30, 39-40, 42, 64, 66, 72, 111, 113-114, 119
Stacy, Helen, 9, 44, 167n
Stalin, Joseph, 22, 150, 161
Stanton, Elizabeth Cady, 78
State v. Kargar, 133
Strasbourg, 40-41
Sudan, 3-4, 45-46, 150, 155
Sullivan, John, 64-65
Supreme Court, India, 118-119
Supreme Court, Spain, 153
Supreme Court, U.S., 10, 13, 28, 37, 41, 61, 79-80, 83, 90-94, 134
surveillance, government, 89-91, 96-98, 105-107
Sweden, 28, 39, 48, 53, 55, 58, 71, 84, 114, 124-126, 130, 160
swine flu, as example of globalization of risk, 142, 144
Switzerland, 21, 41, 52, 58, 71, 78, 122, 125, 128, 137
Syria, 43

T

Taiwan, 22, 70, 72, 82, 126
Tamanaha, Brian, 169n
Tanguy, 53
Tate, Neal, 11-12
Taylor, Charles, 154
technological revolution, 15, 49
technology, 15, 49, 54, 56, 66, 72, 74, 90-91, 95, 101, 106, 108, 126, 129, 139, 141, 160-163
technology, resistance against, 56
terrorism, 9, 35, 56, 66, 91, 96, 105, 107-108, 144, 153, 162-163
Thailand, 17, 71, 78, 126, 132
Thatcher, Margaret, 63
The Lonely Crowd, 50, 174n
Three Penny Opera, 114

Tibet, 139, 153
Tokyo War Crimes trials, 45, 147, 156
torture, 30, 32, 35, 47, 71, 107, 150, 151, 153
Torture Victim Protection Act, U.S., 153
transparency, of government actions, 99
tribunals, international. *See* international tribunals
Turkey, 23, 24, 124, 135, 145

U

Uganda, 45
United Arab Emirates, 78
United Nations (UN), 4, 17, 29-33, 38-39, 45-46, 82, 112, 120-121, 139, 143, 154-155, 160
United States, religious devotion in, 58
Universal Declaration of Human Rights (UDHR), 30-31, 39, 43, 69-70, 89
universal jurisdiction, 145, 151-154
unreasonable searches and seizures, 12, 89-90
Upham, Frank, 20
Uruguay, 22, 44
USA Patriot Act, 107

V

Venezuela, 44
Vo v. City of Garden Grove, 96
vote, right to, 2-3, 7-9, 14, 25, 28, 49, 77-78, 80, 82, 86, 99, 134, 159

W

warrant, search, 90
warrantless searches. *See* privacy; warrant, search; wiretapping
Warren, Samuel, 92, 95, 98, 103, 180n
Weber, Max, 20
welfare state, 28, 112, 114, 117, 119, 144
Whitman, James, 104
wiretapping, 89-91, 107
See also surveillance, government; Fourth Amendment
Wisconsin v. Yoder, 138

women's rights. *See* equality, gender;
   gender violence
World Bank, 20
World Court. *See* International Court
   of Justice
World War II, 1, 10, 11, 17, 22, 29, 45,
   63, 81, 85, 103, 145

Y

yellow journalism, 95
Yugoslavia, 24

qp

Visit us at *www.quidprobooks.com*.